IN THE LAND OF THE TIAN SHAN MOUNTAINS

Muhammad Idrees

INDIES UNITED PUBLISHING HOUSE, LLC

ISBN: 978-1-64456-147-8
Library of Congress Control Number: 2020938695

INDIES UNITED PUBLISHING HOUSE, LLC
P.O. BOX 3071
QUINCY, IL 62305-3071
www.indiesunited.net

This book is dedicated to the beautiful and lovely country of Kyrgyzstan and the loving people who live there.

Reviews

"Muhammad Idrees wrote a wonderful book about his year and a half long journey in Kyrgyzstan from the perspective of a young, observant Afghan intellectual. His sharp eyes help illuminate rich impressions. His subjective journey offers an enjoyable read. He helps understand why those who travel to Central Asia or are fortunate to live there for a longer time, feel they belong there and when they leave feel to have left their hearts behind."

Pal Dunay, Former Director of the OSCE Academy, Bishkek, Kyrgyzstan

"Typically, most travel narratives in the English reading market are Americans or Brits wandering about. Here we have an Afghan studying in Kyrgyzstan, showing that 'being a stranger in strange land' is not a western phenomenon. With humor and insight, the reader joins the author in his journey to a new land. *In the Land of the Tian Shan Mountains* is an engaging book that will grab the reader's attention and not let go".

Timothy May, University of North Georgia.

"A riveting memoir that doubles as a travelogue, this culturally astute story follows one man's journey of Kyrgystan, evoking respect and love for the country."

Jennie Rosenblum - JennieReads

Acknowledgements

It is not easy to write a book in English when it is not your first language, and such was the case with me. I started writing "In the Land of the Tian Shan Mountains" for English readers, however, I did not know how much effort and hard work I needed to shape my idea practically. After I completed the manuscript followed by rounds of edits, I approached more than one hundred publishers and literary agents but none of them showed any interest except the one who wanted to charge me with money that I could not afford. It took me more than a year looking for someone to publish my book but my efforts did not bear any fruits. Next I decided to self-publish it and as a first step I needed to find an editor. I contacted two Indian editors (who worked together) but after paying in advance, they did not do their job and I could do nothing but to look for another option.

After that bitter experience, I was lucky enough to find Gina Casto and Jennie Rosenblum who did the editing task carefully and always advised me whenever I needed. Furthermore, Jennie also believed in me and introduced me to the owner of Indies United Publishing House, Lisa Orban who agreed to publish my book. But the series of thanks I owe to people does not stop here.

I would like to thank the OSCE Academy in Bishkek for providing me the opportunity of studying there. All professors, academy staff, directors and deputy directors and my classmates were very kind during all that time and I really appreciate their love and assistance. The former OSCE Academy director Dr. Pal Dunay has been very kind and helpful whenever I sought his help. Gregory Dunn supervised my dissertation and he guided and helped me successfully complete my dissertation. Jawed Nazari and Rustam were helpful in finding the accommodation when I first arrived. Abid Stanikzai and Masood had been very cooperative throughout my studies.

I think I would not have been able to gather so much information and visit different places without the help of my doctor friends that I made there. I thank Iqbal Hashmi (Baacha), Zahoor Khan, Hasan Khan, Noor Khan, Hanif, Younis and Abid Khan for their support and love during my stay in Kyrgyzstan.

I owe special thanks to Amanullah Imran, Dr. Fazal Hadi Wardag, Farmanullah Bismil and Hafizullah Ghashtalai for reviewing the manuscript and providing me with their useful feedback and comments.

Thanks to Aisha Naushad and Sedra Afzali for helping me out with the translation of words in the English language.

I also want to thank my friends from UNFPA-Kabul who always supported me and appreciated my writing. I did not name each person as the list will get longer. But would specifically add Ms. Bella Tristram who always allocated time for me despite her being very busy and helped me whenever I needed any assistance regarding the writing processes.

Thanks to Najibullah Zirak and Waseem Ahmad who believed in me and always encouraged me to write; I owe many thanks to the founder of Indies United Publishing House for providing me with a plaform to publish my work.

Muhammad Idrees

TABLE OF CONTENTS

Preface

THIS IS the story of the year and a half that I spent in Kyrgyzstan.

My journey started at the beginning of 2014 and continued until late 2015. The story begins with my acceptance of the OSCE Academy Scholarship. I remember that day vividly. It was a weekend in late October and the sun had already dipped low on the horizon, disappearing from the window of my room. Switching on my laptop, I began to check new emails, noticing one, I clicked on it. I was overjoyed when I opened my email and found the acceptance letter for my master's studies. However, my excitement was slowly replaced with fear and worry.

As I read it many times, allowing the words to sink in, the apprehension of leaving my job hovered in my mind. I was completely lost in thought when, after an hour, my mother made her usual visit to my room, calling me for dinner. I glanced around at my surroundings and found my books scattered on the carpet occupying more than half of the space. I got up to leave my room for the one where my mom and dad were waiting for me.

"I have been accepted to a scholarship program for the master's studies in Kyrgyzstan. I need to reply to them within a week to let them know whether I am interested or not."

First, there was a long pause, and then both of them asked for information about the country, program, stipend, and duration. Although I was free to make my own decisions, I felt a sense of panic listening to them talk about the risks I was taking in preferring higher studies over a job and income, and their words still come to my mind today.

Later, when I consulted my friends and colleagues, they expressed more or less the same concerns, but as they had neither heard of the opportunity nor the country, it was difficult to accept their advice.

I decided it was I who should make the final decision. Two days before the deadline for the offer, I made up my mind. I felt confident in my decision and became determined to take advantage of the offer in hand and pursue my studies. I resigned from my job and got ready for the rich and memorable cultural experience that I believed I was sure to gain.

During all that time in Kyrgyzstan, I tried to immerse myself in the country, to get as much information as I could about its culture, society, and history, as well as the overall atmosphere. I made new friends and acquaintances and traveled through nearly the entire country. During my visits to different parts of Kyrgyzstan, I closely watched the lifestyles of people and studied their cultures and traditions. This book is an attempt to share those varied experiences, the highs and lows, as well as the weird and wonderful stories with readers.

I had no intention of writing this book when I began this journey, but whenever I discussed my interesting experiences with my friends or sometimes when I would post on social media, I always received positive feedback. Upon posting new and interesting information and stories about the lifestyle and culture of the people of Kyrgyzstan, my friends and colleagues in different parts of the world showed interest. At the same time, I discovered that most of my friends and colleagues had little or no knowledge of that undiscovered gem in the world. A country about which not enough has been written, even though it possesses beautiful snowy mountains with fantastic green pastures, and fabulous waterfalls, as well as a unique culture and tradition of hospitality.

Kyrgyzstan is an attraction for travelers who seek peace of mind in nature, those who love hiking and skiing, and those who dare to face the real adventure that life has to offer. Moreover, it occupies an important geostrategic position in the region. Being the only democracy in Central Asia, Kyrgyzstan is the focus of big powers and regional players. The idea and motivation behind writing this book were to write something from an Afghan point of view. This book contains my experiences, and I have tried my utmost to write it with complete honesty.

Before leaving my home for Kyrgyzstan, a Google search on the internet provided me with some brief information about the country. Mostly I read about the ethnic violence and revolutions which painted the country as one experiencing political upheavals. At the same time, my parents had trouble pronouncing the name. They called it *Kurdistan, Turkistan,* etc.

I had applied for the OSCE Academy Master's Studies Scholarship in April 2013. In September 2013, I got an email from the Academy about the written test, which was to take place in late September. The Academy had also sent the format of the test along with the venue: Gawharshad Institute of Higher Studies on Darulaman Road, Kabul. The test was scheduled at nine in the morning, and on the same day, an interview was to take place. At that time, I was working for UNFPA, and I was assigned some new responsibilities for our SDES project, which was a challenge in itself. The workload was so demanding and heavy, requiring me to work even during my off days.

It was a hot day, as I recall, and I got permission from my supervisor to sit for the exam. The written test consisted of English grammar and economics-related multiple-choice questions with a long essay testing both knowledge of the English language and economics. I had three hours to finish the test.

While solving the questions, I did not find them difficult, and so, I was done in less than two hours. I went back to my office to finish the urgent work waiting for me and was to check again after 1 p.m. to see if I was selected for an interview.

At 1:30 p.m., when I arrived at the Institute, I found candidates checking their names on the notice board. Sweating profusely, I made space for myself to try to see my name on the list. I was thrilled to find that indeed, my name was third from the top.

After following the directions given on the notice board, I found that the venue for the interview was on the second floor, where nine other candidates were also waiting. The waiting lounge was a wide room with enough sofas and chairs for the candidates, but without air-conditioning, it was very hot. I found a vacant seat in the corner where two other candidates were busy discussing the possible interview questions. The remaining candidates did not seem familiar with each other and appeared to be looking to establish new friendships. After a while, a man with a list in his hands entered the room and announced a name, and one of the two guys sitting near me stood up and went with him. While I waited my turn, the other gentleman struck up a conversation with me. After we exchanged some information regarding our work, studies, and future plans, my name was announced, and I followed the person to the interview room.

Dr. Maxim, then Director of the OSCE Academy, Elham, Afghan Alumni and then Director of Gawharshad Institute, were sitting behind a table with bundles of exam papers and students' applications. Dr. Maxim asked questions, which were fairly simple: *"What is your plan for the next five years?" "Why are you interested in this scholarship?" "How will you contribute to the development of Afghanistan after you return and...?"* After Dr. Maxim finished his questions, he looked to Elham and asked if he had any questions. Thankfully, he did not.

After receiving the acceptance letter for the program in late

October, I learned that the two young men I was sitting near in the waiting lounge were also among the successful candidates. However, they canceled the offer in its final stage and thus out of four scholarships, only two Afghans got the chance to study there.

The scholarship offer to study Economic Governance and Development at the OSCE Academy in Bishkek included round trip travel costs, 180 Euros stipend per month, 100 Euros housing allowance, and basic medical insurance. The Academy started processing my visa and sent me the schedule for my studies. After the two candidates canceled the offer, I learned from the Academy that the other candidate who accepted the scholarship offer was Iqbal.

A couple of days later, our office arranged a farewell party for me. After that, I was officially done with the UNFPA after three years of dedicated service, and I started preparing for Kyrgyzstan. Before leaving for Bishkek, our Academy sent us the email of our senior fellow, Masood in case we needed to ask any questions or help. He had finished his course-work and was leaving for Kabul to complete his dissertation and internship. A few days before my departure, I met Masood and another graduate of the Academy Abid Stanikzai. After meeting them in Kabul, I was more confident in my decision.

Chapter 1

From Kabul to Bishkek

It was my first time traveling out of the country, and therefore I was nervous. A weird and unexplainable kind of fear began mounting over me, and I worried about how I would handle all the challenges ahead. The Academy had already completed the processing of my visa, and my flight from Kabul to Bishkek was scheduled on January 9, 2014, through Dubai. There were no direct flights from Kabul to Bishkek, and almost all of the flights were scheduled through Dubai. My flight was at 6 p.m. from Kabul to Dubai by FlyDubai Airline and then from Dubai to Bishkek with the same airline after a four-hour layover.

Students going to Bishkek do not usually get their visas on their passports; it was the same in my case. My visa was issued upon arrival, and I was provided a reference letter by the Consular Department of the Ministry of Foreign Affairs of Kyrgyzstan along with the invitation letter from the OSCE Academy.

The Kabul International Airport (KIA), sometimes often referred to by foreigners as the "Killed in Action (KIA)" airport, has been renamed as Hamid Karzai International Airport (HKIA). Passengers have to pass through five to six checkpoints before boarding the plane. After crossing the roundabout on the main airport road, there is a checkpoint at the start of the small road that goes to the airport. All passengers get out of the vehicle and take a walking route where they are searched by police. The driver stays by his car, and other group of policemen search him along with his vehicle. From there onward, the car moves forward, and the passengers get back in the car until it turns right where there is another checkpoint. The luggage is unloaded there and passed through the baggage scanner. Passengers also pass through a body scanner followed by a body search. From there, after crossing the carpark and the main waiting hall, you show your ticket to another police officer before proceeding to the terminal area either by walking or on a bus. Before entering the terminal, you must go through another round of baggage and body scanners along with security guards who again check you and your luggage, and sometimes you may also confront a German shepherd or Belgian Malinois checking your luggage. After that, you finally queue up, weigh your luggage, and get your boarding pass.

At the boarding counter, the person responsible checked my passport and reference visa but was not satisfied. I showed him the invitation letter, but the creases on his forehead were not giving me a green signal. I explained to him that the Kyrgyz Embassy did not issue visas for students, that they get their visa upon arrival. He looked at me, but instead of issuing the boarding pass, he referred me to the border police officer standing a short distance away from him. The border police officer asked me about the purpose of my visit but was also not satisfied when I answered that I was going for studies. He shook his head in disappointment and told me to follow him.

While walking a few steps, I noticed a tall, muscular man with a big mustache coming down the stairs from the second floor. The officer greeted this man and quickly told him my story. When I replied to his question that I was going to study, he told the officer to allow me through. Later, I came to know that the big man was the airport police chief. I also realized if the airport staff teases you, pointing out problems in your legal documents, it means they want to be paid some money. The officer had no excuse then.

We went back to the authorized person, and the officer told him to issue me the boarding pass. After getting the pass, I moved to the second floor and queued to get my passport stamped with "Exit." Within a few minutes, the immigration officer stamped my passport and I moved to yet another spot for yet another body and hand-luggage search. I took off my shoes and put them, along with my coat, belt, mobile, and wallet in the tray, which passed through the scanner, and after a few minutes, I was in the lounge waiting for my flight.

At that point, I was relieved because I had been through an extensive body search and interrogation, but I had to face another worry - acrophobia. That was the main reason why traveling by plane was always scary for me. The flight was delayed by thirty minutes and after a while, I saw Iqbal, who I had seen during the interview, and then befriended through emails and social media while waiting for this time to arrive. He also had passed through the same messy interrogation and body searches.

After getting on the plane, the flight attendant did not welcome me with a smile; instead, she checked my boarding pass and showed me my seat in a quite bizarre way. Later, I discovered the reason why.

The flight from Kabul to Dubai was full of Afghan laborers going to Dubai. Their rough physical appearance, hardened hands, and worn clothes revealed the degree of the hard lives they had been living. Because of the language barrier, these workers often have problems with flight attendants. The plane was half-full, and as I watched some of the passengers board, I noticed most had problems finding their seats, and then with the assistance of the flight attendant, the dispute would get resolved.

The plane had a total of six rows of seats, three to each side. Following the instructions of the flight attendant and after putting my hand luggage in the cabin, I sat in the left row between two bearded men discussing their bosses, referring to them as the kindest and they being the most trusted employees. This discussion continued throughout the journey.

While sandwiched between the two and unwillingly listening to their stories, and still waiting for the flight to fully board, a group of five people attempted to attract my attention. Confused and lost, they could not find their seats. The problem got bigger when the flight attendant found them their seats, but they did not want to leave each other because they were one family, and their seats were not together. With the interference of other passengers the group finally agreed to sit separately, but during the entire flight, they were exchanging conversations.

After all passengers were finally seated, the flight attendant began showing passengers one by one how to knot their seat belts, and some passengers enjoyed that demonstration with mischievous smiles. After the doors of the plane were closed, the flight attendant started announcing the precautionary measures in both Arabic and English, but no one was listening. Her colleague reminded each passenger to switch off their phones but with no result at all.

Overall, the atmosphere on the plane was similar to a noisy classroom full of naughty students, and for a while I forgot that I was on an airplane. After a few minutes, the plane was ready to take off, and it started moving slowly on the runway. The passenger to my left was on a call to his family. The flight attendant warned him several times to switch off his phone, but he talked one by one to each member of his family whom he just left. After a little while, when the plane gained momentum, my right hand held the armrest of the seat firmly while my left fist was clenched with my eyes closed as we left the ground. I recited the verses from the Holy Quran and tried to go back to my childhood memories to keep myself calm and relaxed.

As the plane left the ground, the man on the call proudly conveyed the message to his family that he was talking to them from the air. With each upward move, my heart sank until the plane attained a maximum height, and then straightened out. After the plane's movement became straight and still, the passengers untied their seat belts. Some passengers preferred to rest, some talked amongst themselves, while others stared down at the wild landscapes as the plane was still in the Afghan territory. The neighbor to my right put his feet on his seat and had put a small piece of cloth on his face for a short nap; while the one to my left was checking his mobile signal to see if he could once again connect with his family. I preferred to take a short nap, however, not long after, the angry shouting of a passenger pulled me awake.

A thin, older passenger, who stood up from his seat, was screaming and complaining against discriminatory behavior by the crew. "What is going on in this plane?" "I have also paid for the ticket." "Why am I not served food and beverages the way others are served?" "This is discrimination…"

I understood the reason behind his anger, but he did not know that FlyDubai Airline did not serve passengers food or drinks unless they buy it. Being seated in front of me, I explained to him that the airline did not provide food or beverages for free during the flight; therefore, one has to buy their meal and pay on the spot. After hearing my explanation, he calmed down but still did not like the way the airline was dealing with their passengers.

I checked the screen in front of me, and less than an hour was left before our arrival. When I glanced at the other passengers, I found many of them busy talking while a few enjoyed being engaged with the flight attendants. Their faces were fresh, and they seemed happy and excited. I discovered, however, that these brief happy and relaxing moments would soon be over after they get back to their work. In fact, behind each worker or laborer, there was a story.

They go for the hardest kind of jobs in the burning heat of Dubai. They stay there for years to earn money to pay off debts or feed extended families. Among them, a few looked very young and excited, but soon they would start missing their families and loved ones. They quickly realize the reality of Dubai, which is work, work, and more work. The delusive, tall, and fancy buildings were not for them because they have to sleep in a room shared with ten to twelve others. Sometimes, people living in the same room do not meet for months because of their varying shifts. Although all these facts had already been told to them by their senior fellows, their young minds did not accept them as facts until they see and face them. But those who had already experienced the hard life of years of working in Dubai had wrinkles and creases dominating their faces and foreheads looking much older than their real ages. Whether young or old, experienced or immature, their purpose for this journey was to work and send money back home from the day they arrive.

After approximately two and a half hours of flying, the plane started hovering over the city of Dubai. Lights indicated that the colorful nightlife seemed to be in full swing. Before we touched the ground when the flight attendant was about to give safety instructions to passengers, I saw some young men with their faces stuck to the window, eagerly looking through it. When the plane landed but not yet at a complete stop, most of the passengers stood up from their seats and started taking down their luggage from overhead. The flight attendant, who was stuck in the back, but wanted to go to the front area, was shouting and asking them to remain seated and allow her to pass. By then, I completely understood why she did not greet passengers with a smile. It was very difficult to smile under such circumstances.

After getting off the plane, most of the passengers entered Dubai while a few had transit flights. My next flight was scheduled to depart from Terminal 2, so Iqbal and I headed toward the terminal from where we would fly to Bishkek.

Before entering the terminal, the immigration officer checked our passports, reference visas, and tickets. The tall busy man who appeared to be Indian or Pakistani from his hard accent and physical features, told us to wait while he called somewhere and informed someone about our reference visas, passports, and ticket numbers. After about fifteen minutes, he received a call and allowed us to enter the waiting lounge.

For the first time, I saw a huge crowd of people belonging to different parts of the world. People there belonged to different ethnicities, religions, cultures, and countries. They were eating, drinking, shopping, talking, and walking around in the terminal. Some were tense, some excited, some updating their Facebook statuses, while others continuously checked the time for their flight and waited for their flight announcements.

Opposite of the large waiting lounge at one end of the terminal, I saw shops selling perfumes, chocolates, and dates, souvenirs, gifts, etc. These shops were crowded with people, a few of them buyers, many just hanging around killing time. On the other end of the terminal was a chain of fast-food restaurants selling sandwiches, burgers, pizzas, and Pakistani and Indian food. I chose to walk around the terminal and explore while Iqbal preferred to get some rest. I passed through the souvenir shops and peeked in for a quick look before going to the part where the fast-food cafes sat. People queued to get food from those cafes representing the big names in the fast-food world. I bought a burger from one and sat on a chair with a small table. I ate my burger in a hurry, not wanting to miss my connecting flight, and when I checked the time, I saw I still had an hour and a half left before it would be time to board again.

Before going back to the spot where Iqbal waited, I visited the most important place one should always look for anywhere. The toilets of the terminal were neat and clean, and despite being so crowded, the cleaners were continuously busy doing their job. Inside, I did not find any kind of abusive language, dirty poetry, porn-cartoons, or telephone numbers offering sex on the walls like in the public toilets in Kabul. After getting out from there, I noticed the same crowd of people moving like bees. Before going to the part of the terminal where we would get into the bus for the plane going to Bishkek, I decided to get some water from the refrigerators at the corner.

After approaching, a little man with a Charlie Chaplin-style

7

mustache and South Asian physical features was cleaning the floor and I talked to him in Urdu.

"How can I get some water out of the refrigerator?" I asked.

He looked at me and then demonstrated the entire process of how to get any cold drink out of it. Thus, I put two Dirham coins in the refrigerator that offered different types of soft drinks and pressed the code of the drink I wanted, I received a half liter of water. When I returned to Iqbal, he was holding the same half liter of water, which he bought for seven Dirhams from a nearby shop. I realized to my delight that my language skills helped me save money.

After the airport officials announced our flight, Iqbal and I queued up, and once again, the officials checked our documents and allowed us to board a big bus, which took us to the plane headed for Bishkek. We spent more than four hours in the air, and finally landed at Manas International Airport to much cheering and clapping of the Kyrgyz passengers.

The atmosphere at Manas airport was completely different from Dubai. When landing in Dubai, one can feel its liveliness and colorful life some hundreds of feet above the ground. But at Manas Airport, there was complete silence, darkness and severe cold with a temperature of -6°C.

We did not line up with the other passengers, but instead we moved to the Consular Department's window toward the left, where we needed to get our visas. The seat was empty, and I waited by the window. I saw in the queue where the last person disappeared after the customs officer stamped his passport. After some minutes of silence, the visa officer appeared. He looked rather harassed like I was solely responsible for disturbing him. He sat on his chair, and I slowly forwarded him our passports. He did not say anything, just took our reference visas, stamped our passports with a one month visa, and said "seventy dollars" in English. I paid the money, and we moved toward the customs officer, who comparatively was in a good mood because he pronounced the word *"student"* for us and let us in after I nodded my head. He stamped our passports with *"Entry."* We got our luggage without any problem from the carousel and got out of the terminal, where we were surrounded by a number of persistent taxi drivers pulling our luggage. We did not understand a single word they were speaking.

Iqbal had already got the mobile number of Jawed—an Afghan colleague studying in the Politics and Security Group—whom he had already communicated with about our arrival. One of the taxi drivers who had taken hold of one of our bags handed over his mobile phone when Iqbal gestured that he needed a mobile to make a call. Jawed gave Iqbal the address of his apartment and warned him not to pay more than 700 som. The taxi driver was hopeful that we would ride in his taxi as we had called from his mobile. When Iqbal told the address to the taxi driver, he said "1000" in English while in reply Iqbal wrote "700" on his mobile and showed it to him. The taxi driver shook his head in a negative gesture and wrote back "1000." After some minutes of negotiation through the mobile, the driver finally agreed on a sum of 800 som, and we set off in his car for Jawed's apartment.

It was almost dawn when our car started moving toward Bishkek City. Although the snow had covered both sides of the road, the land looked agricultural. It was very cold, but inside the car, the heater was on. I was sleepy, and my eyes kept closing. Everything appeared no different than if we had been passing through a village in Afghanistan. So at that moment, I did not feel that I was out of my country. After forty minutes, the driver again called Jawed because we were already in that area. The driver found his building, it was a tall building probably six stories high, and Jawed, along with his friends, lived on the fifth floor. When we arrived it was very early in the morning, and all the others were sleeping except him. Jawed had a semester break and was doing his assignments. He told us to get some rest and went into the other room, saying we would talk at lunch.

After he left the room, his study table drew my attention. Books and notes were scattered on the table, revealing that he had been very busy with his studies. There were colorful sticky notes on the cupboard indicating various deadlines and reminders, which had me wondering that I should be ready for the Academy's adventure.

We slept for a few hours, waking around noon. Besides Jawed, the other guys living in the apartment were Waheed, and Hashmi (Afghanistan), Rustam (Tajikistan), and Ruslan (Turkmenistan).

Another resident, Azad had left for Kabul during his semester break. In the Politics and Security class, there were five Afghans in total—four males and one female, Fatima. Hashmi prepared a delicious lunch for us, including *chay* and eggs together with tomatoes. The classes at the Academy were scheduled to begin in three days, so within that time we needed to find a place to live.

After eating, Jawed, Rustam, Iqbal, and I went out. Our first sights of the city were beautiful. The city was green, clean, and people of every variety were moving in a rush. Children and youth were prominent, and that picture is still preserved in my memory. Rustam helped us buy Kyrgyz sim cards. From there, we went to two real estate agencies to find an apartment for us. As a temporary solution, there was an apartment on a daily basis at 1500 som/night. It was located in the center of the city in a tall building away from the Academy. It was a modern apartment at a far distance from the Academy, with every facility. Until we could find a proper place, it served as a temporary solution.

Lost in Bishkek

I was shocked and overwhelmed at seeing so many young women walking on the roadside. The weather was freezing cold, and most of them had warm black coats. As night was approaching, their steps were faster than normal, and getting into a *marshrutka* would be difficult. I had not seen so many young women in one place in my entire life, and all this seemed so exciting and shocking to me. At that time, due to my limited knowledge, I thought they were either Kyrgyz or Russians, who were easily identifiable because of their physical features. Later, I learned that there were more than fifty ethnicities living in the country.

Those commuting ladies included students, public and private servants, ladies working in shopping malls, and those returning from their shopping with large, full bags. Some were in groups and some walked alone, while there were a few couples. There were also a good number of them either eating burgers or sandwiches in front of small fast-food chains on both sides of the road or busy talking. I had come from a country where you see mostly men everywhere, but here it was the opposite. I was seeing young ladies more than men, which further beautified the city. There were elderly women and men too walking on the roadside, but young ladies were dominant, and that was the reason they caught my profound attention.

After a little while, it started snowing, and they started rushing toward the bus stop to get into the *marshrutka*, taking them home. That was the center of the city, and it was my first evening. Walking alongside the main road, the shopping malls and food cafes were identifiable by colorful lights. There was no traffic jam, no loud horns, or unpleasant exhaust fumes, and the cars were moving smoothly in a rather disciplined way. Walking around and enjoying myself, looking here and there with excitement, I was trying not to go too far and keep in mind the way I had come from.

I stood at the crossroad and looked at both sides; the left one seemed more attractive with lots of people and colorful lights. I turned left and was confident enough not to lose my way. That side was more interesting, and as I walked through, I saw groups of teens smoking and gossiping along the road-side, while many others belonging to different age groups were enjoying their meals and coffees inside the restaurants and coffee houses. I was also looking for a restaurant I could dine in, and the criterion was simple—the more crowded a restaurant is, the better it is.

After covering some distance, a café with its large wooden door and transparent window glass where I could see people busy eating their food seemed a good place to eat. I entered, and a skinny little waitress welcomed me with a pleasant smile. She led me to a small table for two in the middle of the café where others around were busy eating. The menu was written in Russian, but luckily, it had photos of the dishes, and it was easy for me to look through and choose. After ordering my dinner, I put my apartment's key on the table and enjoyed the most freedom ever, where I could go home anytime without anybody asking me where and with whom I had been. The environment of the café was calm. The waiting staff served the customers who seemed to be enjoying the food and environment. After some time, the café was getting quieter, as people were gradually leaving and heading for their homes. I ate a delicious lamb *shashlik*, paid my bill, and exited the café with a full belly.

Outside it was quieter than before, and the busy streets full of life were calm. Because of snowfall, the weather was bitter cold. After stepping out of the café, I realized that I had, indeed, lost my way. I got confused and could not remember the way back to my apartment. I did not even know the name of the place where my apartment was, which instantly caused me concern. I checked my mobile to call Jawed or Rustam, who knew the address, but unfortunately, I had not saved their mobile numbers. That left me no other option than to contact Masood in Kabul by text message to see if he could contact one of them to get my address.

The snowfall intensified, and the low battery signal of my mobile further scared me into wondering how I would communicate with anyone to find my way home. I sent a message to Masood, told him my situation, and left him my mobile

12

number. In the meantime, the steadily falling snow, accompanied by the chilled breeze, was hitting my face between my muffler and cap. I quickly went from a situation of excitement, joy, and freedom to one of anxiety and fear, wondering where I would spend my night.

Walking randomly in different directions further confused me, and by this time, I knew I was completely lost. During those chaotic moments where my nose and I were both running, the sound of a loud explosion accompanied by fireworks startled me so badly that I misunderstood them for bomb explosions or firing bullets. Scared, nervous, and shivering with cold, I began to search for a safe place to take cover, but when I realized everyone around me was acting normal, I instantly realized that I was wrong. Later, I understood that they were weekend firework celebrations.

In the meantime, I received a call from Jawed laughingly asked me what I was doing out at that time of night. My mobile battery was almost dead and prevented me from narrating to him the entire story then and there, besides the fact that I was starting to freeze. I got my address in a hurry and let out a big sigh of relief. After hailing a taxi, I realized that it was just two streets away from where I had been moving up and down.

When I arrived back at the temporary apartment, I turned the key in the lock and opened the door as quietly as I could. Iqbal was sleeping soundly with the television still on, and its remote lying in his left hand, half protruding from the blanket. I changed my clothes, looked in the mirror, and found my ears and nose still red with remnants of the cold and fear. With relief washing over me, I thanked God for bringing me back home and went to bed.

OSCE Academy, Bishkek

I woke up at 7 a.m. and started preparing for the Academy. I took a shower, and when I came out of the bathroom, an appetizing aroma filled my nostrils. Following the smell, I saw Iqbal busy cooking eggs with tomatoes for breakfast. After eating breakfast, I took out my water-proof shoes from my luggage. This made me remember the words of the shopkeeper in the second-hand shoe market in Kabul when a week before my departure, I went to buy shoes that could resist snow and water.

"This pair of shoes is particularly for the cold weather like in Siberia, and I think they deserve a gentleman like you."

Stepping out of the apartment building, the whole area looked like it was covered with a thick white blanket. In the freezing weather, I had covered myself with warm clothes from head to toe, and my mouth and nose were also covered with a muffler. However, the exhalation out of my nose fogged up on my eyeglasses resulting in a blurred view, so I got my nose out of the muffler.

Iqbal and I started looking for a taxi to take us to the Academy as we were beginning the first day of our Master's Program. At the end of the street, a taxi driver watched our steps moving toward him. The middle-aged driver, wearing glasses balanced on the tip of his nose, wound down the car window. Iqbal showed him the address written on a piece of paper followed by the number 100 on his mobile as the expected fair of a taxi because none of us spoke Russian or Kyrgyz. The taxi driver said something in the Kyrgyz language and was annoyed as to why his countryman was communicating in such a strange way as both of them shared the same physical features. He mistook Iqbal for a local. In the meanwhile, the driver raised his left eyebrow and let us sit in the taxi.

After being driven to the end of the street of our apartment, the taxi moved on to Prospect Mira, also called Prospect Manas, named after the legendary Kyrgyz hero Manas whom I will talk about in the coming chapters. Both sides of the road were white with snow, and children, as well as university students and office workers, rushing eagerly to their various destinations. The taxi covered some distance and then turned left onto Akhunbaev Street, and after passing the Dolce Vita restaurant, which later became my favorite eating place, we turned right onto a side street, which led straight to the OSCE Academy.

When we got out of the taxi, we found ourselves in front of a large blue gate with a smaller door on its left. I had quite a bigger image of the OSCE Academy in my mind, but I found the building very small and situated at the end of a very quiet looking street.

As a typical rule, Academy students who came from other countries preferred to stay closer to the Academy; while Afghans specifically needed to stay close because of the language barrier and unfamiliarity problems.

We opened the door and entered a small room, where a security guard sat at a desk behind a thick glass screen. The security guard did not allow us to pass through the next door and called the administration to verify our identities. When I peeked through the window glass, I saw a half-eaten samsa with some of its ingredients out on a piece of newspaper beside a half-filled cup of green tea. Beside the meal, there was an old yellow landline phone, a showbiz magazine, and a long thick register for registering the visitors.

After receiving confirmation and checking our passports, the guard allowed us inside. Entering through the security door, I found myself in a vast open area. To the left, there was a canteen where a middle-aged lady, her head covered with a white handkerchief, was quickly taking vegetables and other products inside its kitchen, and a teenage girl was calmly helping her out. A little further ahead, next to the canteen was an open area with a table tennis court and carpark. Directly in front of us were two small plastic tables with wooden benches under the bare branches of trees protecting them from the sun during hot summer days. To the right was a lawn with dried and leafless bushes and small trees all around, and a little further ahead was the Academy's prestigious building. Following the guard's instructions, we went to the second floor of the building. After checking the door plates, we found our classroom at the very end of the corridor, thanks to the Economic Governance and Development sign, written in bold letters.

When we entered, all our classmates were already present and sitting in pairs except two ladies sitting alone in the first two rows to the left of the class. This left Iqbal and me with only two vacant places for our seats. Iqbal greeted all with a loud "good morning" and chose the second row while I sat in the front. There was a total of seventeen students in our class—four young men and thirteen young ladies representing all Central Asian states and Afghanistan.

After a while, when everyone had arrived, a tall ethnic Kyrgyz lady wearing a black business suit with a white shirt giving her a more official appearance, came to the classroom. Zarina was her name, and she was the student affairs coordinator. She briefed us on the overall course and told us that she would send us the schedule for the first semester.

Sitting warm and excited, I did not know that the rooms were kept warm with a central heating system, and one had to take off heavy winter clothes and hang them on a stand in the corner of the class. Zarina left after completing her presentation and returned a short while later with a middle-aged Russian man wearing glasses. I already knew Dr. Maxim because he was the one who interviewed me in Kabul.

Dr. Maxim gave a short introductory speech about the Academy, its studies, and general rules and procedures. From there on, each student introduced him or herself briefly. Each introduction was different than the other. Some nervous and stressed, some confident, while a few others over-confident to the level of sounding aggressive. After our introduction, Zarina told us to finish submitting our educational documents for their Russian translation to get registered with the government. Following her last and important announcement, everybody was out of class and queued in front of Karina's (the finance assistant) office to get their monthly stipend.

OSCE Academy was established in 2002 by the mutual cooperation of the Kyrgyz government and the OSCE organization as the center for postgraduate studies, regional dialogue, and research analysis. In 2004, the Academy started a master's program in politics and security for the Central Asian countries. In 2008, Afghanistan was included in this program, and in 2011, the Academy started another master's program of economic governance and development. Currently, the OSCE Academy provides two master's program opportunities for Central Asian countries and Afghanistan[1]. The Academy does not charge any fee. Instead, it provides a monthly grant of 300 Euros (200 Euros monthly stipend to all and 100 Euros accommodation expenses for non-Kyrgyz students). Every year OSCE Academy conducts and hosts various training programs and seminars in the fields of education, media development, conflict resolution, management, and post-conflict development. By 2016, more than 300 students had graduated from the programs of politics and security and economic governance and development. The graduates of OSCE Academy have obtained prestigious positions in both academic and professional careers. Only in Afghanistan, the OSCE Academy's graduates are occupying important positions in government institutions, international organizations, and academia.

OSCE Academy Bishkek has been playing a crucial role in the capacity building of Afghans. The Academy not only provides scholarship opportunities for Afghan students in the academic spheres mentioned above, but it also provides Afghans with an opportunity to participate in various professional training, workshops, and conferences in different professional and academic arenas and build up their capacities. Afghans who graduated from the Academy, also enjoy important academic and professional positions within and outside of Afghanistan.

After three nights in that temporary apartment, Iqbal and I rented a new apartment near our Academy, where we stayed for a month. That one-room apartment was a luxury for me. Like most of the apartments in Bishkek, it had an adequate toilet, spacious kitchen (with all the necessary requirements such as a refrigerator and kitchen equipment) along with furniture, sofas, beds, cupboards, a carpet and even blankets with a monthly rent of 15000 som (about $250).

[1]"History of the Academy", OSCE Academy in Bishkek, accessed May 16, 2016, http://osce-academy.net/en/about/history/

OSCE Academy, Bishkek, Kyrgyzstan

First Days and Nights

It started snowing for the third time in two weeks since I arrived in Bishkek. At first, it snowed very heavily, with cotton balls falling at a rapid pace, and then it slackened. Our classes finished for that day, and I was occupied staring out through the window of my classroom at the view outside.

I saw houses built in the cape-cod style where snow does not stay for long, and the people of the city did not appear to be worried about how to remove the snow from the tops of their roofs. Their houses are kept warm because of the central heating systems. Unlike Kabul, where the poor people of the city do not welcome snow because keeping their houses or tents warm is not an easy task. Even the lower-middle or middle classes face problems in keeping their houses warm. People in Kabul usually rely on wood, coal, gas, and electricity for heating their homes, and due to an overloaded electricity network, there is always a power shortage in winter. Only the *Mikrorayon* built by the Soviets has the central heating system. In winter, after the sunset, the air looks polluted like clouds of fogs because of the smoke from households. But Bishkek was different. It looked white and bright in winter.

After the snowfall stopped, I packed up my laptop and books and left for my apartment. There was dead silence as I passed through the corridor, and I could hear the crunchy sound as my water-proof shoes echoed. I wondered how within a matter of hours, the busy and crowded place became so quiet. I left the Academy by tossing a goodbye to the security guard.

After the first two exciting weeks, severe homesickness started hovering over me. Although the country, city, people, Academy and studies, and everything else was new, I was missing my home. It was the first time that I was away from home, and I did not know how to cope with the situation. I took random walks with no purpose around my neighborhood, tried to talk to people, mostly young ladies, and spent time in the cafes, but nothing

19

helped. I even packed my luggage twice or maybe even three times and was about to leave for home, but my family and friends supported me during that stressful time. Whenever I would talk to them by phone or Skype, they always motivated me not to forget that my main purpose for being there was to study and obtain my master's degree.

During my third week in Bishkek, Rafik (my colleague in Afghanistan who belonged to Kyrgyzstan) invited me to dinner at the Dolce Vita restaurant located a very short distance from our Academy. Dolce Vita also served as a meeting spot for most of the Academy's foreign guests. I had a very good time with Rafik. He asked about all UNFPA-Kabul staff one by one. During our discussion, I complained about homesickness and mentioned going back home.

Understanding my situation, Rafik told me about one of his friends who had a job assignment in a remote area of Kyrgyzstan for a couple of years in the early 1990s. "You are lucky that you can communicate with your family through Skype or telephone. During that time, communication through emails was not yet possible, and that region did not yet have the facility of the telephone. Therefore, writing letters was the only way to communicate with the outer world." I recognized Rafik's sympathy, and he added with a meaningful smile, "Be patient. Wait until the summer comes, which is very interesting with lots of undressing in Bishkek."

He was right. Later in summer, the city became greener, and the women's clothes became shorter and transparent, giving an attractive sexy look to the city.

Our class environment was very friendly in the beginning, and everybody was eager to get to know each other. During our breaks and free time, we discussed each other's social and academic interests, future plans, and the experience of Bishkek and the Academy. In a very short time, we became acquainted with each other, but later our classmates could not keep up the friendly network of cooperation and coordination. Everybody either became isolated or split into groups of two or three. Working on assignments became like a secret mission where no one helped others. In addition, it seemed the connection between two people was confined to personal gain. For example, if he/she could help me with a particular subject. The main reason behind this was the competition. Everybody wanted to be at the top to benefit from the internship opportunities in Geneva and Oslo. Each year three to four students from the economic group and seven to eight from the politics group were accepted for the internship at the Geneva Center for Security Policy (GCSP) and Norwegian Institute of International Affairs (NUPI). Thus, the competition began, and everyone was busy trying hard to take the lead in class and meet the criteria for better opportunities.

The fifteen months master's program of the OSCE Academy also included a two month internship period, and the final dissertation must be written during that period. During these fifteen months, the Academy keeps its students so busy that they cannot find any time for other activities like sports, visiting historical places, or sightseeing. Students even spend their weekends doing assignments, and that is the reason that those students who are in Kyrgyzstan for the first time cannot enjoy it fully; there is no opportunity to see the unique culture and breathtaking landscapes of that pearl on earth.

I was also expecting some extra-curricular activities like pre-studies seminars, academic orientations, visiting important government or historical places, etc. before our studies started. But from the very first day, we had our semester schedule, and classes began. The teaching mechanism in the Academy was very interesting and productive. For example, the total 100 marks were divided into presentations, home assignments, group works, attendance, mid-term, and final term exams. So, one had to cope with deadlines of assignments and be continuously active in and outside the classroom to succeed in their studies.

All the classes were going well, but I, along with a few other students, had problems in micro and macroeconomics classes because of the harder mathematics and mathematical problems. About half of our classmates were from the American University of Central Asia (AUCA), and they already had studied more or less the same micro and macroeconomics in their bachelor's program under the same teacher therefore, being a majority, they would tell the teacher to skip certain chapters or topics and go forward, not considering the background of other students. The teacher's style was so fast that I was seeing chapters running in front of my eyes without any understanding. Throughout the semester I struggled with these two subjects, and thus I was unable to devote enough time to my other subjects.

After about three weeks, one of our classmates dropped out, probably due to the problems with some subjects. Besides these troublesome subjects, I really enjoyed Dina's academic writing class, who was a very hard-working teacher. Throughout our course, we also had extensive short and long modules, from one week to one month long.

In Bishkek, people mostly speak Russian and Kyrgyz languages, but Russian is more dominant, and my biggest problem was the complete unfamiliarity with either language while most people did not know any English. In Kyrgyzstan, when someone does not speak the local languages, he or she can face lots of problems on a daily basis. For example, when shopkeepers or taxi drivers come to know that you are a foreigner and new in the city, they would often charge you double or triple. Moreover, in restaurants or shops, it would be difficult to buy and order the food you want, and as a solution, you have to rely on gestures and body language.

It was my third weekend and after finishing my classes on Friday, I did not go to my apartment. Instead I chose to walk along the road I saw every day full of cars and people when I would come to my Academy in the early mornings. I decided to discover where that road would lead and how interesting it would be walking along.

Prospect Mira also called Prospect Manas, was the longest road connecting the two ends of the city. Walking downward toward the center of the city, I was not sure how far I would go. Most of the people coming my way were students, full of energy, talking, and laughing. They had books in their hands while my mind was occupied with thoughts of finding a restaurant for my lunch. I passed Manas Cinema, and because of its huge old building with many young boys and girls around, I mistook it for a university. After covering some distance, I entered a crowded café with many young men and women eating there. It was located on the main road lined with universities (Bishkek Humanities University, Kyrgyz Technical University, and Manas University); therefore, most of the visitors were students.

The short waitress asked me in a hurry in Russian what I wanted while her eyes were stuck on the other customers. "Chicken Burger," I replied. She became more attentive and repeated those words again, and my reply was the same, "Chicken Burger."

She shook her head, left me, and returned shortly with a colleague who was supposed to translate for her. Once again, I pronounced "Chicken Burger" and was confident enough that my problem would be solved this time. But the waitress showed such annoyance that I became doubtful about my language abilities. I looked around for any possible help, but nothing appeared to be available, so I tried a different approach. I acted like a hen clucking to make her understand what I wanted. After several attempts of imitating a hen flapping its wings, both of them understood what I wanted, and they said together with a smile "*koritsa.*" After some minutes, the first waitress came back with two chicken legs without the burger, and that was absolutely okay for me. Thus "*koritsa*" was the first Russian word I learned.

That experience reminded me of another story when one of my friends went to a shop to buy an ice-cream in Spain. The problem was that the female shopkeeper did not understand English and my friend did not understand Spanish. Eventually, he tried to make her understand with a gesture of licking the air with his tongue, which the lady misunderstood for some sexual act. He very nearly got himself in trouble for sexual harassment because the lady thought he wanted something else. But my imitation of a hen made the two waitresses laugh, and I was relieved that I not only got some chicken to eat but also brought laughter to some faces.

During this time, I had only those few, short explorations beyond going to the Academy and back to my accommodation. I still could not communicate with taxi drivers or shopkeepers because I did not understand the language of the city. My

Academy kept me busy with studies, but I was still curious to explore the city, and this one particular weekend, I planned to do just that.

Bishkek Park was the name I heard whenever I would ask my classmates for recommendations of local places to visit. I had developed quite a big and crowded picture in my mind with lots of play equipment, clean air, and grassy land. I went to a nearby taxi, standing on the main road and told the driver, "Bishkek Park," and showed him the digit 100 on my mobile as the possible fare, and he agreed.

As the taxi drove along Prospect Mira, I studied the passing view of busy shops and shopping centers, old public offices in cube-shaped buildings with their windows protruding constructed during the Soviet time, and residential buildings mostly old but a few new as well. After driving some distance, the taxi turned right and stopped in front of a big shopping mall. The driver pointed with his hand to get out. I was puzzled and thought he brought me to the wrong place, but when I saw Bishkek Park written with big bold letters on top of the mall, I realized that I was wrong, leaving me with no other choice but to visit that big shopping center.

Upon entering, I smelled a wave of perfumes and found the inside of the mall very attractive and lively, with lots of people busy shopping, hanging out, and enjoying their meals. There were shops of clothing, shoes, and jewelry on both sides. From my later visits, I learned that the products inside the shops were mostly Chinese and Turkish, but there were also European and American brand products.

Moving forward, toward the dead-end, there was a fast-food restaurant with a big fountain at the center in front of shops with a children's play area at its side. After completing my round-trip, I went up to the second floor on the escalator. The second floor also had shops with similar items for sale, and on the third floor, there were mostly Turkish restaurants, a cinema, and a play place or game zone for children. The fourth and top floor was a bowling club while the underground had a skating rink and some shops around. I enjoyed my time in the mall and looked for shops and restaurants where I thought I would want to shop and eat, but as it was my first time, I was confused as to which café to choose because they all looked very similar. Eventually, I randomly chose one, and it was easy to decide the food because the menu had photos of the dishes. I ordered *Iskender Kebab*.

After eating my food, I exited the mall to find that it was already dark outside. Right in front of the mall, three or four taxi drivers waited with their vehicles for the very last customers to come out. I noticed a few people were walking along the road-side, exhaling warm breath into the cold night air, and the traffic was also reduced.

I did not want to get a taxi to go home; instead I wanted to walk and see the night view of the city. Walking a few yards to the left was the Prospect Mira, and turning left again after walking a few steps was a coffee shop at the corner near the Russian Embassy with quite a good number of people inside. It was Sierra coffee, a fancy coffee place popular among foreigners and locals. So whenever people wanted to meet, the best place was that coffee house. People visited it for meetings, discussions, relaxing, and drinking coffee. Its walls were decorated with paintings and photos reflecting the traditional and tourist places of the country. In one corner, there was a world map on the wall with needles pinned from visitors representing their countries. I looked through it and found needles from almost every country. My country also had two needles pinned, and therefore I did not make any addition to it.

Not being a coffee drinker or addict, seeing so many coffee names like Americano, Latte, Cappuccino... on the board made me wonder which one to choose. The beautiful Russian waitress with her hair dyed red and wearing a black shirt with Sierra Coffee written in bold letters across it greeted me with her beautiful smile.

"How can I help you, Sir?"

"I want coffee."

"Which one, Americano, Latte...?" She pointed to the blackboard with many names of coffee written on it with different colors.

It was difficult for me to decide since most of the names on the board seemed unfamiliar to me. Seeing my confusion, she suggested, "I think coffee with milk will be okay."

"Yes, please."

She quickly entered the price of the coffee and gave me the

receipt. I paid for it, and the lady asked for my name, which she had to announce when the coffee was ready. After a couple of minutes, she called out my name, and I got my coffee. There were not many people in the café at this time, so many chairs were empty. I chose to sit near the glass from where I could see the view outside. A few people were there just to hang out while some students and foreigners were discussing their business stuff as well. It was a tasty coffee like *milk-chay*.

After finishing, I went outside and saw both *marshrutkas* and taxis. Although *marshrutka* was far cheaper than a taxi, I was not familiar with the transportation system and thus chose to take a taxi back to my apartment.

Besides the language barrier, food and toilet seats were some of the other problems I had to cope with. I also struggled with cooking because neither Iqbal nor I had any experience. We could only find sandwiches, burgers, and pizzas in restaurants and cafes, which were neither economical nor healthy. The Kyrgyz traditional food was good and similar to Afghan food, but I could not find them in every restaurant. Also, I did not know where we could find a good restaurant for traditional Kyrgyz food. At that time, I was only familiar with the Italian Dolce Vita Restaurant and Shashlik Café near our Academy. Luckily, I soon found King Burger on Akhunbaev Abaeva, a walk of about ten minutes from the Academy. King Burger was not the franchise of the American Burger King fast food chain but a restaurant owned by a Pakistani whose customers were mostly Indian and Pakistani students, and I began visiting it once or twice a week.

The toilet seats were different than the ones I was used to in Kabul where one would sit in a squat position, but the problem with toilets in Bishkek was that they were seat toilets. I was not familiar with how to use it. I used them in a squat position but this was full of risk. If I fell off its edges, I might have faced terrible results in the form of fracturing a bone. Later, I learned how to use them.

Inside View of Bishkek Park

My Neighborhood

After spending a month in the rented apartment, we (Daler, Firdavs, Iqbal, and I) decided to look for another apartment near the Academy where we could live together. Living together provided us with many advantages. We could study together, conduct academic discussions and also solve the issue of cooking. Everybody equally liked the idea as the language was the main problem for Iqbal and me while Daler and Firdavs were coming from the center by *marshrutka,* which always took a lot of their time.

Daler took the responsibility to talk with the agents in the real estate offices to find an apartment at an affordable price. After a couple of days, Daler found an apartment with two rooms and one big hall or lounge with a monthly rent of $400. When we went to see its condition and location, it was not worth $400. It did not have any furniture, kitchen equipment, or beds. The old building lacked a main security lock, and the rooms' locks were mostly broken. Iqbal and I showed our unwillingness, but Daler insisted that it was not easy to find a good place in such a short time near the Academy. Unwillingly, we eventually agreed, but the next problem to solve was who would stay in the rooms and who would share the lounge.

Firdavs did not like the place and withdrew from the very beginning, leaving Daler, Iqbal, and I to choose. Daler announced that he had a girlfriend, so he should get a room. We respected his situation, and that left Iqbal and me to debate over the remaining bedroom. Unfortunately for me, Iqbal had already done his homework and came up with tens of reasons why he deserved the room. Thus, I had to stay in the lounge. Later, we found out that Daler had no girlfriend, and it was his tactic to get the room.

The landlady who promised to bring all the necessary things came up with old beds, furniture, and kitchen equipment. As our classes had already begun, wasting our time on finding such things was not a good idea. We compromised and adjusted to using whatever we had.

I was greatly relieved after the problem of accommodation was solved. However, living in the lounge had many disadvantages. The main one was that I was always disturbed by the movements of my colleagues. Whether they were going to and from the kitchen, toilet, bathroom, or outside, I was disturbed because they had to pass through the lounge. There was one advantage, however, for a lazy person like me. Whenever they would start moving around in the mornings in preparation for the Academy, I would be awakened.

As it turned out, some of the reasons we had decided to live together did not become a practical reality. Daler was already familiar with the city because he had studied for his bachelor's degree from the AUCA. He therefore spent the majority of his time outside of the apartment with his friends. Iqbal and I, being new in the city, would stay home, but we did not agree about cooking as neither of us had any experience. Sometimes, when one of us would give it a try, the result would be so annoying with either too much oil, not properly cooked food, or over-cooked food. Finally, we started relying on eggs.

One day I switched on my laptop and started chatting with one of my friends, Sayed Mohammad, after a very long time. When he learned that I had come to Bishkek, he told me that he had spent a lot of time in Bishkek and had many friends there. He had a car business in Bishkek some years ago. He took my mobile number, and after some minutes I got a call from a person by the name of Arif, who was my friend's business partner in Bishkek. After a brief talk with Arif, we agreed to meet that same evening.

After I told him the address, Arif came to the main road, Akhunbaev, and he took me to the center of the city. He was a short man with a dark brown complexion and was responsible for Sayed's Toyota Company in Bishkek. They imported used cars from Japan and sold them in Bishkek. Some Pakistani businessmen and students were making a good profit out of that. A businessman would import cars from Japan, and even before arrival, the students would buy vehicles they would later sell. On each car they would make a profit somewhere between $500 to $1000. The demand for Japanese cars rose because they were cheaper, newer, and their spare parts readily available. That business worked really well from 2006 to 2014, but later, it went down due to an increase in taxes. When it was no longer profitable, people started looking for other businesses.

The sun was setting, and the time for *Maghrib* prayer was getting nearer. We went to the Central Mosque to offer prayer. It was one of the biggest mosques in Bishkek. After offering prayer, outside the mosque, some Chechens with long red beards and tough, strong bodies approached us and started talking to Arif. Arif introduced me, and they were very happy after learning that I was from Afghanistan. Giving me a thorough look, the tallest among them asked me why I had no beard. His mood was to ask some more questions and get acquainted, but it was getting late. Later I came to know that because of their activities like spreading radicalization and Islamic extremism, encouraging people to fight in Syria and Iraq, and much more in and outside the country, the government was continually keeping a close eye on them.

From there onward, we went to Ala Too Ploshad and took some photos. Arif insisted I dine with him at the restaurant, but I had classes the next day, so I needed to go home. He was very friendly and told me to call him without hesitation if I needed any help.

People gathered for Friday Prayer in Central Mosque

From my Academy, moving west on Akhunbaev street, a large street dissected it northward. To the right side of the street, there were four-story residential apartments while to the left were streets lined with buildings, both residential and offices. After passing three blocks of apartments, the next small path to the right led to another series of apartments. The last building had the number 44 written with bold black paint on its exterior sidewall and was my new home. My apartment was on the third floor. It was an old building and the entrance gate did not have a lock, so it stayed open all the time. The paint on the exterior walls was peeling and weathered, and most of the bricks were visible. The balconies were mostly filled with useless stuff with their fences broken. In front of our building, there were three or four old trash bins. Each night these bins would be filled with trash, and early in the morning, the municipality vehicles would come to take them. Like every other apartment, at the front of the building, there was a small area for children to play. Opposite to our building was a new building, and the area in between was concrete, where children usually played football or skated. The distance between the Academy and my new apartment was about a five-minute walk. There was also a shortcut through an area with trees, a play spot for children, a social center for *babushkas*, and a parking place, and most of the time, I would use that shorter route.

My neighborhood was old but calm and quiet. From morning until late afternoon or sometimes evening, I stayed at the Academy, while only on weekends, I stayed home. I rarely saw most of my neighbors, although I did meet a few. On the second floor, an old lady lived alone with tens of cats and dogs. Whenever she opened her door, an unpleasant smell would waft out and spread all over the building. That smell was terrible and sometimes quite unbearable. Her army of cats and dogs would also accompany her wherever she went. She talked either to herself or to her army while scratching her unkempt white hair. I would always see her wearing a long dirty blue coat, which once would have been a fashionable coat in the city. The neighbor next to the old lady complained about her because the disgusting smell would enter into neighboring homes and linger twenty-four hours a day. Luckily, we were on the third floor—one floor above. Still, it was so bad that while passing through the second floor, the smell of my cologne would vanish. There was no way to escape or avoid the unpleasantness.

The Domkom also lived on the second floor. She was a kind lady and had a son named Max. Whenever she wanted to communicate with us, when Daler was not around, her son Max would translate for her. Max's knowledge of English was limited to *hello, how are you?* and *goodbye*, but still, he was always enthusiastic about translation. Max had a freckle-faced friend, Anthon, who sported a ponytail, and sometimes they both would play in the concrete area in front of the new building. Unlike Max, Anthon was skinny. They had other friends as well, and they would play football together in the late afternoon hours. Sometimes I would manage to get out and watch them play. Anthon knew how to skate and had a skateboard, which he shared with his friend, Max.

I also became a friend, and sometimes I would buy them ice cream, which they would rarely accept. Here it is not the tradition among children to accept gifts or anything from strangers. Unlike the Western world, communicating with them is not considered suspicious because interaction with children is always perceived in the sense of love and affection. On occasion, I would give them money too, a practice which I stopped after knowing that it was not considered good in their culture. I remember one day when I was giving Anthon some money, his father appeared in the street and Anthon disappeared without accepting it.

On the park route, I also enjoyed the social center of *babushkas*. I sometimes had the opportunity to communicate with *privet* and *kak dela*. Most of the *babushkas* talked and gossiped there while some also came with their grandchildren and pets. In Kyrgyzstan, the family holds an important position in a person's social life. Most of the families irrespective of their ethnicities live together, and parents and grandparents have a respectable place. I often saw grandmas along with their grandchildren walking or shopping. Due to Western influence, homes for the aged ones are becoming popular, but a grandma and a grandpa still have a special place in their societies, and this tradition is stricter in rural areas.

A snowy view of my Neighborhood

A snowy view of my Neighborhood

While passing through that shortcut I would come across an old damp house covered with bushes and trees that looked eerie and mysterious. Over the space of a few days, I noticed a frail old lady always standing outside the door of her house. I would usually ignore her but watch her out of the corner of my eye as I passed by. To me, she looked scary and suspicious. Sometimes she would beckon with her hand for me to come to her, but since I was new in the city and I didn't want to be cut into pieces and disposed of in a dumpster somewhere, like in a Hollywood horror movie, I would never comply. However, I began to wonder if perhaps she might need help or maybe wanted to tell me something.

One particular day, it was a different case, and that evening when she waved me over as I was returning, I dared to go to her. When I approached her, she said something that I did not understand, but she gestured for me to come inside and eat something. I accepted. It was almost dark when I entered her home, which was quiet and gloomy. The passage was narrow and dark, with its walls cracked and damaged, giving the impression that no one had lived there for quite a long time. The door to the living room opened with a creak, and I entered the dimly lit room.

The golden tooth of the old lady sparkled as she smiled and gestured with her hand for me to sit as she went to the kitchen. I must admit to being nervous as I glanced around at the walls, the door, and furniture, which further increased my fear because it all looked as though it came from centuries before.

There was a wooden table in the corner with a dusty 'Pirates of the Caribbean' ship lying on it along with a wooden chair at its front. The couches in the middle of the room had thick layers of dust all around, as well. I cleaned some dust from a couch and made some space to sit. The walls of the room were bare except for a picture of a scary skeleton holding a cigarette in its mouth. It nearly scared me to death when a black cat suddenly fell on the couch opposite me with a loud and extended *meow!*

After a while, the old lady brought tea in a very old kettle and shouted, "Mini Mini." At that moment, I felt a little relieved. I assumed other people also lived there and "Mini" was perhaps her daughter or granddaughter, and whoever it was would appear at any moment to come to pour tea for me. But that relief was short-lived as a small monkey soon entered the room, who first hugged the lady, then pulled the cat's tail. The cat reacted by letting out a loud meow and left the room with its tail raised in an angry huff. Mini poured tea into my cup and then started concerning me with her gestures and showing me her teeth. The old lady went back to the kitchen and reappeared with a platter of rice and meat. But before I started eating, for some reason, I looked down at her feet and noticed that they were deformed and inverted.

Suddenly, I understood the situation and realized I was in the wrong place. My heart started beating fast, and my body was shivering with fear. I was trying to remain normal and not let her know what I had seen. She passed me the platter while I was thinking about how to escape. Terrified and embarrassed, when I tried to take some rice, my spoon touched a hard substance in the middle of the plate, and as soon as I took it out, I was shocked to see that it was a human palm.

I bolted up out of my seat and started running toward the door. The old lady jumped up and tried to catch me. I ran through the narrow hallway I had come through, and she threw the palm, which started to chase me.

As soon as I got out of the house, I continued running toward my apartment. I ran through bushes and small trees, and whenever I looked back, I saw the palm was still following me. I ran fast, and it ran faster, and was quickly catching up to me. About the time the palm was closing in on me, it extended itself to catch me. And then I woke up.

Scared and sweating, I looked all around me, not sure it was actually a dream. I switched on the light and drank a glass of water and sat upright, still scared. I looked at my watch and saw it was 3 a.m. I checked for Daler and Iqbal in their rooms, and they were both sleeping soundly. Feeling calmer, I went back to my bed and, after some minutes, fell asleep again.

A page from my diary

"Today, I had a narrow escape from a very tragic incident. It was late afternoon, and I was sitting on my bed working on an assignment when suddenly I saw flames outside the window of my room. Reacting quickly and horrified, I jumped out of bed thinking the flames had come from the kitchen, which was attached to the lounge where I was staying. But after checking the kitchen, I realized that the flames were coming from the window of the stairwell between the second and third floors.

Daler was not home, and I shouted at Iqbal to get ready for an escape. Following my instincts, I quickly gathered up my educational documents, money, and laptop. In the meantime,

Iqbal came out of his room, totally unaware of the situation. When I told him what was going on, he quickly got his laptop, and we both left the apartment to save ourselves.

Outside the apartment, all we could see was smoke and fumes. When we reached the second floor, our *Domkom,* and her son, Max, were putting out the fire with buckets of water they would bring from their apartment. When Max saw us escaping, he screamed, *"Ogan ogan…"* to draw our attention. But being terrified we couldn't see any other option but to escape. After reaching the first floor, we realized that the situation was not that bad so we returned to the second floor and helped Max and his mother to extinguish the fire. After a few minutes, the fire was put out, but by this time, the smoke had already saturated the interior, making it appear as though the entire building had caught fire.

Later, we learned that a drug-addict had lit the fire by burning some papers and cartons on the stair landing between the second and third floors. As the window of the stairwell opening outside was near the window of my lounge, within seconds, its flames approached the neighboring windows. There was a serious risk that if we had not put out the fire on time, the gas lines passing through the walls of the building carrying gas to different apartments could have caught fire.

When I came back to my room, it was covered in black soot from the smoke, which it took me all evening to clean. After that incident, the *Domkom* started collecting money to install a lock to ensure the security of the building. But unfortunately, we did not see the lock as long as we lived there.

"Happy Ending"

Unlike Kabul, the hairdressers in Bishkek were mostly females. I asked my colleagues from the Politics Group where I could get a haircut, and they showed me a hair salon situated near the Academy.

When I entered the saloon, the lady administrator stood up and showed me the way to the main hall where four beautiful ladies were busy manicuring, hair-dying, hair cutting, etc. The owner of the salon came forward and greeted me in English. She seemed between forty and forty-five years old. First, she gave me a clean white towel and took me to another chair with a washbasin on its top. After I adjusted my head into the basin, she opened the warm water. I felt quite relaxed as she started massaging the shampoo into my hair. It was the first time I felt female hands on my body.

After washing my hair, she showed me to another chair in front of a big mirror attached to the wall. She started the haircut in such a focused way that I felt like a celebrity. My previous experiences had been pretty much nothing like this. They included no taking care of hygiene, no prior or post-cutting washing of hair, no smiles… I even remember one time when I protested to the barber in Peshawar for using a used razor, he replied, "I have used this only for one person before you."

But Bishkek was very different. During the haircut, she checked my hair directly and also through the mirror to see if it was right. She would even seek my satisfaction by asking if I was happy with the way it looked. After the haircut, she took me once again to the wash-basin and washed my hair once more.

After I came back to my seat, she asked me. "Where are you from?"

"Afghanistan," I answered, almost whispering.

"Ah, I worked in Afghanistan for five years at the Bagram Airbase."

I realized then the reason behind her good English. The

American Base she referred to was located in Parwan Province of Afghanistan.

"Okay, so how did you find Afghanistan?" I asked.

"It was good, but we were not allowed to go out of the base. I used to work as a hairdresser for the military personnel only."

She again checked if there was any further adjustment needed, and then she used a hair-dryer to dry my hair. When that was done, she used a gel to give me a good style. I had not received such a luxurious haircut in my entire life and was curious about what would happen next. She put both hands on my shoulders and said: "We also have a massage facility here. If you want a massage to relax, we have a very good masseur."

The words "massage" and "relax" had a strange effect on me. I was at once aroused and reminded of the stories of my doctor friend who would go to Thailand on a business trip and return with "massage stories" that had the "happy endings," and these were the most interesting ones. All my other colleagues would listen to his stories so eagerly, and the effects were different on different colleagues, and in the same way, the reactions would also come out differently. That day, those stories freshened my mind once again. In the mirror, in front of me, I could see girls working, and I began trying to guess which one would be the massage expert. I was lost in my reverie when the mild tone of the hairdresser brought me back to reality.

"Do you want to try it?" She held the chair with her right hand, bent her upper body down, and looked into my eyes. Once again, I was feeling a female very close, and I accepted her proposal. There was a small door at the end of the hall. We entered through the door and down a narrow corridor to another room. The room looked much like an operation theatre with two beds separated by a blue curtain. There were some bottles of oil and lubricants on a small table in a corner.

"I will send you the "massagist" in five minutes," She said as she left the room, and I sat on the table wondering which of the pretty women I had seen earlier would come. Would it be the one sitting in the corner with the red dress or the other who was checking her mobile. Either of them would be acceptable to me. I was happy and watching the door when a tall, muscular Russian entered the room and said something in Russian. I was not expecting him in that prohibited area and felt embarrassed when he spoke. He repeated his words again, and when he realized that I did not understand what he was saying, he went out and came back with the hairdresser.

"This is Alexander, one of the best massagists in Bishkek." She said those words firmly, I believe, to convince me to get ready for the massage.

"Is he the only one working?" I was trying to make her understand that I did not want a massage from a male. All my colorful imagination faded away after she said, "Yes," and I started thinking of how I could get myself out of this situation. They did not have any "Natasha" for a massage and I did not want a massage from Alexander. I made the excuse of misunderstanding and left the salon.

Later, when I visited some other hair salons, I met a couple of hairdressers who had worked either in the American bases in Afghanistan or the Manas Airbase in Bishkek. They told me that most of the ladies working in those bases either as hairdressers or helpers were from Kyrgyzstan and were earning good money. A handful of the American soldiers in the bases inside Afghanistan or Manas Airbase had married Kyrgyz ladies and took them to the U.S., but the withdrawal of American forces from Afghanistan resulted in closing their bases. This lead to the shrinkage of business opportunities in Afghanistan. It not only left many Afghans jobless but also left the Kyrgyz associated with them unemployed.

In the same way, Manas Airbase founded in 2001 was working as a transit center for the U.S. military personnel[2] and had provided many job and business opportunities to the people of Kyrgyzstan. There were reports that upon each take-off and landing, $10,000 was paid to the Kyrgyz government that went mostly into corrupt pockets. But after the closure of Manas Airbase in 2014, there were neither of those opportunities, nor Americans. From then onward, the job or business market was not very good, and those connected to Manas Airbase were struggling to find jobs in the local market.

Among them, those who had already made some money started small businesses or bought properties. The hairdressers working in the American bases were earning $20 to $30 per haircut, and most of the time, along with a generous tip, they could make as much as $50 or more. Those ladies started working in an ordinary hair salon in Bishkek, charging no more than $5 per client for a haircut. Thanks to ladies whose manicure and hair-dying charges would help, they were able to meet their living expenses.

After the haircut, I went home. I was in the mood to spend my weekend watching an Indian movie. Indian movies were very popular in Central Asia, and can be watched with the translation to Russian and local languages. During the Soviet reign, when American movies were banned, people enjoyed watching Indian movies. In the 1980s, the Indian actor, Mithun Chakraborty was their favorite, and those days it was Shahrukh Khan. They liked the songs of the movies, and without knowing the meaning, they could even sing some of them. The dominant aspect they liked in Indian movies was their happy endings wherein the end, the actor and actress got united despite passing through difficult circumstances and lived a happy life. I was also in search of a movie that could flavor my weekend and possibly had a "Happy Ending" to it.

[2]Joshua Kucera, "U.S. Checked in Central Asia", The New York Times, accessed Nov.17, 2017 (Nov.04, 2013),
http://www.nytimes.com/2013/11/05/opinion/us-checked-in-central-asia.html?rref=collection%2Ftimestopic%2FTransit%20Center%20at%20Manas

Valentine's Day
with Doctors

An unknown number appeared on my mobile.

"Hello, I am Tariq, Sayed's friend. He gave me your mobile number and asked me to call you and find out if you need anything since you are new in the city."

Before I spoke to thank him, he invited me to dinner. Because of his emphasizing tone, I accepted the invitation and was overjoyed by his generosity and kindness.

In the evening, he picked me up at the Akhunbaev Road. He was sitting in his car near the *Narudni* with its front lights flashing on and off as he told me he would do over the phone. Tariq was of medium height, brown-complexioned, and was from the district Dir of Khyber Pakhtunkhwa Province of Pakistan. He had covered his head with a very warm hat, and later he told me that he had a hair transplant.

Like many Afghans visiting any foreign country for the first time, I was eager to visit a disco or nightclub, but I could not make that request at the very first meeting. So, I sat with him silently in his car as he drove along the streets of the city, and I watched the changing scene while he chatted and provided me with information about each area as we passed through it.

After driving some distance, he parked the car in front of an area with big shops and shopping malls somewhere in the downtown. All the shopping malls, shops, and cafes were crowded with people, and the colorful gift packages, red pillows, and balloons in the shape of hearts were visible from their transparent glasses. I followed Tariq to a place where young men and women were dancing to the loud beats of the music. Inside it was partially dark, and the colorful lights revolving in different directions made me think that it was a disco.

"Thank you very much for bringing me here. You heard the voice of my heart without me telling you."

41

"Well, actually, this is a famous Pakistani pizza restaurant," he replied.

I had obviously misunderstood the place, but anyway, it was not less than a disco. I was excited and checking out each customer, mostly ladies loaded with heavy makeup from head to toe. Inside the restaurant was also decorated with red balloons with 14 on them, and I remembered it was Valentine's Day.

This day is celebrated in most parts of the world nowadays on February 14 by showing love and affection to each other. In countries like Afghanistan and Kyrgyzstan, not many people know about this day. Being a Western celebration, this day also found its way to Kyrgyzstan under Western influence but is only confined to the capital among the elite or upper-middle class. Similarly, in Afghanistan, very few people, specifically only the youth who have been to foreign countries, know about that day.

I watched young couples enjoying their happy moments in different ways. "Please do not stare at people as they mind it," Tariq said. "They do not like the eyes of foreigners on them." He looked uncomfortable when he said these words. Understanding the situation, I tried to limit my spying to watching them from the corner of my eye because I could not stop myself from looking at them altogether.

After eating the spicy pizza, Tariq took me to visit his friends living in a students' hostel. It was a dark street lined with apartments on both sides. He parked the car to one side, and there were three big buildings to the left. Two were hostels for students studying in Kyrgyz State Medical Academy and the third one, a medical center. We entered the first building (an older five-story building), and Tariq went inside a small room with transparent glass where an older chubby lady with an angry look was checking those crossing through a rusty old Soviet waist-high turnstile making a creaking sound whenever someone would pass. After a five minute chat, Tariq waved his hand asking me to enter that room with him. The woman looked at me with an angry expression on her face and said something to Tariq. Tariq asked me to show her my identity card. The lady checked my ID card, looked at me bizarrely, and Tariq told me to follow him after getting her approval.

From the dirty old stairs and stained walls, we went to the

fourth floor where Tariq's friends were living. That building totally represented India and Pakistan in the Central Asian atmosphere. With the smell of *masala* and spicy food, the Indian and Pakistani students walking and talking, I felt like I was somewhere in Pakistan or India.

To the right end of the corridor, we entered a room and saw two guys completely focused on their smartphones, while a tall guy greeted us first was busy preparing *milk-chay*. The two serious looking guys were Liaqat and Khurshed, who stayed busy again with their mobiles after greeting us, while the tall skinny guy, Hasan engaged with Tariq. When the *chay* was ready, a short guy with a long red beard entered the room. After he came in, everybody started talking to him, and Hasan began serving the *chay*.

He was Kiramat and was one year senior to the others. He was a religious person, and besides studies, he was also involved in religious activities as part of *Tablighi Jamaat*. Besides other Islamic countries, this group was also active in Kyrgyzstan and would travel to different parts of the country to deliver the message of Islam. Kiramat being part of that group had a respectable place both among the students and his peers. He always dressed up religiously and closely kept eyes on his friends not to get involved in any un-Islamic activity like drinking alcohol or keeping relationships without getting married. He even interfered if he found any of his friends or colleagues involved in suspicious activities. Thus he had an essential role in keeping his friends and colleagues on the right track. They all belonged to the Buner District of Khyber Pakhtunkhwa.

During our discussion, they asked me about my purpose for visiting, the nature of my scholarship, and the studies in the Academy. I also discovered that many Pakistani and Indian students were studying medicine in Kyrgyzstan. These were the future doctors who would work for the wellbeing of humans, and interestingly, I met them on Valentine's Day.

While drinking *chay*, a skinny man with dark brown coloring entered the room. He looked like a drug-addict. He greeted all with a verbal *salam* and sat on a wooden chair in the corner of the room. Hasan served him with a cup of *chay*. His name was Asal Shah. During a very brief time with him, approximately five minutes, he asked me some very straight questions like how long had I been staying in Bishkek and whether I had a girlfriend. After hearing my reply, Asal Shah appeared relieved and advised me to stay away from girls in Bishkek. He was about to prolong the discussion when I interrupted that I would have my classes in the morning and therefore I needed to go. Asal Shah is a very special character, and we will meet him again later in the book, so you'll want to keep on reading.

After a few days, I again received a call from Tariq. He had gotten married to a Kyrgyz lady and was leaving for Pakistan with her. He wanted to introduce me to some of his other friends. I made an excuse because I had some deadlines for my assignments. I wished him a safe journey and happy life.

Chapter 2

Kyrgyzstan at a Glance

Kyrgyzstan is a Central Asian country that came into being in 1991 after the disintegration of the USSR. Bishkek is its capital located in the north of the country. Founded in 1878, its original name was Pishpek. During the Soviet Union period, its name was changed to Frunze. The Frunze name was given after the Bolshevik military leader Mikhail Frunze. In 1991, Frunze was changed to Bishkek by the Kyrgyz parliament. The city is located at about 800 meters above sea level and is surrounded by Ala Too ranges, which further extend to the Tian Shan Mountains. This city is the administrative unit of Chuy Province[3]. Bishkek City has all the facilities of a modern city but at cheaper rates. The city represents the Western, Soviet, and Kyrgyz styles. The old buildings, monuments, and statues give it a Soviet color, while bars, discos, restaurants, and shopping malls give it a Western swing and Kyrgyz babushkas and elderly men wearing kalpak give it a Kyrgyz flavor. Thus in that small city, one can find the Kyrgyz, Soviet and Western features providing colorful attractions. It is a small and clean city with a good transportation system all around. In Bishkek City, people mostly live in apartments. Apartment buildings vary in size ranging from five stories to even eighteen floors. All the apartments have electricity, gas, and a heating system. The monthly cost of electricity and gas is also very low— 200 to 300 som per month while the heating system in winter costs from 1000 to 1500 som per month.

About 90% of the country is mountainous; the Tian Shan Mountains make up a large part of its mountain ranges. This country has all four seasons. During winter the temperature drops below the freezing point reaching as low as -25°C in the northern parts of the country, while in summer the temperature rises to as much as 45°C.

Kyrgyzstan is famous for its natural beauty with snowy

mountains, green pastures, vast lakes, and flowing rivers. Its clean air, sound and secure environment, diverse and unique culture, and cheap living expenses attract tourists from all over the world. However it still has to do more in attracting tourists as most people do not know about it. Kyrgyzstan is a country comprised of diverse ethnicities. Besides the Kyrgyz majority, the other ethnicities living are Uzbeks, Russians, Dungans, Uyghurs, Kazakhs, Turks, Ukrainians, Koreans, Germans, Tatars, Tajiks, and others. Russian and Kyrgyz are the official languages of the country.

The total population of Kyrgyzstan is almost equal to the population of Kabul Province—5.5 to 6 million. About 75% are Muslims, 20% Orthodox Christians, and the rest belonging to other religions[4].

Kyrgyzstan is a country of natural beauty, making it very attractive to tourists. It has the biggest natural walnut forest in Arslanbob, Sulayman Too (Sulayman Mountain) in Osh, Issyk Kul Lake in Issyk Kul Province, and Jailoos (pastures), mountains and waterfalls. Its diverse multi-ethnicity, unique tradition, and proud history further beautify the country. About the beauty of the country, Philip Shishkin writes in his book Restless Valley that according to a legend, the Kyrgyz were asleep when God was distributing lands to the peoples of the Earth. When the Kyrgyz woke up landless, they pleaded with God to give them at least something. God took pity on the helpless Kyrgyz and gave them a patch of land that he had initially planned to keep for himself. And that is the reason that you see it as a piece of heaven surrounded by mountains. Kyrgyzstan shares its border with three other Central Asian countries [Kazakhstan, Tajikistan and Uzbeksitan] and China. The famous Issyk Kul Lake appears like a large blue spot giving it the look of a tear on the map[5].

Kyrgyzstan is a small country and not many foreigners live in this country because of the lack of economic and business opportunities it offers. A handful of businessmen, mostly Turks, Russians, Chinese, and few Indians and Pakistanis, have their businesses in Kyrgyzstan. Most of the people around the world do not know about this undercover jewel on earth; therefore, a large number of tourists are from Russia and Kazakhstan. They usually visit the country during the summer to enjoy the beauty of Issyk

Kul. The number of tourists from Western countries is very little compared to the natural tourist opportunities the country provides.

Students make up a large percentage of foreigners, mainly from Kazakhstan, Turkey, China, and Afghanistan but the number of Indian and Pakistani students is in the thousands. There were approximately ten thousand Indians and two thousand Pakistani students studying mainly medicine at Kyrgyz State Medical University, International School of Medicine, and Kyrgyz-Russian Slavic University in Bishkek, Osh State Medical University (Osh City), Jalalabad Medical University (Jalalabad City) and Asian Medical Institute (Kant City). The stories I heard of bringing the foreign students to Kyrgyzstan were full of greed for the sole purpose of earning money. Some contractors brought students to Kyrgyzstan, took their money, and disappeared. Some of the students were admitted to a university that did not have any legal recognition. Baacha told me that the promises made by his agent in Pakistan were all lies.

"The agent charged double for everything, which I later realized, but I could not do anything about it."

But some contractors considered both profit and students' priorities. Let's take the case of the International School of Medicine (ISM)—a private university hosting thousands of Indians and Pakistani students. The Indian contractor or agent of ISM had arranged a separate hostel, transportation, food, and accommodation facilities for the students he brought from India, and thus, the number of Indian students was growing each year.

The other problem that foreigners, specifically the Indians and Pakistani students, faced was the street crime. Easily identifiable from their looks, color, and places where they lived, the criminals attacked them and snatched their mobiles and money. Almost every Indian and Pakistani I met shared the story of theft, physical harassment or robbery. The logic behind this was that the local criminals knew that these students possessed money because they got their money in large amounts from their families for their fees and living expenses. Although the level of crime has gotten better compared to the past, still possible risks exist.

Overall, Kyrgyzstan was a peaceful country, but sometimes one could face theft or the incident of snatching mobiles or wallets especially in late night hours. The wallet snatching or theft could also happen somewhere in the evening in the street while pickpocketing can happen in marshrutka or bazaars.

Kyrgyzstan is a Central Asian country sandwiched between important countries in the region. Due to its geostrategic importance, it has become the focal point of superpowers and regional players. China not only shares its border but is an important economic partner of Kyrgyzstan. It aims to develop both political and economic relations with Central Asian countries through Silk Road economic projects focusing on political cooperation, international trade, and investment. Energy trade is also one of the important factors of Chinese interest in the region.

Moreover, Kyrgyzstan is part of One Belt One Road (OBOR), which aims to construct roads and highways, pipelines and logistics infrastructure. Through this route, goods will be exported from China to Europe, Caucasus, and the Middle East, while the gas from Turkmenistan and Uzbekistan will flow to China. In 2014, out of a total of $211 million in foreign direct investments in Kyrgyzstan, the Chinese share was $108 million. China also provided grants and loans of $274.4 million and $1.8 billion respectively[6]. By expanding its economic activities in Kyrgyzstan, China wants to be influential as a crucial economic partner. Dordoy, the biggest bazaar of the country, is full of Chinese goods, and from there, those goods are re-exported to other Central Asian countries. China is also deeply concerned about the growing radicalization and militancy in Kyrgyzstan, posing a threat to the bordering Xinxiang Province having a majority of Muslim Uyghur population. Moreover, a large number of Chinese marry the local girls, get Kyrgyz citizenship, buy properties, and expand their businesses.

Unlike the Chinese, ethnic Russians started leaving Kyrgyzstan for Russia after the Soviet Union broke down, and it continues even now. Russians do not seem interested in staying in Kyrgyzstan. I had become acquainted with a few Russians during my studies, and most of them left for Russia by the end of my studies. The reasons they gave me were the poor economic opportunities that the country provided. In order to be employed in the government, international organizations and the private sector, one needs to know the Kyrgyz language, which made the

Russian populace ineligible.

The USSR once ruled Central Asia entirely, but after its disintegration, the Russian Federation was struggling to restore the economy. After Vladimir Putin came into power, Russia began developing its political, economic and diplomatic relations with Central Asia. The American war against terrorism, followed by establishing Manas Airbase, made the Russians setting up their military base in Kant a few miles away from Bishkek in 2003. Although Russia supported the U.S. war on terrorism in Afghanistan, it later put pressure on Kyrgyzstan to close down Manas Airbase until it finally did close in 2014. Last year, the Kyrgyz President Almazbek Atambaev even suggested another Russian base in the southern part of the country[7]. Russia's growing interest in the country is not one-sided, and Kyrgyzstan also sees Russia as its important strategic partner. I could not understand the Russian strategy toward the region, and largely it seemed like a responsive strategy against the developments by U.S. and China.

The U.S., although present thousands of miles away from Kyrgyzstan, marked its physical presence with the war against terrorism in Afghanistan by opening Manas Airbase in Bishkek. Using soft power is also the American priority to influence local society. The American University of Central Asia (AUCA) founded in the early 1990s, was not only providing quality education opportunities to the students of Kyrgyzstan and other Central Asian countries, but also educating them about democratic values, human rights, freedom of speech and more. The American presence aims to strengthen the democracy in the country while its military presence declined considerably after the closure of Manas Airbase in 2014. Hundreds of Western NGOs are working in Kyrgyzstan with the motive to work for human rights, democracy, and the rule of law.

After the withdrawal of American forces and the closure of Manas Airbase, the relationships between both countries sort of cooled down, but the rise of radicalization, militancy, drug-trafficking, and illegal human movements have compelled the U.S. to stay active in Central Asian politics. All three superpowers (China, Russia, and the U.S.) focus on maintaining their presence in the region not only because of the rivalry against one another but also to root out some of the shared problems like militancy, drug-trafficking, and corruption.

Turkey is another important country for Kyrgyzstan from both economic and political points of view. Both countries not only share the common historical, cultural, and linguistic roots, but they have the same ancestral origins too. During the last couple of years, Turkey has been trying to get an influential position in Central Asia. Besides the economic and diplomatic relationships, Turkey has been focusing on the soft power strategy. Turkish schools and the prestigious Manas University are serving a pivotal role in providing quality education to Kyrgyz students. Moreover, Turkey also facilitated the exchange of students, as well as teaching staff for enhancing their capacities[8]. Turks have been involved in establishing huge businesses in Kyrgyzstan, and most of the big shopping centers in the city belong to them.

India is also eager to set up its economic and diplomatic relationships with Central Asia, and Kyrgyzstan is one among them where the Indian interest has lately grown considerably. Kyrgyzstan is not only hosting thousands of Indian students, but it also got India's attention for investment purposes. Kyrgyz landscapes provide a fantastic opportunity for Indian tourists as well as the Bollywood filmmakers to shoot their films at much cheaper rates.

Furthermore, Kyrgyzstan shares its border with three of the Central Asian countries, with the exception of Turkmenistan. The northern neighbor Kazakhstan is an important country enriched with natural resources like oil, gas, coal, and other precious minerals. Kyrgyz and Kazakh are considered brothers living in two different countries, therefore their people are very close to each other. Both of the countries are members of important regional treaties like CSTO, SCO, Customs Union, and others.

Tajikistan and Uzbekistan are the two southern neighbors, and both countries have their own importance in terms of trade, water and border management, and regional cooperation. On the one hand, there exists a window of opportunity to be established with these two countries; on the other hand, there are also some issues like growing radicalization, drug-trafficking, and corruption threatening these three countries. Ferghana Valley, present in

Tajikistan, Kyrgyzstan, and Uzbekistan, is considered an important geostrategic position.

Kyrgyzstan occupies an important geostrategic, transit, economic, and political position in Central Asia. It is the only democracy in the region, and it is moving ahead very carefully not to challenge any super or regional power. Therefore, it should be very careful in keeping the right balance between those players in order not to provoke anyone's interest or worries if it is to shine as a prosperous, democratic country.

Kyrgyzstan does not possess hydro-carbon resources, but it can use its hydropower energy for booming its economic prosperity. CASA-1000 is an important energy trade initiative connecting Central Asia with South Asia, where electricity from Kyrgyzstan and Tajikistan will be exported to Afghanistan and Pakistan. Despite its movement toward development, it is also facing problems like drug-trafficking, religious extremism, and border disputes. Moreover, weak institutions, corruption, and poor human rights records are threats to the country.

[3]"Bishkek city", Oriental Express Central Asia, accessed May 20, 2016, http://www.kyrgyzstan.orexca.com/bishkek_kyrgyzstan.shtml
[4]The World Factbook, Kyrgyzstan, CIA, (May 17, 2016), accessed May 20, 2016,
https://www.cia.gov/library/publications/the-world-factbook/geos/kg.html
[5]Philip Shishkin, Restless Valley, Yale University Press, New Haven and London (2013) P.4
[6]Dinara Taldybayeva, "Prospects for China-Kyrgyzstan Economic Relations in the Framework of the Silk Road Economic Belt Project", HKTDC (March 28, 2017), accessed Oct.14, 2017, http://china-trade-research.hktdc.com/business-news/article/The-Belt-and-Road-Initiative/Prospects-for-China-Kyrgyzstan-Economic-Relations-in-the-Framework-of-the-Silk-Road-Economic-Belt-Project/obor/en/1/1X000000/1X0A9JIX.htm
[7]Catherine Putz, "What About that Proposed Second Russian Base in Kyrgyzstan?", The Diplomat, (March 07, 2018), accessed March 25, 2018,
https://thediplomat.com/2018/03/what-about-that-proposed-second-russian-base-in-kyrgyzstan/
[8]Dinara Murzaeva, "Kyrgyzstan-Turkey Relations: Cooperation in Political and Educational spheres", Review of European Studies, Vol.6,

No.3 (2014), accessed Dec. 22, 2017,
http://www.ccsenet.org/journal/index.php/res/article/view/39511/218
96

Nowruz in Bishkek

A Pakistani went to Norway and applied for asylum, representing himself as an Afghan. Being well-prepared, he answered all of the questions correctly but was struck by a final deadly question.

"Tell us, what do you know about Nowruz?"

"Nowruz was a very good man, and he fought very bravely against the Soviet forces," the Pakistani replied. The following day he was deported.

But here, I am talking about the Nowruz, the New Year, celebrated in many countries like Afghanistan, Azerbaijan, Iran, Central Asia, and some Gulf countries, along with some parts of India and Pakistan. The word Nowruz literally means "New Day" in the Persian language and is the New Year believed to be celebrated some 3000 years ago. Its celebration date is March 21, which the UN observes as the international Nowruz Day. Ferdowsi, the writer of the famous book Shahnameh, mentions that the first Nowruz was celebrated by King Jamshed, and that year had its roots in the ancient religion of Zoroastrian. During the reign of King Jamshed, civilization was founded, and everyone had their own role in society. After all his work, it was time to celebrate and that first day of spring was celebrated as Nowruz[9]. The different customs and rituals of Nowruz, which are common in almost all the countries, include cleaning the house days or a week before the Nowruz day, buying new clothes, and visiting friends and family members.

Nowruz is also celebrated in Kyrgyzstan with great enthusiasm. The women clean their houses and cook traditional food like borsok, plov, and beshbarmak. They also visit family members and friends. In the morning, the old women smoke dry juniper plants to remove the evil spirits from the house. They spell "Alas, alas ar baleden kalas" (Away all disasters and misfortunes), and this is resounded over the members of the family. In Ala Too Ploshad, people get together and celebrate this New Year. In rural areas, Nowruz is celebrated with greater pomp and show than in the cities.

Our Academy celebrated Nowruz Day on the 20th of March. An email was sent to all students with the schedule of the Nowruz asking them to make a contribution to Nowruz events by preparing traditional food, songs, poems, or any other traditional activity related to Nowruz and present on that day. One day before, we, the Afghan colleagues, sat together and assigned each one of us a responsibility. Fatema took the responsibility of preparing Bolani and Haft Mewa, for Nowruz. The evening before the event, Fatema, Azad, and I went together to Beta-Store-1 on Chuy to buy dry fruits and pots for serving the food. We found all the necessary stuff for our event.

I really liked the Beta Store, which had individual portions for every item, i.e., from food to grocery, clothes, and everyday necessities. While we were there, I was hungry and bought some slices of pizza. After we paid the bill, I remembered that I should have bought a carpet cleaner for my room. I entered again and took the piece of pizza inside the store, and I started eating. After I found the carpet cleaner, I came to the cashier to pay. A security guard approached me and said something which I did not understand. He repeated the same sentences again, but I still could not figure out what he was trying to say. He called upon his other colleague, and like a thief or someone suspicious, they took me to the security room.

I became nervous and did not know what they would do to me. Inside the room, there were many monitors showing different parts of the store. I was not sure what the problem was until they showed me my video when I was eating a slice of pizza at the mall. I understood the situation, but the problem was how to explain to them that I had already paid for the pizza and re-entered the mall.

I tried hard with my gestures and body language to convey my message. They took me back to the counter, and there again, I tried to explain to the lady cashier that I had already paid for that slice of pizza, which was already in my stomach, and the receipt could be somewhere in the trash bins near the cashier's desk.

Finally, they believed, and I was released and relieved, but I learned two very important things from that incident. First, I should be careful while shopping and always keep receipts for a short while, and second, I really needed to learn the Russian language!

While all this drama was taking place with me, Azad and Fatema started looking for me until I got out of the mall and told them the entire story.

From there we went to meet some Afghan female students studying at the American University of Central Asia from whom we wanted to borrow the national flag, equipment for making bolani, and traditional Afghan clothes for Fatema. Their apartment was somewhere in the center, and when we entered we found them studying for their exams. They were busy, and the stress of exams was obvious on their faces. They served us with chay, and beyond that, we did not want to disturb them, so we got out of there and left for our apartments.

The next day, the Nowruz event began at 11 a.m.. Most of the students were wearing the traditional clothes of their countries, and they looked awesome. Besides Academy students, there were also fifteen students from the University of St. Andrews, U.K, on a visit in the framework of cooperation between the two institutions. The stage was controlled by students from the politics group, and Fazilat, my classmate from Uzbekistan, was representing our class. The day began with the brief introduction of Nowruz followed by the presentations of different groups of students showing how Nowruz was celebrated in their countries. A Kyrgyz female student from the politics group removed the evil spirits from us by saying "Alas, alas ar baleden kalas" (Away all disasters and misfortunes), and then she served everyone with borsok followed by a group of Kyrgyz students who sang their traditional song. Ruslan from Turkmenistan read a poem about Nowruz, and a professor from the University of St. Andrews read its English translation. Our classmate Firdavs played guitar with his guest-friend, who sang a Tajiki song. Students from Uzbekistan and Kazakhstan represented their country in terms of traditional dances. Jawed from our team explained how Nowruz was celebrated in our country, followed by the traditional dance. The students from St. Andrews University also participated in a round dance like the Turkish one. Next, the most important part of the day began with the announcement for lunch. The lunch had two channels of food. First was the plov and meat prepared by the

Academy, and second was the traditional food served on long tables from the students of each Central Asian country and Afghanistan. The event was very interesting, and the guest students appeared to very much enjoy it. They discovered how Nowruz was celebrated in Central Asia and Afghanistan. That colorful and enjoyable event finished at about 4 p.m..

[9]"New Year's Celebrations Nowruz", Asian Art Museum, accessed March 03, 2016,
http://education.asianart.org/sites/asianart.org/files/resource-downloads/Nowruz_Teacher_Packet.pdf

*Students and Faculties from the OSCE Academy
and University of St. Andrews on Nowruz Day*

A Day in Bishkek

I spent most of my weekends at home, busy doing assignments or homework from the class. Some weekends, I also watched movies at night and would get up late in the morning while other weekends included visiting Bishkek Park or Sierra Coffee simply to hangout.

One weekend, in particular, I attempted to explore the city. I planned to try something different. That Sunday morning, after eating fried eggs with green tea, which was my usual breakfast during the weekends, I got out of the apartment. I walked toward the nearby bus stop, unsure which way to go. It was a quiet and silent morning, and only a few people were out in the streets. When I went to the main road, the traffic was far less than the normal business days.

At the bus stop, I saw teenage boys and girls dressed in jeans and shirts, two babushkas in their long dresses and their heads covered with a small white sheet of cloth having colorful circular patches and an old man dressed well in his old suit waiting for their marshrutka to take them to their destination. The marshrutkas would stop to drop off or take on passengers from the bus stop. I was still not sure which one to get on, and during that time four marshrutkas and a bus passed us. Before the fifth one arrived, I made up my mind and got on. I looked over every passenger with an eagle eye and chose the second last seat near the window.

The local means of transportation in Kyrgyzstan are buses, marshrutkas, and taxies. In Bishkek City, buses and marshrutkas go to different stations passing through different locations. The fare for the bus and marshrutka is between 8 and 10 som, respectively, and is the same if you want to go one stop or many. The fare of marshrutka after 9 p.m. increases to 12 som. In buses, the pensioners and disabled ones travel free by showing their I.D cards from 9 a.m. to 4 p.m..

There is a very good culture; when a bus or marshrutka is

crowded, and there is no seat available, the younger ones always vacate their seats to the elder ones without considering their gender. For example, a young lady can vacate her seat to an older man while in Afghanistan usually, it is males who offer seats for elderly males, and females (of any age).

If you are a foreigner in Kyrgyzstan and not acquainted well with the local languages, my advice would be to travel by taxi. There is a network of different companies providing taxis. They have special numbers, for example, 180, 1485, 387, etc. You call on any of these numbers, tell your address and they send you the nearby taxi. The taxis that you get on the spot could charge you more, or criminal-minded taxi-drivers might steal your money or luggage, therefore being a foreigner, one should be very cautious.

As I occupied the seat, I was enjoying the view of the city from the window, while the marshrutka would bounce me whenever there would be jumps or speed-breakers. Our marshrukta was moving on the Prospect Manas, and I had already become acquainted with that road. After passing the Russian Embassy with Sierra Coffee to its right, it entered into the city center, and from there it turned left, and I was seeing this part of the city for the first time, while the road to the right went toward Bishkek Park.

There were shops and apartments to both sides, and passengers would get off to head in different locations, which almost emptied the marshrutka. As the final stop approached, I was still not sure where to get off. The driver said something to me, probably asking where I wanted to depart. I left my seat and said, "Zdes Astanavitsa" (stop here). After I got off the marshrutka, I found a residential area where I saw shops on both sides of the road. Life was normal, but not many people were walking along the roadsides.

I crossed the road heading to the left and entered the residential area. Unlike Kabul, the front areas of the apartments possessed the facilities like small parks and playgrounds for children with trees that would give a green look during spring and summer. The balconies of some of the flats were decorated with dried branches of small trees while others were simple. Over some balconies, there were ropes upon which clothes were hung for drying. Similarly, the front areas of some of the apartments were decorated with plants and trees, while some were rather simple.

As I passed through various apartments, I found babushkas in long dresses and thick coats involved in some very serious discussion in front of their apartments. A little farther on, a young mother was teaching her son how to start walking in the play area for children and many other children were playing football. There were also some mothers who had brought their children outside in the fresh air. The apartments there were mostly five-stories high, and that region was called Toktogola. As I walked, I noticed people and their lifestyles. Talking babushkas, playing children, clean households, and a calm environment were the interesting features of that part of the city.

After covering some distance, I found my way to a bazarchik where vendors, mostly old ladies occupying small spaces, were selling fruits, vegetables, milk, yogurts, and some selling homemade woolen socks and gloves. There were also some young girls selling popcorns and sweet corns which would be replaced by cold drinks like jarma and chalap during the summers. Unlike Afghanistan, where women cannot work in bazaars or as shopkeepers, the women of Kyrgyzstan, making up half of the population of the country, were working shoulder to shoulder with their men, while in some cases they were ahead of men. Besides the bazarchik, there was a super-store and a meat shop. The meat shop was clean with pieces of meat placed in different portions of a display fridge, all clean and without stains of blood. Later I also saw meat shops in Osh and Ortosai bazaars where hunks of meat hung from hooks in and outside the shops stained with blood giving exactly the same picture of a butcher's shop anywhere in Afghanistan.

After passing through the bazaarchik a little ahead was Begemot, a small fast-food canteen. I was hungry by this time and bought a chicken burger without having to imitate a hen because I knew how to say chicken burger in the Russian language. After finishing my lunch on the roadside, I still had time until it got dark. I had in my mind the way back to the Prospect Mira and from there I could easily go home. Walking through the apartments, sometimes through small streets, I saw people going home and I felt envious over their fate that they would join their families for the dinner while I would go to a place where books and assignments waited for me. I was more than 600 miles away from my home in a city where, indeed, there was not fear of fighting or blasts, but I was missing my home, my streets and the fearsome city where life was always at risk. These were the feelings every normal and patriotic human being has when he/she is away from his homeland.

After crossing the last row of apartments, I was back on Prospect Mira and I went straight to Sierra Coffee. There was a good number of both foreigners and locals enjoying their talks and coffee. I got one medium-size Cappuccino that had become my favorite. Last time, when I changed it for an Americano, it was not only small in quantity but also severely bitter. I was enjoying my coffee when I heard an interesting conversation.

"But your English is not like Americans." A lady spoke the words in a typical Kyrgyz accent.

"Because I spent a lot of time in Dubai and other countries." This came from a male voice in an African accent but I did not turn my head and continued drinking my coffee.

"So, what do you do in Bishkek?" This was the next question the lady asked.

"I have come here to start some business and I need some young female staff."

Until the last sip of my coffee, I realized from the conversation that the man was a businessman, and the lady was a would-be employee in his office. But before leaving the café when I looked at them, I found a Kyrgyz lady sitting with a dark-skinned skinny guy. Later, I met that guy who pretended to be American and discovered he was actually from Somalia studying medicine in Bishkek. It was one of his flirting tricks to identify himself as American.

Outside it was already dark with chilling cold. The coffee lady helped me to call a taxi and within some minutes, the taxi arrived. In Kyrgyzstan, the taxi drivers are very talkative. Even if they know that you don't understand their language, they will talk to you. The taxi driver spoke a little English, and after knowing that I was from Afghanistan, he suddenly switched to a political topic.

"I had spent one year in Afghanistan as a soldier. We entered into Afghanistan to support the state and the government. We favored a system that we believed in equally for ourselves and

61

yourselves… We wanted to serve the Afghan people… But Mujahedeen did not allow us…"

"You came with tanks and imposed the system which was against the religion and culture of Afghan people, and in return, you expected to win the hearts of Afghans…"

"Look what Americans are doing in Afghanistan. They kill people, torture people naked with dogs, raid houses at nights… Even if we came with tanks, we did not do such atrocities…"

The taxi had already made a stop in front of our apartment, and when I looked at the meter reader, I saw that our discussion lasted for nearly thirty minutes, and further prolonging the discussion meant I should pay more for it. During that discussion, he was the obvious winner because after I got out of his taxi, I paid 350 som, 200 som for the discussion.

Upon entering the apartment, Iqbal was busy cooking eggs with tomatoes. "Where were you all day? I called your mobile, but you did not reply," he said with a meaningful smile. I checked my mobile and had two miscalls from him, and the reason was that I was busy exploring the city. I answered that I had been to the center of the city, which probably did not convince him. I was exhausted and wanted to sleep. I went to bed, recalling all the activities of the day and fell asleep.

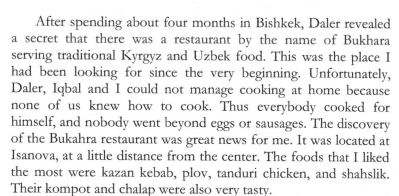

After spending about four months in Bishkek, Daler revealed a secret that there was a restaurant by the name of Bukhara serving traditional Kyrgyz and Uzbek food. This was the place I had been looking for since the very beginning. Unfortunately, Daler, Iqbal and I could not manage cooking at home because none of us knew how to cook. Thus everybody cooked for himself, and nobody went beyond eggs or sausages. The discovery of the Bukahra restaurant was great news for me. It was located at Isanova, at a little distance from the center. The foods that I liked the most were kazan kebab, plov, tanduri chicken, and shahslik. Their kompot and chalap were also very tasty.

The restaurant was also decorated in a traditional way. It had two halls separating smokers and non-smokers. The walls of the restaurant were painted with the historical places and monuments of Uzbekistan. The tables were covered with handmade tablecloths showing the traditional artwork of the country.

During my first visits to the restaurant, ordering my food was also very interesting. The restaurant's menu was in Russian, so I would go table to table to see what others were eating and would tell the waitress to bring that food for me. That interesting style of ordering food would make the waitresses laugh and the visitors annoyed. Later, I memorized the names of the food, which I liked the most until they managed to print their menu in the English language.

What's Up....!

It was 11 p.m. when I entered into Retro-Metro—a disco club located on Prospect Manas. I was not alone as I had the company of Asal Shah. Late afternoon that day, I visited my doctor friends to go somewhere and hangout, but they were preparing for their exam. So instead, I planned with Asal Shah to go out and spend the weekend, although I realized my friends were not happy when Shah was telling me that he knew some very good places in the city that provided good entertainment. Thus it was him who first introduced me to the night-life of Bishkek.

The club was for those over twenty-five years old. Before entering the main gate, two young Kyrgyz men came out, one furiously jostled me with his shoulder. Later I came to find out that such acts were normal to foreigners, especially in such places, and the situation could get worse if the foreigners had Kyrgyz girls with them. Shah bought two tickets from the window-service, followed by stamping our wrists visible only when the security man would shine a specific light on the stamp.

Upon entering, I felt the beats of loud music pulsated throughout my body. Shah led me toward the bar side, and I saw he had a good relationship with everyone from security to bar staff, who greeted him warmheartedly. Everything I saw was new and interesting. Different people from different age groups were dancing, drinking, enjoying their time and celebrating the weekend. In front of the bar, there was a row of ten stools followed by a small space and then another row of stools with a long table. Opposite the bar was the dance floor, and all around were a number of tables, some with chairs and some with couches.

My eyes were watching everything and everyone with great excitement because for the first time in my life, I was seeing females in short sexy dresses dancing and toasting with wine and vodka. Before, I had seen such scenes only in movies.

I glanced around at different people present in the club. In the corner to the left, a group of five cheerful girls conversing with excitement and moving their bodies with the beats of music attracted my attention. They looked overjoyed and delighted. When they liked a song, one or two stood up and danced with eagerness. I was just imagining that the busy life after graduation did not allow them to meet often, and they were meeting after a long time in that small city.

To the very right was the DJ, loudspeakers, and stage with people sitting beneath. I saw a group of young men and women celebrating the birthday of their friend. The birthday girl had blonde hair and was wearing a red dress and a white crown, and had received many gifts and flowers and appeared to be enjoying her celebration.

I next saw three overweight men who looked to be Turks and over the age of sixty, sitting with two young girls, probably the age of their granddaughters near the dance floor smoking shisha (hookah). Two among them with big tummies and chins hanging down were busy talking and toasting with those girls while the third one, who was not very fat, was looking hungrily in search of young beauty.

The dance floor was full of men and women, some dancing with those whom they had come with while some were approaching the opposite sex to start up a relationship.

An older lady, possibly above the age of sixty, was dancing fast in Michael Jackson style, but no one was noticing her because she had already spent her youth days and was not attractive enough for anyone to care. Some men appeared happy to have made a successful pairing while some were still struggling.

After some time, more ladies loaded with tons of makeup on their faces arrived. A few found vacant stools while most of them stood near the bar. This was a group of prostitutes looking for the clients. Anyone who could afford them was acceptable, but foreigners and the older ones were the best options. Instead of enjoying the music, their gazes were searching for possible partners for the rest of the night.

Two waitresses were holding an ethnic Russian looking fellow somewhere in his fifties by both his arms, bringing him toward a table in a very respectable way. He was blind and wearing black shades. Shah later told me that he had seen that guy here many times over the last five to six years. Apparently, the man enjoyed the disco just by sitting there.

Completing a full scan of the club, I found a vacant seat nearby. After reallocating my gaze, I found Shah dancing with that older lady whom I talked about earlier. In the beginning, I was enjoying the loud music with people dancing to its beats, but later, the smoke of shisha and cigarettes and the smell of alcohol became intolerable. I left the hall and went out to breathe some fresh air. The outside area of the club had benches where some of the ladies were sitting while some stood by the gate, busy talking and smoking. The atmosphere there was quiet and starting a conversation with any of them was not a bad idea. I tried my luck with the ladies standing near the gate, but "No English" were the only two words I heard in return. Feeling hopeless, I went to the last bench where a young blonde lady was sitting smoking a cigarette. She was beautiful with a serious look, and the word "hello" came out of my mouth unintentionally. Contrary to my expectation, she replied to me with the same "hello." I was very happy to finally find someone interested in talking.

"Do you speak English?" I asked with a smile. She puffed the smoke of the cigarette into the air and replied.

"Yes, I do."

I was overwhelmed after knowing that she spoke English. In our brief chat, I learned that she had come from Kazakhstan to Bishkek for studies. Next, I wanted to know whether she had come with her friends, boyfriend, or colleagues to the club.

"Are you alone?" I asked and looked eagerly at her for the reply.

She again puffed smoke into the air and told me that she had come with her friend and was waiting for her to come out.

In the meantime, her friend came out of the club and waved to her friend, and she stood up. I built my confidence and asked for her mobile number as my final try. I did not believe her when she said that she did not have a mobile number and then added, "What's up?"

"Nothing," I replied.

She walked toward her friend and said again, "What's Up?" showing me her mobile.

I looked here and there and again replied with confusion, "Nothing."

After hearing the second time, "Nothing," she smiled, got into the taxi with her friend, and left me confused and puzzled.

I went back into the club, still feeling confused. About an hour later, I saw some prominent changes in the club. Those men who were just looking eager for a dance before I left the hall were now romancing with ladies. A few of the men and women had turned into zombies appearing dead drunk. I realized that I was the strangest kind of Homo sapiens in that hall as I was not drinking, dancing, or dating, but simply watching people and things with annoyance. I waved my hand several times to Shah to remind him that it was the time to leave but could not get his attention because he was enjoying his romantic moments with that old lady. In the meantime, the waitress rushed toward me and gave me the receipt of Shah's drinks. After paying the bill, I went to the dance floor and grabbed him by the hand to get his attention and convince him it was time to go home because the bill had already made me angry.

After getting into the taxi, I realized that Shah was still in the disco with that lady. I looked through the taxi window, and Bishkek was sleeping soundly. I thought for a while about how weekends differed between Kabul and Bishkek. In Kabul, people's entertaining activity is to visit their relatives or friends or get together around Qargha Lake or mountain picnic in Paghman. If you are with your wife or other women of your family then you have to tolerate the staring eyes of the males who continuously stare at your females until they or you leave. But in Bishkek, besides visiting friends and family members on weekends, people also go to bars, discos, and other entertaining places. The taxi stopped, and the voice of the driver brought me back to Bishkek.

So that was the story of one of the particular weekends that I had spent with Shah in the disco. Besides the tall snowy mountains, deep blue lakes and rich culture which attract tourists from different parts of the world, the nightlife of Kyrgyzstan is also very interesting, especially in Bishkek. There are tens of discos, pubs, and bars which provide fabulous entertaining opportunities for people belonging to different age groups and categories of life. The entry to these clubs varies from 0 to 500 som. If you are a foreigner and want to go to a club, you can have a pretty good time there, but you should be careful about the internal environment because sometimes there could be a fight, or some people can cause problems outside the club if they know you are a foreigner. On weekends some people drink too much therefore one has to be careful not to get in any trouble. Europeans and Americans who visit Bishkek find very cheap entertainment in bars and nightclubs while enjoying the same entertainment in their home countries would have been very expensive.

It was almost dawn when I dropped Shah at his hostel's gate. After arriving home, I returned to thinking about the "what's up" puzzle and could not figure out what the lady meant by it. Later on, I learned about the WhatsApp application. I installed it on my mobile because my classmates had created a class-group and started communicating through it. After losing this important opportunity, I wanted to cry over my ignorance. Its importance was further realized during the exams, but by that time, I had installed it.

The Island of Democracy

Kyrgyzstan, also called the island of democracy, is the only Central Asian country that sustains democracy. Despite the two revolutions in 2005 and 2010, the country continued its democratic journey. The country is facing multiple problems like drug-trafficking, radicalization and terrorism, trafficking in humans, law and order issues, nepotism, weak institutions, and corruption, but the important thing was that democracy ruled the country. We studied all the above issues in our coursework, but corruption attracted my attention the most, and I call it the mother of problems.

In fact, not just in Kyrgyzstan but in the entire region of Central Asia, corruption was transforming into the popular culture. Luckily, the OSCE Academy included modules like good governance and economic governance, focusing on tackling the issue of corruption to produce highly skilled, efficient, and honest graduates in both public and private sectors.

That was a very important learning experience for me because it not only included the theories of governance, development, and strategies for eradicating corruption but also focused the life experiences of the students. The most interesting part of the module was when everyone would tell captivating stories of corruption from their life experiences, and most of them were terrible and shocking. From the discussions and others experiences, I came to understand that corruption was one of the main problems that Central Asia faced.

Corruption is usually associated with civil war, dictatorship, and terrorism, but Kyrgyzstan did not face any civil war, dictatorship, or the notable problems of terrorism, but still, the situation was bad. In Kyrgyzstan, corruption existed in every sector, from the police to courts and from education to health. But the disastrous situation of corruption in the higher education sector was very surprising for me.

For example, my classmates shared stories that in universities, one had to pay in order to get good grades on exams and even if a person was intelligent or hardworking, he/she had to pay, if not in all, but definitely in some subjects.

Moreover, the stories of my doctor friends were even more shocking and embarrassing. One day I saw them collecting money for their professor to pass them in the exams, and the process of money collection was such that the professor even negotiated the amount of money to be paid with the president of students. The worst I heard was that medical degrees were available for sale at $10,000 to $12,000. Now imagine a person sitting opposite to you having a stethoscope in his ears listening to you and prescribing medication is not a doctor but has bought the degree.

Although Afghanistan ranked ahead of Kyrgyzstan in corruption, the education or higher education sectors had not been that corrupt. Most of the professors or teaching staff mark students based on merit without any expectation, although exceptions would definitely exist.

In our class, everybody shared their unpleasant experiences. Saule, who typically would not speak unless necessary said, "My brother was the most intelligent student in his class, but one of his teachers was not passing him in his subject because he had not paid him the money. At first, my brother would not agree to pay, but in the end, he had no other option, and so he did."

Aigul, a kind lady told us the story of the kindergarten where her daughters were admitted. She complained about the staff because they were creating problems about getting paid.

Personally, I had been the victim of corruption when I finished my college in Pakistan and was looking for admission to the university. Afghan refugees had their own quota seats in Pakistani colleges and universities. Afghan Commisionerate was established in 1979 by the federal government of Pakistan to facilitate the refugees coming from Afghanistan, and besides other assistance, it also took care of the education of refugees[10]. When I went there to submit my application for the university, a skinny bearded clerk who was responsible for accepting the applications told me that I was late and therefore could not be considered that year.

Inexperienced and immature, I believed him and resigned myself to waiting for the next year. The following year, I went before the application process started because I did not want to be late again. There I met some other students who told me that I would miss another year too if I did not pay him. I paid the man some money then and saved myself a place for that year, but he had ruined my precious year before.

One day during our class break, I started telling Aijan, my classmate, a story about a corrupt public officer in Kabul who was addicted to taking bribes. One day a very poor man came to this public officer's office and asked for his legal work to be done, but the officer demanded money in return. The poor man said that he hardly made a living, but the officer did not accept that excuse. The officer said, "I understand you are a poor man, so give me 2000 Afghani (Afghan currency)." The poor man replied that he had nothing to give. The officer said, "Okay, make it 1000." But the answer from the poor man was the same. After going back and forth several times, the officer finally understood that the poor man had nothing to give, so he said to him, "Look. I cannot allow you to give nothing. In order to get your work done come and massage me for thirty minutes."

Now, this might be a fabricated story or could be a joke, but I wanted to tell her something humorous. I thought she would find it funny and interesting but contrary to my expectations she got very upset and became very much worried regarding the level of corruption. She expressed her feelings about how bad it was when the poor man had nothing to offer, but still, the officer wanted him to pay.

There I understood that the sense of jokes varies from country to country or society to society. Some jokes could be universal, while some could be a joke in one society, and it could be a straightforward story or a piece of information in another. The same works for sense of humor too. A person having a good sense of humor in one country may not be the same in another country. He could be considered rude or stupid, even though he might have received an appreciation for his humor in his own country.

[10]Commissionerate Afghan Refugees (CAR), Khyber Pakhtunkhwa, Peshawar, accessed Nov.29, 2017,
http://www.kpkcar.org/carnewsite/CAR/index.php/page/about-us

My first semester's exam was coming nearer, and everybody in the class was busy submitting assignments and preparing for the exam. Two weeks before our final-term exam, our Academy informed us by email that a well-known Pakistani author and expert of Afghanistan and Central Asian affairs, Ahmad Rashid would deliver a lecture on the topic, "The West, Afghanistan and Central Asia Looking Beyond the 2014".

As the U.S. and the withdrawal of its allied forces from Afghanistan would start in 2014, fears among the common Afghans started circulating that the country could go again into chaos and civil war. After the closure of American bases and the businesses attached to them, many people became jobless. The prices of real estate fell rapidly, and some took refuge in Europe. The business of human traffickers and travel agencies grew, and Dubai and Istanbul became the destinations of the travelers.

The year 2014 was challenging for Afghans and the presidential elections further confused people. In February and March, electoral campaigns and alliances were the hot topics of discussion.

As 2014 was the year the security would be controlled by Afghan forces, the main problems after the withdrawal were the deteriorating security in the country that was expected because of the failure of peace talks or reconciliation with Taliban. Unemployment (tens of thousands of jobs were created by the foreign troops in Afghanistan), and the fear of civil war were the expected outcomes in the coming years. That was the reason the expert on the topic was invited to present his view on the post—2014 situation in Afghanistan and its possible effects on Central Asia.

The entire conference room, which could barely accommodate sixty people at most, was full of diplomats, academicians, and representatives from various national and international organizations, along with the students from various institutions and universities. During his one hour lecture, Rashid highlighted different issues such as militancy, radicalization, drug and human trafficking, and the flow of refugees from Afghanistan to Central Asia, which according to him, were expected to happen after the withdrawal of U.S. and NATO forces from Afghanistan. The event ended with a questions/answers session. I did not hear anything new because all those worries were already felt by the common people in Afghanistan. At the end of the event, a few students approached the author for his autograph.

Author with Ahmad Rashid

Every individual has a story…in fact, many stories in his or her life. Sad, funny, humorous, tragic, happy…moments come and go, and stay as memories while very few enter into the literary world in the form of novels, dramas, and stories, for people to read and watch. Every individual's life is full of such stories. During my stay in Kyrgyzstan, I met different people, and some of their stories prompted me to write about them. The following is the story of a ninety-year-old ethnic Russian woman who was living alone in my neighborhood. A story of a woman who witnessed many ups and downs in her life.

Vera Fedorova

Vera looked through the window; it was snowing heavily outside. The dark night looked brighter as the lawn was covered with snow like a white sheet. The silence inside the room was broken by the voice of the warden who brought Vera's luggage into the room and showed her to her bed. It was her first night at the old people's home, her new residence. Vera would be sharing that room with three other women who more or less had the same story and would soon become her friends.

In the old people's home, their best times would be spent talking to one another, and the more they talked, the more they would feel content. They had a television too, and the lucky ones would receive visitors. But who would come to Vera, as she had no one left in the city to visit her? The city where she was born, where she grew up, studied and spent all her life was completely strange to her now. Tears oozed from her big blue eyes, and she went to bed with all the drama of her life moving past her eyes.

Vera, a ninety-year-old Russian had been living alone in her apartment for the last fifteen years after her husband died. Her only daughter, who was married, started taking care of her after and would visit her twice and sometimes three or more times a week. Three years later, Vera's daughter also died. Vera was left with a grandson and granddaughter.

Her granddaughter, Mariya, was married too, and she, along with her husband took over the care of Vera until five years ago when they moved to Russia. They wanted to take her with them to Russia, but the doctors would not give permission due to Vera's poor health. After moving to Russia, Mariya would send Vera money through her brother, Andrey, who was then living with Vera.

Everything seemed good until Mariya decided to visit her grandmother. That visit revealed the miserable life of Vera. Upon entering the house, all Mariya could see was garbage and bottles of vodka everywhere. Granny cried and told Mariya that Andrey spent all the money she sent on vodka and gambling. He did not even care about her food. Mariya had no other option but to expel her brother from the house. She gave the responsibility of caring for her granny to her university classmate and friend, Elena, and for the last two years, Elena took care of Vera.

After the disintegration of the former USSR, the ethnic Russians started moving to Russia. The few left in Kyrgystan had businesses or jobs. Elena and her husband also preferred to stay in Kyrgyzstan because of their business. She brought Vera foodstuff every weekend and spent time with her. If Vera had any medical problem, Elena would take her to the hospital. The last time, it was Elena who took Vera to the hospital for her eye operation.

Vera never thought she would face such a fortune at this stage of her life. She had a very happy life in Bishkek when she was young. Being born in Frunze, she was proud to be called Frunzian because that was the hometown of Mikhail Frunze. She was sad when its name was changed to Bishkek after the emergence of independent Kyrgyzstan. But names constantly change, anyhow, and in reality, they do not matter all that much.

She had seen many ups and downs in that small city. As a happy child, she felt the true essence of Bishkek to its fullest terms. Her childhood memories, both at school and home, were the most memorable part of her life. In school, she was an active ballet dancer and had performed in multiple theatres of Bishkek, Moscow, and Saint Petersburg. Then war erupted, leaving desperation and chaos hovering over the people. Those years were the hardest as millions of people were killed. But every night has its dawn. The Soviets became victorious, and since then, they celebrate May 9 as the victory day.

After finishing school, Vera found a job in a factory and fell in love with Nikolai, who also worked there. Vera and Nikolai enjoyed their first days of dating in the greenest city of Central Asia. Within a year, they were married.

She was enjoying her happy life, and there were no worries of any kind because the state took care of its citizens. When her daughter was born, they named her Oksana, and forty days after her birth, Vera arranged a party for her and her husband's relatives and friends. Some years later they were given an apartment by the state, and each year, they would add something new to their little apartment. She remembered the date each item entered her apartment: refrigerator, television, and all the others. That was a beautiful life, enjoying the lively summers in Issyk Kul and Karakol, while during the spring, Bishkek was like heaven on earth.

But then life started changing. First, when the Soviet Union disintegrated. Many of her relatives, friends, and colleagues left the country, but she did not leave Bishkek because that was the city where she was born, where she had spent her childhood and where she felt the most comfortable. It was a very hard time for her. Hunger was knocking at people's doors because the factories shut down, people became unemployed, and even finding a piece of bread became a challenge. Vera baked bread at home and sold the loaves along with her husband in the street. But still, she had her family, relatives, and friends around.

With the passage of time, life continued to worsen. First her husband died; he was hit by a car when crossing the road, followed by the death of her daughter three years later, whose cancer was in the final stage when diagnosed. Her grand-daughter, Mariya, moved to Russia, and her grandson, Andrey, became addicted to gambling and alcohol.

After Andrey was expelled, he would stand outside the building to beg for a few som from his granny. Sometimes Vera would spot him lying dead drunk beneath the trees outside her window, but still she would not open her door to him. Then one day, Andrey left and never came back, and it was Elena who started taking care of her.

Mariya would send money through Elena to assist in caring for Vera. It was Elena who gave her hope. Elena's one hour a week meant the entire world to Vera. All week, she would wait for Elena, who visited every Saturday and brought her foodstuffs for the whole week. Whenever Saturday approached, Vera would not sleep because of her excitement. She would wake up again and again during the night, and during the day she would look forward to her visit.

Although Elena always came at a fixed time between 5 and 6 p.m., Vera's patience would run low all afternoon. During that one hour, Vera would check her watch again and again, but the time always passed so slowly as she waited.

During their brief chats, sometimes Vera would flip through her photo album, and at other times she would talk about the golden period during the Soviet times. But the hardest time was when Elena would have to leave. After her departure, Vera's one room apartment would look so quiet and calm like no one had visited it for months.

During her last visit, when Elena said that her family was moving to Russia, Vera was shocked, and she did not talk to her after hearing that shocking news that day. She was already used to loneliness, but this time, it was accompanied by a sense of hopelessness, and the fear started mounting. That time she did not wave goodbye to Elena from her room's window like she usually did when Elena would step out of the building. That was a kind of understanding between both of them and a unique style of saying goodbye bringing smiles on both faces. Whether it was her fate, or whatever you call it, Vera no longer had anyone to look after her. Elena and her family were going to Moscow. Sometimes, Elena thought of not leaving the country, for the sake of Vera and to be there for her. But that was not possible.

Elena had already informed Mariya about her moving to Russia, so the last option left with Mariya was to admit her granny to an old people's home. After a week, Mariya came to Bishkek for her granny. She did not know how to tell her about going to the old people's home. Granny was very happy with Mariya because they had spent so much time together when Mariya was a child. So after the arrival of Mariya, they spent some very happy days together. But then, the time came…

"Granny! I want to tell you something." After she washed the dishes from breakfast, Mariya sat next to her at a small table in the kitchen and held her hand. Vera's eyes glittered and looked into Mariya's, waiting for her words. "I am going to shift you to a new place where they will take good care of you. You will not be alone, and there will be many other women there who will become your friends."

Mariya said these sentences in one breath because it was a difficult task to tell her about moving to the old people's home, and ever since her arrival, she was looking for the right time and the right words. Vera became like a statue, and she did not say anything, while her eyes were filled with tears.

Mariya had finished all the documentation process for Vera's admission. The last day before leaving her apartment, Vera glanced over her room one last time; she was leaving behind all the possessions of her entire life except her one packed bag, which consisted mostly of her clothes and photographs of her life.

Gloomy and desolate, Vera felt like she was being buried alive. On the way, Mariya told her that the new place would be good for her, and the staff there would take good care of her, but Vera was silent.

After entering the new place, all old eyes were staring at the newcomer. She was taken to her room, and she went near the window that resembled the one she had in her apartment. She looked through the window with all the drama of her life moving past her eyes.

Ala Archa National Park

Five months after my second semester started, our class lecturer, Greg, arranged a trip to Ala Archa National Park for the class. Ala Archa is a nature park with an area about 200 sq. km located in the Tian Shan Mountains, about 40 km from Bishkek City. It has a flowing river surrounded by green mountains providing a good picnic spot and a nice place for hikers, trekkers, mountain climbers, and skiers (in winter). The word Ala Archa means "Variegated Junipers."

Greg had two friends Matthew and Clayton, from the U.S. visiting Kyrgyzstan for the first time. Everybody bought something like fruits, biscuits, chips, cakes, juice, and water, etc. to serve as lunch stuff. At about 9 a.m. we left Bishkek City. The marshrukta first passed Akhunbaev Dushambinskaya and drove on Prospect Mira toward the accommodations of Kyrgyzstan's President Almazbek Atambayev. After awhile the series of apartment buildings disappeared, and I began to see cape-cod style houses on both sides of the road. Further ahead, beautiful landscapes filled the view with a flowing river and green mountains to the sides. I occupied a single window seat and was enjoying the sights of nature when Greg's loud voice pulled everyone's attention.

"Hi Guys, let's make this trip a memorable one, and I will hold my class here in the marshrutka." Everybody cheered and started clapping. I did not hear the second part of his sentence and I misunderstood it for some kind of announcement, a party or a game. Therefore I also clapped with excitement. Later, I regretted my excitement after knowing the real reason behind it. Thus the class started and every fellow discussed his/her research topic with him as he was teaching research method and design.

Every mind inside the marshrutka either became busy with their smartphones searching or discussing the research topics with other fellows. The marshrutka turned into a mobile class. Outside the marshrutka, nature was in full swing but surprised seeing a bus full of people ignoring its beauty. By the time the marshrutka arrived at the entrance gate of Ala Archa park, everyone in the class had discussed his/her research topic. The driver parked the marshrutka at the entrance gate of the park and from there we walked to find a place to sit and eat. Going through hard rocks and trees, we found a place under the shadow of alpine trees near the river.

Everybody shared the food (cookies, fruits, and juices) they had brought. After the casual lunch, some of the colleagues played a game. I do not remember its name but they used some special cards and each player would become king, villain, police, etc. The one who would stay until the end was the winner. A few started taking photos and I went a little far from them to enjoy the nature that had opened its lap to embrace us.

It was a breathtaking view. The sky was filled with clouds and the sun would sometimes peek through. The splashing sound of the flowing river would echo while striking the big rocks. The tall green mountains looked fabulous and the fresh clean air was refreshing to the soul. The temperature there was cooler than Bishkek City, and there were also some other groups of families and friends for a picnic.

At about 4 p.m. we got a call to return, And on the way back we took some group photos. While walking toward our marshrutka I broke the silence by telling some jokes:

One day a man went to a barber and asked him the price of a haircut. The Barber replied, "$20." The guy asked how much for shaving, and the barber replied, "$10." The client finally said, "okay shave my head."

A man went abroad away from his home country. After some years he sent back a photo of him sitting on a donkey mentioning at the bottom of the photo, "The one with a cap is me."

Once a man went to a country where the water was very scarce. He went to a barber shop and asked about shaving his beard. The barber spit on the shaving brush and was about to start shaving when the man asked, "What nonsense is this?" The barber replied, "Sir, there is a shortage of water and as respect, I spit on the brush. Otherwise, I spit directly on the face of other clients."

Whenever I would say my jokes, Greg and his two friends, along with my classmates, would take a pause for a while and then would start laughing. I was happy that my jokes were making them laugh. On the way back to Bishkek, a light rainfall began. I took the front seat beside the driver to shoot some videos. At the back of the marshrutka, my classmates were busy playing a guessing game. One person would think of a person in his/her mind, and others would have to guess the name of the person within twelve questions. Their laughter would echo when someone would guess correctly.

Before sunset we were back in the city where we got off near our Academy. That was the first opportunity where I saw Kyrgyzstan other than Bishkek. I very much enjoyed the nature, the flowing water, the mountains, and the green pastures. It was a wonderful and memorable day and its memories are still refresh in my mind whenever I see those photos.

Ala Archa National Park

Group Photo at Ala Archa National Park

Chapter 3

Burana Tower

After visiting the Ala Archa National Park, my next attempt to see Kyrgyzstan started from the Burana Tower. It was a hot day when I got into a marshrutka going to Tokmok—a small town in the Chuy Province toward the east of Bishkek. At the bus station, I told the driver in a Russian-English mix along with gestures that I wanted to go to Burana Tower. The driver nodded his big head and told me to sit. I was both excited and nervous that I would not arrive without facing any problems.

After all seats of the marshrutka were occupied, the driver started collecting fares from the passengers. The fare from Bishkek to Tokmok was 70 som but I had no change, so I gave a note of 500 som. The driver started giving back the remaining money to those who had given notes of 100, 200, 500 or 1000 som. One by one each of the passengers got back his money except me. I had already heard the stories of local people cheating foreigners, and I thought I was another victim. I was nervous because if the driver would not return my change, how would I say that I had given him 500 som as I could not speak the Russian language. But the driver's gaze searched mine, and as the last in line, he gave me the correct change.

After driving a little way, the marshrutka was out of the city where crops and small houses appeared on both sides of the road. It took me one hour to reach Tokmok. The driver stopped the marshrutka near the roundabout and called me, "Come come…". I left my seat as I was the only one to react. There were three taxis on the side of the road and their drivers were waiting for visitors under the shadow of the trees. After a brief negotiation with one of them, he agreed to 500 som which included a round-trip and an hour or a little more waiting period. The way from the main road to the tower was a small dirt path going through the green crops. After about fifteen minutes, we were at the entrance gate of the tower. From the main entrance gate, another small path led to the tower.

Burana Tower is one of the ancient towers located in Tokmok region at a distance of 80 km from Bishkek City. The area around the tower is filled with a beautiful green view of the valley. There is a museum at a distance of about 20 meters from the tower, while the nearby area is surrounded by different rocks dating back to the 6th to 10th centuries. The access to the roof of the tower is through narrow dark stairs. There is also a hill nearby which looks like it was a temple or a palace from centuries ago. One can go to Burana Tower by different options, for example, either by marshrutka to Tokmok which will cost between 70 to 80 som ($1.5). From Tokmok a round trip to Burana tower could cost 400 to 500 som including the waiting period of the cab (supposedly one hour) or you can go to a tourist company and ask them to schedule a trip for you. There are many tourist companies in Kyrgyzstan which have offices all over the country. The notable ones are the trekking union with an office on Kevskaya Street and the Community Based Tourism (CBT) who have a well-established network of host houses for tourists at a reasonable price.

The tower from the ground up to about five meters is broader than the one which starts above this. From the ground, round metallic stairs in the open area take you to the small entrance door from where another series of stairs made of bricks start. After reaching the second series of stairs, there was complete darkness and the rounded stairs were sandwiched between the walls of the tower.

After climbing some stairs, I felt like I was trapped in a cave with no way to get out. I came down the stairs and the driver who accompanied me was checking out the glory of the tower like he was visiting it for the first time. Expressing my worry, the driver took the lead while I checked the height of the tower, making sure how many stairs to climb more than I did the first time. Following the taxi driver, I reached the top.

A young teenage couple was enjoying the days of their youth, and our arrival did not disturb them at all. I occupied myself with seeing the view of the valley. The small circular area at the top of the tower is about 5.5 square meters, and from there, you can see the entire valley. The tower is about 25 meters high.

No one knows the exact historical background of the tower,

although some sources date it back to about the 10th century, and there is a legend connected to the tower. There was a king and he had a very beautiful daughter whom he loved very much. One day the king called upon the famous fortunetellers to come and tell the fortune of his daughter. All of the fortunetellers told of a happy life ahead for his daughter except one. He said, "I know that you can execute me for the truth I am going to tell you, but the fact is that your daughter will not reach her sixteenth birthday and will die from the bite of a black spider." The king became very sad, and in the hopes of protecting his daughter, he built a high tower and kept her there, isolated inside a room. The girl lived inside that tower, and she was not allowed to go outside; all she could do was look through the closed windows. The servants would bring her food, water, and clothes, whatever she needed, and would make sure that she was safe from spiders.

Finally, when the girl had her sixteenth birthday, the king was very happy that the fortuneteller's prediction had not come to be true. He wanted to celebrate that day and went to her room with some fruit. The moment she accepted the fruit, she fell down on the ground and died. When the king checked the fruit, he found a black spider in it. In grief, the king sobbed so loudly that the tower shook, and its top part fell, creating the ruin which we see today.

Both in Central Asia and South Asia, you would find minarets or towers like Qutub Minar in Delhi (India), Minaret of Jam in Ghor Province of Afghanistan, Kalyan Minaret in Bukhara (Uzbekistan), and Hiran Minar in Sheikhupura, a city in Pakistan depicting a unique style of architecture of the Mughal and Turk dynasties. Each of them is associated with a unique history.

Burana Tower

Bride Kidnapping

A screaming shriek reached my ears, a girl's scream, I thought. I slowed my steps and tried to identify from which direction the screams came, but could not.

I continued my walk but at a quickened pace, and believed I was getting nearer to the screaming. After a few more steps, I saw two young men talking to a young lady who was screaming and crying. I did not want to interfere because I did not know whether they were friends, colleagues, or belonged to a single family. I was about to pass by when I saw those two men started to pull the girl into a car by force. I was astonished because a few people passing by were not interfering.

I could not tolerate that kind of abuse and torture and decided to help, irrespective of the consequences. I hurried toward them, but right before I showed my intentions, I recalled bride kidnapping and realized my intervention could ruin the entire plan. Being a foreigner, I could face some serious consequences. So, I looked here and there and continued my walk. The car left, and I wished them a good life ahead.

What I witnessed could have been a bride kidnapping, a family dispute or maybe something else. But bride kidnapping was a big issue in Kyrgyzstan. Bride kidnapping was part of the Kyrgyz culture since ancient times, but lately, the government made it illegal, setting the punishment at seven years imprisonment. In the past, the kidnapping would take place with the help of horses, but nowadays, cars are used in implementing this evil practice.

In this culture a young man who likes a young woman kidnaps her with the help of his friends, and then the lady has to submit because she is no longer accepted back into her family. Sometimes a man and a woman willing to marry each other act out a bride kidnapping. But in most cases, a girl is kidnapped against her will, and then she must spend the rest of her life in misery. There had also been cases recorded where the kidnapped brides committed suicide. Often, problems like maternal mortality, domestic

89

violence, and other abuses are connected to such an act.

When you bring up this issue with the new generation living in Bishkek, you would think the problem did not exist any longer, but in reality, it does, especially in rural areas. In Kyrgyzstan, the government and the international community are trying to solve this problem by creating awareness, legislation, and its proper implementation. Besides Kyrgyzstan, this tradition is also practiced in Kazakhstan, Chechnya, and some East European and African countries. Afghanistan is one of the worst countries when it comes to women's rights. Killing, rape, and domestic violence are some of the main issues, but some other issues have received the society's approval like handing girls over to grieved or rival parties to settle a conflict or dispute, or forcing early child marriages and honor killings. In some cases, the young ladies are even handed over to men three or four times their age. The main factor behind this is the bridewealth which is paid to the parents of the girl. On one hand girls suffer because of the evil traditions in the country, but on the other hand, young men cannot get married because of the high costs of wedding expenditures. We, the people, are mainly responsible for such practices because we justify them, and we, the people, need to strive to eliminate these evils.

Before my summer vacation had started, I went to Dr. Pal's office and asked if he had time for a meeting. Busy at his work, he pointed with his hand to sit down while his gaze remained stuck on the computer screen. After about two to three minutes, he took his pen and notebook and came to the meeting table.

"I was working on some important documents," he said. "Okay, you have ten minutes to tell me your purpose for coming."

The thought of only ten minutes made me nervous because it appeared he was expecting some academic discussion from me while I had in my mind to discuss what places I should visit in Kyrgyzstan. Puzzled as to how to begin, the fuse in my mind exploded.

"As I have a summer break for one and a half months, I wanted to start learning the Russian language and also to visit different places in the country. I was hoping to get your advice as to what places I should visit."

He put his pen and notebook aside, and I realized that my question was not at all what he expected.

"I do not know much about the places to visit in this country," he replied. "You should talk to Shirbek Juraev (the Deputy Director), he would help you."

I realized that I should sound at least a little academic, so I continued. "Well, the purpose of my traveling is to write about the culture, society, and other interesting aspects of Kyrgyzstan and its people because I think that information would be very new and interesting to people in my country."

"Ah, yes, that will be very interesting, and good luck ahead," Pal said, concluding the meeting. As I was leaving his office, I saw that he immediately became busy again looking at the computer screen.

For the summer holidays, I developed a plan which included joining a fitness club, learning basic Russian, and exploring the beauty of the country. Daler and Iqbal wanted to spend their holidays at home, but the problem was that I could not afford the rent of $400 a month on my own. I told Daler to let the landlady know and see if she would agree to $200 per month for July and August. The landlady agreed on one condition that we would stay after August at $400 per month. We all three agreed, and thus, I spent my summer holidays in the same apartment.

The very first day after my colleagues left Bishkek, I went to the fitness center near my apartment. Determined and full of energy, I exercised for one hour. But the next week my entire body was in such severe pain that I could hardly move my body parts. After that experience, I gave up fitness, and my first plan was not fulfilled. After failing the fitness experience, I did not want my second plan to fail. I went to the London School of Bishkek, a local institution for language studies providing learning opportunities both for foreigners and locals in the Kyrgyz, Russian, and English languages by native speakers. I completed a twenty-day intensive program, which enabled me to speak some basic Russian and solve my day to day problems. During that experience, I became acquainted with other foreigners learning either Russian or Kyrgyz languages.

Happy Eid!
(Ait Merik Bolsun)

Eid is the Islamic festival that comes after the holy month of Ramadan (the ninth month of the Islamic calendar in which Muslims observe fasting before sunrise until sunset). Before talking about Eid, I want to tell how I spent the month of Ramadan in Bishkek. Unlike my previous experiences, this month was totally different in Bishkek. In Peshawar and Kabul, where I spent most of my life, Ramadan is practiced in full terms, and you will not see any restaurant open during the daytime. Not observing fasting (unless having a valid excuse) is not only a sinful act in Islam but is also considered very shameful culturally. During Ramadan, unlike the rest of the eleven months, mosques are full of people, and even those who do not read Salah (prayer) start praying. In fact, Ramadan is the month of patience, and its purpose is not only to refrain from eating and drinking but to be an exemplary Muslim for the rest of the world. The strict observation of this holy month in Peshawar and Kabul is because of sharing the same culture, religion, language and ethnicity. Historically, these two cities were once the winter and summer capitals of the Afghan Durrani Empire. In 1776, Timur Shah Durrani (son of Ahmad Shah Durrani, the founder of modern Afghanistan) chose Peshawar as its winter capital until 1818 when it was captured by Sikh emperor Maharaja Ranjit Singh[11].

In Kyrgyzstan, where the majority of the population is Muslim (75%-80%), but still many of the people do not have enough knowledge about the religion, and that was the reason that I did not see many people fasting. During the Soviet times, people stayed away from the religion but after the disintegration of the USSR, people gradually started taking an interest in the religion and with the majority being Muslims, they respected those a lot who read Salah and kept fasting during the month of Ramadan even if they did not. In mosques, special arrangements were made for the Iftar (breaking the fast). The first twenty days of Ramadan I spent at home and sometimes would go to nearby restaurants. King Burger had announced special Ramadan packages, but I did not find anyone taking their offer. One evening while I was breaking the fast together with the owner of the restaurant, a tall guy rushed into the restaurant and told the owner to serve him with food as he did not break his fast. He was the friend of the owner, and he joined us for food. He was from Lahore and was doing a car business in Bishkek. Like many other Pakistanis, he had his own story.

He was married to an ethnic Russian lady and had been living in Bishkek for the last twelve years. But due to the deteriorating business environment, he was looking for an opportunity to move to any other country—probably Europe or America. During our talk, I asked why he did not eat at home when he had a family.

"My wife is busy taking care of the children, and she could not manage to cook for me at that specific time. But eating here, I also have a good time with my friend." He patted the owner of the restaurant on his shoulder and continued his meal.

"How is the situation in Afghanistan now? Is it improving?" He was hurryingly eating rice spoon after spoon, where half of them would fall from his mouth onto his plate and some onto mine. I started giving my answer but realized in the middle that he was not listening, but rather busy with his food, so I changed the topic.

"How is life in Bishkek, are you planning to go back to Lahore instead of Europe or America?"

"Well, the problem is once you adjust to living abroad, it gets very difficult to go back and live in your country. Two years ago, I went to Lahore, and I was fed-up with guests coming every day to meet with me. Traffic jams, noise, and black-outs made my days terrible." He further added, "I cannot imagine going back to Pakistan as life in Pakistan would be very difficult for my wife."

"Is your wife ethnic Kyrgyz or Russian?"

"My wife is Russian, and she is very kind and caring. Those who marry Kyrgyz either end up getting a divorce or have a very bad time. Russian wives are very sincere, and they will take good care of you."

I was seeing how good she was taking care of him.

Later I learned that those Pakistanis or Indians who married Russian ladies were admiring Russian wives while those who married Kyrgyz ladies were admiring Kyrgyz, and they would each give their own justifications.

I was about to leave when he asked me if I knew the procedure for how to submit an asylum application like some of the Afghan asylum seekers did. I did not have any idea, and I left the place after paying the bill.

[11]"Peshawar, Pakistan", World Heritage Encyclopedia, accessed, Nov.17, 2017, http://www.worldlibrary.org/articles/peshawar,_pakistan

---

All the last week of Ramadan, I had my dinner at the Bukhara restaurant. By this time, I had memorized most of the café's dishes and became familiar with a few waiters and waitresses, and Nurlan was among them. Nurlan, who was in his mid-twenties, had graduated from the Kyrgyz National University, but because of poor employment opportunities, he was working in a restaurant. Before joining Bukhara restaurant, he was working part-time as a receptionist in one of the city's famous hotels. He was a very kind person. He spoke enough English to communicate with me and would always approach me whenever he would see me having problems making myself understood with one of the other waitstaff. Sometimes, when I would stay in the restaurant until late, he would come over to me, and we would discuss different topics, sometimes about my country and sometimes about his. One evening, I told Nurlan I wanted to see Kyrgyzstan and asked what places he would suggest.

"Go to Osh, Jalalabad, Issyk Kul, Lake Sarey Chelek... You can go anywhere. Kyrgyzstan is very beautiful. I wish I could go with you, but I have my job here." He was so excited after knowing that I planned to travel through Kyrgyzstan.

One day before Eid, I was expecting that Baryalai would call me and invite me for lunch or dinner on Eid day. Now, you are probably wondering who Baryalai is.

The first time I met him was during my first week in Bishkek when I was returning home from a nearby shop. He was talking to his younger brother while returning from the gym. Baryalai was in his late twenties while his younger brother was about eighteen-years-old. I followed them after overhearing them talking, and I patted him on his shoulder. After the introduction, we exchanged our mobile numbers with the hope of meeting in the near future. We did not find an opportunity until the day before the Eid when I called him.

"Salam Baryalay Jan. I am Idrees. How are you? I hope everything is fine with you and your family." I said, starting my conversation in a typical Afghan-style, where lots of words and sentences with the same meaning are spoken again and again.

"I am fine."

I was expecting the same back and forth greeting, but the reply from the other side was not welcoming.

"When and where will be the Eid prayer gathering tomorrow?" I asked in a very humble way after noting the tone from the other side.

"The biggest gathering will take place at Ala Too Ploshad at 7 a.m., but it is also read in other mosques in different areas."

I could tell he was about to disconnect the call, but I continued as I was trying to express to him that I wanted to be part of any gathering or get together after the prayer. "What do people do here after reading the prayer, and where do Afghans gather after reading the prayer?"

"This is not Afghanistan, and people do not get together during Eid days. Here, people go back to their work after reading the prayer."

I was not satisfied with his answer, and although he very clearly told me not to bother him again, I made one last attempt. "I would like to see you, greet you on the Eid day and spend some good time together and maybe enjoy the Afghan food with you." This time my accent was very flattering, and my mind was not ready for any refusal. But I will not share what I heard from the other side.

From that day, I did not contact him again. During my last days in Bishkek, I learned that, like many other Afghans, his family was given asylum in Canada and he moved there.

Well prepared, early in the morning, I did not find any signs of Eid like my previous experiences where early in the morning on

Eid day, the voices of Mullahs reciting the verses from the holy Quran are echoed from the mosques everywhere. Men dressed in new or clean clothes rushing toward the mosque while women prepared delicious dishes. But Bishkek was calmer and quieter than any other normal day because it was a public holiday.

After reading the prayer at Ala Too Ploshad, I saw everybody rushing back to their normal lives. The sun had just risen while the shops, shopping malls, and restaurants were usually closed at that time, and I wondered what I should do. The only reasonable option left was to go home and back to sleep.

View of Ala Too Ploshad on Eid Day

People gathered for Eid Prayer near Ala Too Ploshad

Change of Guards on Eid Day, Ala Too Ploshad

I was sleeping when I heard knocking on the door. I thought I was dreaming, but when the knocks became louder and continual, I realized I needed to wake up and see who was at the door.

Peeping through the spy-hole, I did not find anyone. Again, I thought I was having a dream and went back to sleep. But before I laid back down, again the knocking started. Scared, I confirmed through the window that it was not night but day which gave me some relief. Peeping the second time, I saw three children waiting for someone to open the door.

I did, and all three started singing a kind of poem in a fluent rhythm in the Kyrgyz language. I only understood the words "Orozo" and "Ait" (Eid) and realized they wanted "Eidi," the money or gifts typically given to children or youngsters on Eid day by elders. After giving them the Eidi they went away happy.

Eidi is an important part of Eid celebrations for children in Afghanistan. In villages, children go from house to house of their relatives, neighbors, and others close to them and receive Eidi in the form of walnuts, cookies, sweets, and boiled eggs, etc., while in cities, it is usually in the form of money. That money or gifts are very important for children, and they count who gave how much. Some children save that money, while others spend it over time, depending their nature.

I had spent my Eid days both in my native village and in the city when my family was living in Peshawar. In the village, my cousins and I, along with our uncles, would go to our relatives, and we would receive a handmade handkerchief filled with dry fruits and chocolates. In Peshawar, I would go to our relatives' homes greeting Eid and would receive money and then go to the next home.

Sometimes, I regretted going to a house where the male elders were not present because usually men gave the Eidi and it would not be good to revisit that house. Sometimes some miserly guests gave me a very tough time, but I did not leave until I received money from them. I would be sitting in front of the guest to remind him that he was forgetting something. At that time, even when he would take out the handkerchief from his pocket, I would stretch out my hand, which would work as a reminder that I want my Eidi. Finally, that moment would come when I would be successful, but sometimes I stayed unsuccessful too when the guest would be too miserly.

In the evening, my doctor friends invited me to dinner. There I got acquainted with some other fellows, and thus the community of my doctor friends grew further. The White-skinned with Russian features was Iqbal, whom his friends called Baacha. Then there was the muscular, jolly-natured fellow with green eyes named Zahoor Khan, the serious-looking Noor Khan who talked only when needed, and Asal Shah. That evening, I also learned that Kiramat (the religious person who was the active member of Tablighi Jamaat) had received his medical degree, and he had already left for Pakistan.

It was one of the most entertaining times I had had since my arrival in Bishkek. After eating the delicious food that included plov, meat, and desserts prepared by Hasan, over the next few hours, we discussed numerous topics, mostly about their first experiences in Kyrgyzstan.

Baacha told a very interesting story from Ramadan the previous year when they were living in a rented apartment. The landlady of the apartment called them to bring her the monthly rent. As it was 28th of Ramadan, the guys replied, "O Nas ect Oroza, mojhno posle trey dneya" The Russian translation is basically "We are having Oroza (we are fasting), can we please pay after Eid?"

Thirty minutes later the landlady was knocking at their door looking for her daughter Oroza[12]. Later she realized that the guys meant Ramadan by Oroza.

Another interesting story was about Kiramat. A couple of years back, the Imam (chief) of Kaaba[13] had come to Kyrgyzstan for a visit. He had to deliver a religious speech in the central mosque of Bishkek, and the enthusiastic and eager Muslims in the country who wanted to listen and see him started flowing toward the central mosque. So, how could Kiramat miss that opportunity?

He, along with his friends Hasan, Zahoor, Baacha, and Noor, decided to go to the mosque early with the hope of occupying the front area. On that day, Kiramat wore long traditional Arabic dress and Keffiyeh—a head-dress worn by Arabs consisting of a square of fabric fastened by a band around the crown of the head.

While approaching the mosque, in the middle of four muscular and tall guys, the administration of the mosque mistook Kiramat as Imam of Kaaba, and the crowd of people and the Kyrgyz security approached him and took him to the Minbar, a pulpit in the mosque where the Imam stands to deliver sermons or speeches. Confused and nervous, Kiramat did not know what to do at that time. Looking at the huge crowd of people where the front line was reserved for the important people from the government and embassies of Islamic countries, Kiramat did a wise thing.

He announced on the loudspeaker, "Respectable guests. Thank you very much for coming. I appreciate your patience, and the Imam of Kaaba will be here within some minutes." Thus he got himself out of that terrible situation.

I had such a pleasant time with them that I did not leave for my apartment until about 1 a.m..

[12]Oroza is a Kyrgyz female name while it also means Ramadan in the Kyrgyz language.
[13]Kaaba is the holiest and most sacred cube-shaped building (of Muslims) located at the Masjid Al-Haram in the city of Makkah, Saudi Arabia. Muslims face Kaaba for reading their prayers.

John in Bishkek

First time I met him was in the hostel when Tariq introduced me to the students studying medicine who became my friends. At the second meeting, he took me to a disco. The third time was back in the hostel during the Eid dinner. During our fourth meeting, I learned many things about him. I am talking about Asal Shah, who was Shah to his friends and John to the girls in the city. Asal Shah and John are one person, and I will use John from here onward.

John was the most interesting character, and his stories were full of adventure. Unlike the other guys, John had been living in Bishkek for the last fifteen years. He finished six years of studies in medicine in ten years and then stayed to pursue his specialization. He also successfully completed his specialization from a Medical University in Osh City while living in Bishkek. That would be the first-ever achievement in medical sciences that a person living in one city completed his degree in the other without appearing for classes.

After completing all his studies, he did not return to his country but preferred to stay in Bishkek, find a good job, save some money and do some business. Those days he was doing nothing or possibly working for a pharmaceutical company. But one could often find him in parks, shopping malls, discos, and the area around his hostel where he had his own place to sit. He spoke many languages, English, Urdu, Pashto, Dari, Kyrgyz, Russian, Turkish and no one knew where he was originally from. Sometimes he would say that he was a Turk, sometimes he said that his forefathers had migrated from Bukhara, while still other times, he claimed to have a connection with Afghanistan. Later I learned that his family was residing in Pakistan.

One day when I went to visit my friends in the hostel and found their door locked, I saw John coming out of his room. He seemed very happy to see me and took me to his small cube-shaped room. There were half a dozen dirty socks scattered on the floor near the door. John quickly made space between his laptop and blanket for me to sit and went to prepare tea. Above his bed were his pants and shirts hanging down from a hook. Opposite the bed was his roommate's mattress, blanket and a pillow for sleeping, and dirty would not be a proper word to describe them. In one corner of the room, there was a table covered with some pieces of stale bread, a thick old English dictionary with a nail clipper on it, a brown comb with almost half of the teeth missing, and a jug of water. After completing my scan of the room, a cockroach quickly emerged from the pillow of his friend and disappeared in the blanket. I could smell the socks when John came with a kettle and two cups. He sat on the mattress, and the cockroach went back toward the pillow. He was eager to talk to me and share his stories. One of John's stories was of coming to Bishkek.

"My parents wanted me to be a doctor because of the rivalries in our families. My two paternal and four maternal cousins are doctors. That is why they wanted me to be the scapegoat for their wishes. In my mind, I did not have any other options but to become a doctor. But after attempting three times in the entrance exam, I could not qualify to make it through the medical university. After my failures, they did not give up and started looking for opportunities to send me abroad to study medicine. One of our relatives who had studied in Bishkek, came to my father with the idea of sending me here for medicine studies. That person exaggerated everything so much that my father agreed, and thus that person started the admission procedures. After arriving in Kyrgyzstan, I realized that this person was an agent working for his own benefit because he received shares for each individual he brought to Kyrgyzstan. I could not start my studies for one year because the medicine university where I was enrolled did not have legal recognition. I spent the first couple of months along with four other newcomers in a weird old apartment situated in a small town away from Bishkek. The agent took money from us for different reasons, and he warned us not to go outside because being foreigners, we could get into trouble. During the day we would peep out the windows of the apartment, taking care not to be seen by anyone while we talked about our childhood and village life during the nights.

Within the first two to three months, all the other newcomers went back home because they could not cope with the terrible situation. But I stayed, and after a year, I enrolled myself in a legally registered medicine university."

John had some very unique characteristics. For example, he did not remember the address of any place. Even he did not remember where he had been living. When he would go to his own place or anywhere, he would ask or call his friends. The logic behind this was that he had reserved his memory for important things and did not want to fill it with such useless things.

He was very religious when he first came to Kyrgyzstan, and he would be busy praying all the time. For about the first five years, neither did he visit any disco nor try to find a girlfriend. During that time, he remained focused on his studies and kept himself from sin. But after those first five years, everything changed, and he broke all those religious ties and started going to discos and nightclubs, and began dating girls. After some attempts at dating, he succeeded in taking it to the bedroom, which was strictly forbidden in his religion.

After his first experience, he spent one week in the mosque, praying and crying for forgiveness. Although being inexperienced, he would laugh over his first experience later. He did not meet that girl again. But he became an expert in flirting and dating.

Visiting discos and nightclubs became his routine, and like a conqueror, who conquers land after land, he moved ahead. He made relationships with many girls, but no one lived with him for more than a couple of months because of his religious beliefs. In every relationship, he would start feeling guilty after some time and then would become religious. If the girl had been a non-Muslim, he would start preaching his religion. He would scare her with talk of the fire of hell, black poisonous snakes, and scorpions, where she would have to live forever. But the result was not what he expected, and she would leave him. Then after some time passed, again, he would start looking for girls.

John was a short man with dark skin having South Asian features, and one would say even with one's eyes closed that he was a Pakistani or Indian, but he told me another interesting story.

"Everybody who meets me for the first time thinks I am Turk or Russian. I was far cuter and beautiful when I was born. But one day, my mom put me in the swing outside, and a lady came, put her ugly son in the swing and took me with her. Now what you see is not me because that lady took me with her."

His sense of logic had me believing for a while that he was not the real one.

"I also mistook you for an ethnic Russian when I first met you," I told him. John was flying high after I said this, and he poured me some more tea.

John's personality was difficult to understand. The more time I spent with him, the more I realized what a desperate and unpredictable personality he possessed. Fear, fun, doubt, anger, all were not enough to define him. He was a person who was lost fulfilling the wishes of his parents to become a doctor in their family to live with pride among their tribe or clan. At the same time, in return, they did not provide an appropriate platform.

Next, he told me about the very strange relationship between him and his brother and the way he was communicating with him.

"I have a brother who is ten years older than me. As an angry man, no one in the family could even dare to talk to him. When I was young, I wanted to talk to him, discuss different things in a friendly way, but that was impossible. After I came to Bishkek, I created a Facebook ID in the name of my brother and put his photos there. Since then, once or twice a week, usually during the winter, I would stay online with both IDs, my personal and the other for my brother. Each evening, I would chat online with my brother in a friendly way. I talked to him about all the different things I wanted, and there was not any fear. After each chat, I felt relaxed and relieved."

I did not believe this story until he showed me the history of his chats.

John considered himself the expert of Central Asia, specifically Kyrgyzstan. According to him, the people from the former Soviet Socialist Republics were sincere, trustworthy, and family-oriented compared to Western Europe or the U.S.

"They would respect you irrespective of where you come from or which religion you practice. There are many Indians, Pakistanis, Turks, and many others who married girls belonging to different ethnicities in Kyrgyzstan, and they are living a happy life. A few have taken them to their home country where those ladies adopted a completely new lifestyle which they would have never thought of in their life."

I remembered the story of Rina, which I had watched on BBC Pashto television. Rina got married to an Afghan who was studying at a university in Saint Petersburg. She said in her interview that before her marriage, her husband, Abdullah, had told her that he was very poor and lived in a tent in Afghanistan. Rina replied that she loved him, so wealth and money did not matter. After they got married, she came with him to Kabul where she saw that her husband had a good house and a car too. Later her husband became deputy minister, but after the Soviet invasion, they moved to Russia.

She said that her husband was enjoying a good life in Kabul and Kabul was a modern city where girls were driving cars. She had two sons Abdul Rashid and Timor Shah. One was living in Russia and the other in the Czech Republic. Her apartment in Mikrorayon was occupied by someone during the civil war, but she won the case in court, and she now lived there.

When the reporter asked her if she would leave Kabul or would continue living there, she replied that Afghanistan was her home, people loved and respected her, and she had friends there. She would not leave the country.

I also saw her a couple of times traveling by local transportation in Kabul, and she was teaching Russian in a language school.

After hearing so many stories, John showed me his diary, which he wanted to transform into a book. Some of the pages from his diary are as follow:

Bishkek, 2004

It is now 8 o'clock in the evening. Amjad and I have been sitting near the window of our room watching the main road. From nine o'clock until one in the afternoon, I was watching the main road. Five marshrutkas, four cars, and two buses passed. From one o'clock until four Amjad counted three marshrutkas, one bus, and two cars. In total, eight marshrutkas, six cars, and three buses drove through the main road.

Nov. 2008

I met Dr. Steve in a restaurant, and we became friends since then. He is a very generous person, and he often invites me to dinner. During our first chat he asked whether I had a girlfriend and when I answered no, he gave me a smile of satisfaction. Later at the end of every meeting, he would ask whether I had found a girlfriend, and my answer would always be the same, "No." But during our last meeting, he asked me if I had a boyfriend. I was embarrassed by his question, but I think his tongue slipped, and he meant a girlfriend instead. My answer was again, "No," as usual.

Jan. 2009

Dr. Steve invited me to the New Year party in his home. I was very happy. His apartment is in the center of the city in a very calm and elite area. He served good food, and after dinner, he served champagne. After a few toasts, he sat near me and started patting my shoulder and arms whenever he talked. At first I ignored him, but when he came closer and put his hand on my thigh, I became suspicious. Then he tried to kiss and hug me. This was unacceptable to me. I pushed him away, and he tried to catch me. I escaped from him and avoided sexual assault. Now I realize why he was always asking me whether I had a girlfriend and that when I thought he had made a slip of his tongue, he actually did not. Dr. Steve was a sick man, and I will not meet him again.

April 2010, Bishkek

I am hearing sounds of gunshots from time to time for the last couple of days. Sometimes, they become very severe and rapid followed by human screaming, and sometimes they slow down. The news on the television shows that an uprising has taken place against President Bakiyev to oust him from his position. I have been told by my local friends not to go out of the apartment and stay alert even inside. I am very scared of any possible attack by the looters as I was informed by my friends that vandals had looted shops in the city. I do not know what will happen next.

105

Although I had already experienced a similar incident in 2005 when I was living in a hostel with hundreds of other students. But this time, I am alone. I have not gone out of the apartment for the last two days, and I am relying on the food that I had saved. Sometimes, I also hear the screaming sounds followed by a group of people that pass through my apartment building. I realize that they are taking the injured to the hospital. I am mentally very uncomfortable. I have already packed my important stuff for an emergency evacuation. I am afraid of what the looters will do to me when they do not find anything worth looting. Would they kill me? Would they leave me alone? If they kill, what will happen to my body? Will I be buried? Where...? Will my family be informed? These are the questions mounting in my head and every second I spend is full of fear and anxiety.

March 20, 2012, Bishkek

Today I found a new disco and I discovered that some girls go there to enjoy the calm environment because no one disturbs them, but I do not know why males did not disturb them. I did not ask anyone because that was not my business. Upon entering, they showed me two different types of wristbands as the entry marks and asked me which one to stamp. This was the first time I was confronted with two different colors of wristbands, green and pink. I expressed my ignorance and smiled, and the man on the reception tied the pink wristband around my wrist. After entering the club, I found mostly men with a few ladies. Men holding hands and arms around one another were strange for me. But the weirdest thing was when men were approaching me seeing my wristband. One American made my time so terrible that I postponed my plan of flirting with girls and escaped the place. Later, I realized that it was a gay club and I was given the wristband for passive people.

Bishkek, 2014

Today when I went to the toilet for the third time in Bishkek Park, I remembered it was because of the cauliflower that Amjad cooked last night. The second problem was that I still cannot sit normally on the commode, which takes me more time than usual and I have already broken three water-tanks. During my third visit, the number of visitors increased, and I heard knocks on the doors. When no one came out, they got suspicious, especially the one where I was inside. Among them, one person looked from the bottom of the door and did not find the feet touching the ground. "There is no one inside, let me get into it from the top and open the lock," I heard someone said. I could do nothing but sit there. The person peeked through the top and found me sitting like a thief holding the water-tank. That man told them the inside story, and there was big laughter when I got out after doing my job.

After reading some pages from John's diary, it seemed an interesting book which would include John's fifteen years of experiences. I even came up with a title: "John in Bishkek."

I thanked John for his hospitality and thrust out my hand for a handshake. He stood and stepped on the poor cockroach in the middle of the room before extending his hand.

Chapter 4

The Beauty of Southern Kyrgyzstan (Osh, Jalalabad, and Arslanbob)

During my Russian classes, I not only became familiar with some basic Russian but also acquainted with a few Westerners. Among them with brown hair, blue eyes, and at medium height was Kennie from Canada who liked to discuss any topic. She could also communicate fluently with locals in Russian. When I shared with her about my plans to travel to southern Kyrgyzstan, I discovered that she also planned to travel there. Kennie informed me that she and her friend Rachel would be going to Osh somewhere at the end of July or the beginning of August. I agreed and told her that any date was okay for me until the start of my classes in September.

One day before we left for Osh, we all three agreed to meet at the Hyatt Regency, a five-star hotel located in Bishkek City, where there was the office of Kyrgyz Concept dealing in booking and selling flight tickets. The tall Rachel was from the U.S. who did not speak a lot unless needed and was on a short tour of Kyrgyzstan. She and I paid 2800 som each for a one-way ticket from Bishkek to Osh because I wanted to come back by road, and Rachel wanted to go to China from there, while Kennie paid for her round trip. Kennie had also booked our accommodations online.

On August 01, at 8 a.m., we flew on Tezjet Airline from Bishkek, and by 9:30 am we were at the airport in Osh. I did not have to worry about anything because my companions had enough information about the city and places to visit. The good thing was that they always considered the economic factor and thus everything on our trip, including food and transportation, was cheaper. I would have definitely taken a taxi from the airport to Osh City, but having maps in hands and knowing which number *marshrutka* went to the center of the city, my companions were responsible, and I was free from all worries.

We sat in a *marshrutka* going toward Biy Ordo hostel where we planned to stay. The *marshrutka* traveled through green fields, and it was almost similar to the way from Manas Airport to Bishkek City. After about a twenty minute drive, we got off on the main road. We moved to the right, and after crossing two streets, we were at the Biy Ordo hostel. The administrator lady sitting in the entrance of the gate checked our names, passports, and booking and showed us the room where we would stay. She did not bother us with questions like the purpose of our visit, checking the dates on the visa or showing suspicious expressions. That was because the country's overall atmosphere was peaceful and there was no potential threat to anyone.

The foreigners also enjoyed that peaceful environment. Recalling my country, I could not enjoy the same level of liberty as I did in Kyrgyzstan. I could not travel to most parts of the country, while within the small city of Kabul one has to pass through multiple checkpoints. If you are traveling to other provinces, you have your identification documents at all times, and sometimes you can even be interrogated by the security personnel despite having identification documents. Moreover, most of the Afghans traveling to neighboring Pakistan for medical treatment or family visits face lots of problems despite having valid visas. From crossing the border until you get into a hotel or your relative's house, a number of security officials will not only interrogate you but will also take money because it is the money that matters. Likewise, checking into hotels is usually accompanied by so many questions where one feels like a criminal or terrorist. In the same way, Pakistanis coming to Afghanistan face the same problems. It is because of the lack of trust between the two countries and the waves of terrorism and extremism they both face.

I was happy for Kyrgyzstan that the people were living in peace and tranquility. They did not witness the environment of fighting or killings, although the 2010 ethnic violence between Kyrgyz and Uzbek in the Osh region led to the killing of hundreds of people with thousands injured, their properties burned and looted, and the figure of those displaced is hundreds of thousands[14]. But later, after electing the new government, things got better.

Our room consisted of three bunkbeds, a space for six people in total, with a toilet/bathroom but without a lock. When we entered the room, it was filled with the smell of the dirty socks of the three trackers sleeping in their beds. They were occupying the first three beds on the ground, and their big trekking shoes were open on the ground.

We put down our luggage and decided to go out after taking a shower in the lockless bathroom. For the time being, its broken lock was not a problem because if one person among us were inside, the other two would be waiting for his/her turn, and thus no other person could get in. Its long-term solution was to install a new lock in the door but for its short-term solution the person inside should sing a song to ensure his/her presence because a sign hanging outside telling that it's in use could fall down to the ground.

We had the entire day, so we decided to visit Sulayman Mountain. I stayed for two nights at the Biy Ordo hostel where there were tens of other tourists from Europe, America, and Australia besides us.

Kennie wanted to get some money from her account, so first we searched for a bank. Looking at the map, she found the bank was located on the other side of the main road. It took her about thirty minutes to get her money, and we went back to the bus stop where the *marshrutka* was going to the center of the city. Kennie knew the way from the map and thus we got off the *marshrutka* somewhere in the center of the city. From here we could walk to the mountain. There, in a nearby café, we took our breakfast (*chay* with bread) and then moved toward the Sulayman Mountain.

[14]Franco Galdini, "Kyrgyzstan Violence: Four Years On", Aljazeera (July 01, 2014), accessed Oct.08, 2017,
https://www.aljazeera.com/indepth/opinion/2014/06/kyrgyzstan-violence-2010-201463016460195835.html

Local Café in Osh

Sulayman-Too
(Sulayman Mountain)

In Medieval times Osh was one of the largest and oldest cities of Ferghana valley, serving as an important hub for the Silk Road travelers. Osh is the administrative unit of Osh region, which borders China, Tajikistan, and Uzbekistan. It is the largest city after Bishkek. Besides Kyrgyz, Uzbeks make up the second largest ethnic group while the other ethnicities include Tatars, Russians, Tajiks, Dungons, and Turks. It was August and the weather was hotter than in Bishkek, so the sun was directly shining on our foreheads.

The historical and most interesting view for tourists in Osh city is Sulayman Mountain. This mountain is entirely located in Kyrgyzstan, and from its top you can see the full view of Osh City. This is a sacred mountain, which is UNESCO's world heritage site in the country. It attracts not only foreign tourists, but also the locals who visit it because of its sacredness. A series of stairs lead to the top of the mountain. It takes about thirty to forty minutes by walking and there are two entry points to the mountain, so you go up in one way and get down by the other.

This mountain is believed to be the place of the Prophet Sulayman (Solomon), and the shrine on top is believed to be his grave. On top of the mountain, there are many sacred rocks thought to be a cure for different diseases and problems, especially infertility. It is said that Moghul King Babur would also come to this mountain and read Salah (prayer) at his younger age, where now a small mosque has been built.

When we arrived there, a Mullah sitting inside the mosque was explaining the history of the mountain, and people were gathered and listening to him in a very respectful way. Both men and women were among the listeners, and when someone would not listen to Mullah's talk in a respectful way (for example, holding hands like in prayer), the local men and women would remind

114

him/her to do so. The Mullah was busy providing information in the Kyrgyz language, probably about the historical background of the mountain. We stood there for some minutes and listened to the Mullah, which we did not understand. From there onward, there were also small caves or stones called fertility caves or stones, where many ladies got together there and prayed for their fertility. Besides the ladies, a few teenagers were praying in advance. On top was a museum in the form of a cave that contained jars and rocks from ancient times, traditional clothes, gravestones, coins, petroglyphs, and preserved animals. Inside the cave, we felt a bit relieved because it was much colder than the outside.

People praying outside the small mosque on top of Sulayman Mountain

View of Osh City from Sulayman Mountain

Cave Museum on top of Sulayman Mountain

Inside View of Cave Museum

Ancient jars and stones in Cave Museum

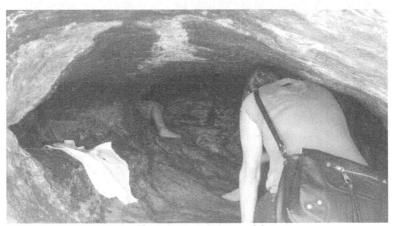

Fertility Cave on top of Sulayman Mountain

On the way back from the mountain, we were accompanied by some Uzbek teenage boys who wanted to take photos with Kennie and Rachel and probably had many things more in their hearts, but language was a barrier. Kennie's Russian was enough to communicate well with them, and an Uzbek teenager had almost fallen in love with her and was continuously following her. First Kennie was smiling and enjoying the attention, but later she felt uncomfortable and wanted to get rid of him. Finally, she became serious, and the guy with his two friends left us disappointed.

117

Thus, that love story of about thirty minutes reached an end.

We climbed down the stairs using the other route, and from there we headed toward the entrance where we had started our journey to the mountain. We came across a number of Uzbek women who were in groups going to a nearby old mosque for reading the prayer. That small one-room mosque was also very old, but I could not figure out when and by whom it was built.

The mosque was locked, and the ladies called upon two men busy talking a little far away to bring the key for the mosque. By the time one of them went to bring the keys, the ladies started talking to us. They were very talkative and wanted to communicate with us. They asked us one by one where we were from. Kennie was the only one among us who could communicate with them. They invited us for *chay* and dinner, and we thanked them for their hospitality. We still had some time before it would get dark, and so we went to a nearby restaurant for our joint lunch and dinner. The restaurant was spacious, and its porch-swing seats were comfortable enough to make us a little relaxed. We ate *shashlik*, fries, and *plov,* and took a taxi back to our hostel.

During the day, I had followed my friends, but after the sunset, I got out of the hostel for a walk in the streets of Osh to see the normal life. Children were playing as I walked. A little ahead were some female shopkeepers sitting and gossiping in front of their shops. After a little way, I found another street that horizontally bisected the one I was on, which joined the main road to the left.

I felt the time in Osh did not pass at the same speed as in Bishkek. It was a slower pace. People were returning to their homes as darkness was dominating. Turning left toward the main road, the number of cars had shrunk compared to the daytime. I stood for a while watching the traffic on the road, and then started following the same route I had come through.

The shops at both sides of the street had pyramids of watermelons and melons. I entered the shop, said *"zdrastvoyty"* to the lady shopkeeper and asked the prices of watermelons and melons outside. They were at much lower prices than Bishkek. The shopkeeper was Tajik, and after knowing my nationality, her mood was to extend the conversation, but it was getting late. I bought a watermelon and a melon from her and said goodbye.

When I came back, Kennie and Rachel were sitting with two other tourists, each from Australia and New Zealand, in the green lawn of the hostel that had covered wooden benches. That was the right time to enjoy the fruits I had brought. I went to the kitchen and got a knife and cut the melon and watermelon into pieces for my friends.

Tall with a height of around six feet five inches and muscular body was Tyler from New Zealand. He told me that a few hours earlier an American family approached him asking if it would be okay to travel to Afghanistan as they had planned to go by road from Osh to Tajikistan and then Afghanistan. According to him, the family did not have any information about Afghanistan and thus were looking forward to the suggestions of tourists. My answer was very straightforward.

"Visiting Afghanistan as a tourist is full of risks and dangers. The insecurity has spread all over the country. Taliban, ISIS, warlords, criminals... One cannot name any single threat or danger as there are many and complex in nature." I felt satisfied that my words would reach that family and they would cancel their plan of traveling to Afghanistan. But at the same time, I was saddened by preventing people from entering my country. Afghanistan was once a hub for tourists. Tourists from Europe to America visited this country and enjoyed a peaceful Afghanistan. Generous hospitality, unique culture, mountainous terrain, clean air, and multi-ethnicity made Afghanistan a worth-seeing place on earth. But prolonged war has negatively affected every dynamic of the Afghan society.

It was a quarter to ten when Kennie and Rachel went to bed, and Tyler got busy loading credit on his mobile. The other tourist was an Aussie with a reddish face and small eyes. He looked to be in his early thirties and was wearing brown shorts and a red t-shirt. He and I were left on the benches opposite to each other.

"How do you find Kyrgyzstan?" I asked, beginning a friendly chat.

"Wait," he said, "I am a little busy." He turned his face and became busy reading the *Lonely Planet*. Although, when I brought the melons, I saw him the most excited, with his eyes glittering like he was seeing them for the first time. But then he became like a total stranger. I cleaned the table and left the heap of melon and watermelon skins in front of him and went to my room without saying goodnight.

I was trying hard, but she realized.

"Is it your first time?"

"No, this is not my first time. Actually I have tried it many times in Bishkek," I replied, but she was not satisfied. I tried to bring her closer to my lips but being so hot I could not tolerate. After a bit of struggle, I brought the bowl close to my mouth and sipped its soup, and the long noodles also entered my mouth. This was *laghman* from Osh, a popular Central Asian food. We also have a very beautiful province by the name of *Laghman* in Afghanistan, located in the eastern part of our country. Looking at the empty bowl, the waitress was satisfied that I liked her *laghman*.

My journey to *laghman* was not that easy. I woke up early in the morning while the others were still sleeping or maybe laying with their eyes closed. I washed my face and went outside for breakfast. In the search for famous and traditional food, I made my way to the main road. There were a few restaurants or cafes on the right side of the road, and they had just started preparing for their customers. None of the cafés or restaurants had crowds of customers like I had seen in Kabul, Peshawar, and Lahore before. After a short peek, I passed two of them while the third one seemed better because there were some people sitting in the chairs on the sidewalk.

I sat outside in an open area with small tables each for four people. It also had a small hall inside. When I asked the waitress, I learned that the available breakfast was *laghman, manti,* and *shorpo*. I ordered *laghman* with green tea. After ordering my food, all of the people sitting stood up and started preparing *laghman*. I realized that all the sitting people that I thought to be customers were actually workers of the café, and I was their first customer of the day. While waiting I watched the entire process of making *laghman*. One guy was stretching and preparing the long noodles in his hands while the others were busy preparing meat, and the elderly lady was cutting onions and coriander, etc. After about thirty minutes, my *laghman* was ready, and I was eating it with sips of green tea.

Laghman from Osh

This café was near the hostel, and when I came back, I found Kennie and Rachel sitting on the benches in the corner of the lawn, taking their breakfasts. There were also other tourists sitting on the benches. A group of four German tourists where one guy's hair was very long and due to multiple twists against each other, his hair looked like twisted ropes. A couple from Sweden and an American whose thin beard around his cheeks gave him a goat look, were sitting on the next bench. In another corner, the Aussie was counting Kyrgyz money and probably calculating for the rest of his expedition. A little farther away was a parking area where there were probably four Harley Davidson old bikes loaded with luggage. I took my camera and started taking photos with their permission. The one with rope hair became a little suspicious when I zoomed my camera toward his hair and took some shots. He was satisfied after I answered that I wanted to save the photos just for my personal album.

After some minutes, Kennie and Rachel were ready to see the other worth-seeing places in the city. The first place they decided to go was the three-story yurt near Sulayman Mountain. We got into a *marshrutka* in front of our hostel, which took us to the yurt. The Aussie who ate my melons last night was already there wearing the same shorts and t-shirt.

On the ground floor, there were petroglyphs of ancient times, animal skins, swords and shields, rugs, *shyrdak*, and preserved animals. I took out my camera and was about to take photos when the caretaker lady came forward and asked for 100 som for unlimited photos. She also said if I wanted to take photos with traditional clothes and war costumes including a sword, head mask, and shield, I should pay 100 more for using them. The Aussie appeared to be looking at different items but was, in fact, listening to our conversation and made some calculations. When I paid 200 som for taking photos with swords, shields, chainmail helmet, and mace, the Aussie paid too.

On the second floor, there were some sculptures and paintings of famous Kyrgyz people, and Kurmanjan Datka was one among them. Kurmanjan, also known as the queen of the south, was a powerful and influential lady of the 19th century from southern Kyrgyzstan. At her young age, she rebelled against the local custom when she was given in marriage to a man she did not want to marry. Later, she married Alimbek Datka, who was the governor of Andijon Province in the Kokand Khanate. After her husband's assassination, she became the governor. She was a very wise lady. Unlike her husband and her sons who fought against the Russian Tsar, she cleverly persuaded people not to fight against the powerful Tsar and thus saved her people from a great disaster[15]. A film has also been made on her life by the name of "Kurmanjan" highlighting her struggle. The third story was almost empty with some paintings. The size of the stories also got smaller with the ground story the biggest one and the third floor the smallest.

[15]Qishloq Ovozi, "Who was Kurmanjan Datka and what does she mean to the Kyrgyz people?" Radio Free Europe (Dec.31, 2014), accessed Jan.04, 2017, https://www.rferl.org/a/qishloq-ovozi-who-was-kurmanjan-datka/26770979.html

Three-story Yurt

Sculpture of Alembek Datka

Sculpture of Kurmanjaan Datka

From there we moved to Osh Bazar—the oldest bazaar in Kyrgyzstan—about 3000 years old. Osh Bazaar was very crowded, and its sections were specified for different items and products. A river flowed at the rear of the bazaar. Inside the bazaar, we found a small café where we took our lunch. The café had run out of *laghman,* and the *plot* was not included in the menu, so we all three ordered *shashlik.*

View of Osh Bazaar

Women Shopkeepers in Osh Bazaar

Women Selling bread in Osh Bazaar

Bread from Osh

After lunch, when we had seen almost all the main points of the bazaar, we walked on the main road toward our hostel. We passed through another big mosque—Amina Mosque. Osh has many big mosques compared to Bishkek, showing the increased level of religiosity. It was a hot day, and people were busy in their daily lives. We passed through the gigantic statute of Kanykei, Manas's wife, who was a very wise woman too. The apartment behind the statue was very beautiful. Walking along the main road, the apartments to the sides were a beautiful view. At about 5 p.m. we arrived back at the hostel.

Statue of Kanykei, Manas's Wife

The next morning, Rachel planned to leave for China, but that evening, she received the bad news that the border had been closed. In fact, that evening, a tragic incident took place in the Uyghur majority province Xinxiang. The Mullah of the mosque was killed, which erupted tensions in the region. We did not know the exact nature of the incident, but there were reports of border closure. Rachel was nervous whether she should leave for the Kyrgyz-China border in the morning. That evening, Rachel and Kennie preferred to take their dinner in the hostel and I met Tyler out on the lawn and asked if he wanted to go out for dinner. As I was totally ignorant about the city, I left it up to him to decide where to go. He had already spent a week in Osh and knew a cafe famous for local food. We rented a taxi which drove us along the main road followed by wide streets to the café. The cafe was large and crowded, with most of the tables for four people. Busy waitstaff were serving the food to the customers. After looking all around, a group of three people left a table attached to the window from where the road was visible, and we sat there. As it was getting late, I realized that the café was running out of the main dishes, so we quickly accepted the waiter's suggestion of *shashlik* and salad with *kompot*. Tyler had come to Osh without staying in Bishkek. He was working for a car repair company as a technician in New Zealand and stayed busy most of the time chatting with his girlfriend, who had not joined him for the trip. I invited him to come to Bishkek, but he was not sure and told me that his girlfriend wanted him to get back to New Zealand soon; therefore he was planning to leave Kyrgyzstan.

After we got out of the restaurant, there was no taxi nearby. We walked toward our left where there were a few cars, hoping to find a taxi. On the way, while we were walking, a car came to an aggressive stop, and some guys got out acting as though they planned on attacking or kidnapping us. Tyler very quickly made a boxing position and got ready to fight. But my reaction was different. Adrenaline sent me into a fight or flight reaction, and I was favoring the latter one. But those guys had nothing to do with us, and they entered a shop. A few yards ahead, we found a taxi that took us to our hostel.

Later in the hostel, I asked Tyler, "What would you have done had they really attacked us?"

"I am a boxer and was ready to fight had something bad happened," he said. "What would you have done?"

"Of course, I would fight." I said these words firmly, looked here and there, said goodnight to Tyler, and entered my room.

The Story of a Soviet Soldier in Afghanistan

Early in the morning, Rachel was packing her luggage as she had got the good news that the Kyrgyz-Chinese border had reopened after the incident of Imam's killing. She was getting prepared to leave for China. Kennie was busy writing in her diary. She wrote in her diary two times a day: before going to bed and after waking up. I guess the latter one was the plan for the rest of the day. She was staying for the third day because she wanted to see the Sunday livestock bazaar. I departed from them and went to Tyler's room to say goodbye. The door was locked, and after several knocks, when the door was not opened, I left the place. Either he was sleeping, or he had gone outside very earlier. I paid my two nights due and left the hostel.

On the road, the Aussie was standing with his two big bags and headphones in his ears. He was completely indifferent, but I had known from Kennie that he was also going to Jalalabad if I wanted to join him. Looking at this luggage, I thought he might have been waiting for a taxi to take him to the bus station, but I was wrong, and we got into the same *marshrutka*. He made space for his long rectangular bag behind the driver's seat and took the other one with him to the back seat. I stood beside the bag with a teenage boy whose mother was sitting in the front seat like a statue. The young boy was looking at me, and because of his friendly expression, I said "hello" with a smile.

"Hello, *Ty Otkuda*," he said, which translated to where are you from?

"Afghanistan."

He looked at me thoroughly and then said something, but I did not understand. *"Moi dyadya voyeval vy Afghanistane,"* He repeated. The second time he spoke the words slowly and clearly. But I could not get the meaning, and I shook my head. He repeated the same sentence two more times, which helped me to

128

memorize the sentence. Other passengers in the *marshrutka* were looking at us but unable to help us. Finally, he acted like using AK-47 and then said something to his mom, "Mama…"

Probably that this guy (me) is from Afghanistan. His mom listened to him, looked at me and continued her statue pose.

At that time, I did not know the meaning of his sentence, but I realized that he wanted to tell me something about the fighting in Afghanistan. Later when I asked my friends for the translation, I discovered it was "My uncle fought in Afghanistan."

In Kyrgyzstan, I met a number of people who had spent time in Afghanistan. They included soldiers, technicians, engineers, and other skilled people of Soviet times and employees of international organizations and hairdressers after the Taliban were ousted from the power. Every foreigner who came to Afghanistan had his/her own unique stories with different experiences. Afghanistan is a land where whether you come as a friend or foe, you cannot leave without being impressed by the land, people, culture, hospitality, and the simple life there.

Despite that the communication between that young boy and me was not understandable. I found him enthusiastic to tell me something. His uncle might have told him about his Afghan friends, culture, jokes, food, and the lifestyle of people. In Kyrgyzstan, luckily, people did not experience war and fighting, and therefore they cannot imagine how brutal and merciless it is. They did not know how a bomb from a plane or placed in a car or anywhere else kills tens of people. How a mother feels when she sends her children to school, but they do not return. And in some cases people even disappear, the pieces of their bodies not even recognizable. In the beginning, when I would tell the stories of fighting to my class fellows, they did not understand. They asked me strange questions like, "Why did people fight there?" "Don't they understand fighting is not good for them?" "Did you see fighting?" Later I stopped telling such stories.

The Aussie stood from his seat, and I understood that we had arrived at the bus station. It was not a proper bus station but a few cars waiting for the passengers. Upon our arrival, three to four drivers approached us in seconds and started pulling us along with our luggage to their cars. The Aussie moved forward to talk to them. He once again took his *Lonely Planet*, checked the rates and started bargaining with the drivers. I was standing quietly because whatever price he bargained was absolutely acceptable for me. The advantage of Western foreigners during that trip was that they carried maps and the *Lonely Planet* book to find places and directions. They find cheaper means of everything and haggle on prices using the travel book. We two sat in the car, and within a short time, other passengers also came, and the car started its journey.

The drivers I saw were nearly the same wherever they were. They use different tricks to deceive passengers. I remember when I was going from Kabul to Jalalabad, I paid Afs.100 more than others because the driver negotiated with everyone differently. On the next trip, when I figured out that trick, I talked to the passengers about the fares, but they were already asked by the driver to tell 100 Afs more, and thus, at the end once again, I paid more than others. In some cases, the drivers even gave some money in advance to one or two passengers, so when it is time to pay, everybody could pay the same amount, and the next guy will not understand that he has been deceived.

The way from Osh to Jalalabad City presented beautiful scenery of houses and crops to both sides of the road. Trees along the road looked like they were guarding the road, and the green crops, mostly maize, along with small steep hills, were comforting to the eyes. There were no big buildings or apartments, and mostly, the houses were one story. After about an hour's journey, the car passed by a local bazaar. The road onward was smooth, and the journey was enjoyable.

Do you have Hashish?

Two hours into the journey, we arrived in Jalalabad, the capital city of Jalalabad region located in the south-west of the country. The Aussie went on his way with his headphones in his ears without saying goodbye. Jalalabad is an ancient, beautiful, calm, and clean city. In the past, traders and merchants would pass through it along the Silk Road. It is the third-largest city in Kyrgyzstan.

The city was attractive at first sight. I walked along the main road and entered the bazaar, taking photos of shops and shopkeepers. Women wore long traditional dress while elderly men had Kyrgyz *kalpaks* on their heads. Unlike other tourists with their maps and guidebooks and their experience in traveling, I was worried where I would stay because I had no information about the city nor anyone to help me. I just heard its name and thought it would be an interesting place to visit, and I was right.

I went to a nearby café and ordered green tea. I was just thinking about finding accommodations when two female tourists passed by the café. I rushed outside, said hello and asked if they would help me in finding a place to stay. The response was friendly. They told me they had just arrived in Jalalabad and were staying overnight and the next morning planned to move on to Osh. The three of us entered the café, where I had left my luggage. I poured some green tea in their cups. They told me about Community-based tourism (CBT) that provided affordable accommodations all over Kyrgyzstan. It benefits both tourists and the local communities as travelers get cheaper and safer accommodations and the locals make money. That was the first time I heard about this setup.

While leaving the café, the waitress asked me where I was from. When I answered Afghanistan, she asked, *"Gashish est?"* which translates to "Do you have hashish?" I was embarrassed by the question. I replied, *"Nyet"* (No), and then added, *"Ya Student."* I am a student.

She stared at me for a while and seemed disappointed with my answer. I did not know if she really wanted hashish or was checking if I was in the drug business. Later my friends told me that hashish and heroin were in high demand because of limited availability and high prices. Some people also have links with the police, identifying those selling drugs and informing on them. I was disappointed because it was the third time that I was identified either by hashish, war, or guns. Since my arrival in Kyrgyzstan, despite my limited interaction with people, often the first thing they thought of when they heard I was from Afghanistan was drugs, war, and weapons. We went out of the restaurant and left her looking at us disappointedly.

Saskia and Eline were from the Netherlands, and they were teaching at a school there. They were friends and colleagues and, like many other tourists, were attracted by the natural beauty of Kyrgyzstan. They had the phone numbers of the CBT office in Jalalabad, and they called and told them we were standing at the entrance of a bazaar. After a couple of minutes, the CBT's representative came and took us to their home. It was about a five-minute drive from the main bazaar. On the way, I saw children and adults wearing white caps, rushing to the mosque for prayer.

Like many other houses, it was a one-story building with a small garden with flowers, a vegetable garden, and trees. Grapevines were arranged as a ceiling with the help of a metal rod in the garage, and the unripe grapes were hanging over our heads. The house had two separate parts for the guests and the family. It belonged to an Uzbek family, and an elderly lady showed us to our rooms. They were clean, and the attached bathrooms had clean towels and new soaps. We were asked if we had taken our meal or if we wanted food. As we wanted to explore the city, eating out was a better idea. Saskia said that first, we should visit Ayoub's Spring and I happily accepted her suggestion. The CBT's driver charged us 60 som and took us to the place where shared taxis were going to Ayoub's Spring. I liked the honesty of the CBT staff and the way they dealt with the tourists. From there we got into a shared taxi charging 20 som each to the spring of Ayoub.

View of Bazaar in Jalalabad

The Spring of Ayoub

The Spring of Ayoub is a distance of 2-3 kilometers from the center of Jalalabad, located on a hill with many small trees all around. There is a legend related to the spring that connects it to Prophet Ayoub (Job). It is believed that Prophet Ayoub was cured of different diseases and became healthier and younger after he bathed in its water.

Prophet Ayoub was very famous for his patience. He was rich and generous, and he would always feed and clothe the needy ones. He was blessed with many children, fields, and pastures and cattle and held a respectable place among his people. He was obedient to God and always busy worshipping.

One day, Satan was looking for an opportunity, so he started whispering among people that Prophet Ayoub had been blessed by God, but if God took all those blessings from him, he would no longer worship his God. God also wanted to test his prophet and show to Satan and the people that Ayoub was among His obedient prophets and would worship Him even if He took away all those blessings. Now it was time for the test.

All of his children and his cattle were killed and his lands destroyed. In his life, he faced many disasters. He was expelled from the village for being evil and unfortunate. Ayoub and his wife, Rahima, went hungry, sick, and homeless. During these difficult times, only Rahima stayed by his side. After a long, tough life, God accepted his prayers and sent down an angel from the sky. The angel asked Ayoub to stomp his foot on the ground. When he did so, cold fresh water emerged from the ground, and Ayoub was told to wash in it so all his wounds would be healed. He was successful in the test, and God bestowed upon him all his blessings again; his children were brought back to life.

Nowadays, local people and tourists come to Ayoub Spring to cover their bodies with mud and take a sunbath for an hour or more. After, they clean themselves with muddy water and finally take a shower in the salty mountain water. It is believed these activities are beneficial for the skin and diseases.

After entering, I saw girls and women collecting salty water from the mountains coming down a narrow stream. A little ahead was a small café with tables and chairs in an open area, along with traditional wooden *tapchans* covered with rugs and mattresses where families were eating and relaxing. Moving downward to the left were different small places, and seeing people gathered putting mud on their bodies was a very interesting scene for me. I turned left while Saskia and Eline moved ahead where there was a separate place for females.

The young males were wearing underwear while some old men were completely naked, getting the full advantage of that opportunity. I also went through the entire process of covering my body with muddy water, took a sunbath for a while and then removed the mud with the help of salty water. After taking my shower, I came to the main place where women were busy collecting the mountain's salty water. Saskia and Eline also came after a while. They also passed through the whole process and looked excited.

Hill covered with trees near the Spring of Ayoub

A place near the Spring of Ayoub where people cover themselves with mud

Young men cover themselves with mud

We made our way to the place where cars were going back to the center of the city. Besides Kyrgyzstan's snowy mountains, green pastures, beautiful lakes and rivers, and their unique culture, it also possesses sacred places like caves, stones, and springs scattered throughout the country. These attract people hoping for a cure to physical and spiritual illnesses, infertility and to provide hope for wealth, wisdom and good fortune. In fact, such places with a religious or legendary connection are everywhere in one way or another, and people have a strong belief in going there to solve their problems. In Bukhara, Uzbekistan, there is also a spring by the name of Chashma-Ayoub (Ayoub Spring), where it is believed that Prophet Ayoub stomped the ground.

The Dutch ladies had already found out about a famous local restaurant—I forget its name—and we went there. It was a very big restaurant with live music and a huge outside area with beautiful water fountains at different spots throughout the outer area. Half of the restaurant was a big area in a hall shape, with tables and chairs, with its top covered and opened from its side. The other half had wooden tapchans covered from the top, with rugs on its floor and mattresses at its four sides. A pleasant cold breeze would bring some tiny drops from the fountain on our faces. We walked inside the restaurant, enjoyed the live music, watched some families dancing around and then ate our dinner in the quiet open area. During the dinner, they asked me about Afghanistan.

Saskia knew about the "Afghan Mobile Mini Circus for Children" and looked happy that they had started to provide some sort of entertaining activities for the children in Afghanistan. It reflected her feelings for the children that they should have entertainments and sports activities in their early age. Unfortunately, schools in my country were burned, bombed, demolished, and stay closed because of threats, and those that stayed open did not fulfill the educational standards. I was happy that both of the teachers were curious to know about life in Afghanistan.

"In Afghanistan, mostly, people stay in joint or extended families. Young men and women get married at the will of their parents. Elderly people have a respectable position in the society. Life in villages is more pure and healthier compared to cities. In the capital city Kabul, every morning, children go to schools, students go to universities, servants from public and private sectors go to their offices. Shopkeepers open their shops and life goes on. Besides the fear of bomb blasts and suicide attacks, people enjoy their lives. Youngsters visit their relatives and friends during the weekend. They play sports like soccer and cricket. Bowling clubs and swimming pools are also becoming popular among teenagers. They also visit Baghe Bala, Babur garden, Kargha Lake, and Paghman hillside along with their families or friends and enjoy their time. But during winter, the outdoor activities usually cease because of the snow and cold."

My description of Afghanistan and specifically Kabul seemed interesting for them. But I was curious to know about life in Europe. I remembered when any of our relatives would come from Europe or U.S., they would tell us stories of the tall buildings, clean roads, advanced technology, and trains with bullet speed, but the old people's houses always attracted my attention. I wondered why people sent their old parents to those houses. Who fed them? Who took care of them? It seemed like a materialistic society to me, and I would feel proud that we do not send our elder ones to those houses. However that is another discussion as to how they are treated in those homes.

"Well, it is not like what you people think. We do not send them because we want to get rid of them, but because we want to take better care of them. During the day we go to our jobs, and no one stays at home to take care of them. There they have doctors, nurses, and caretakers. Moreover, we visit them regularly, and sometimes we take them out for a picnic." Her information showed me the other side of the mirror because due to limited information, I had made up a different mindset.

Eline and Saskia were tall and strong ladies. Eline was taller at a little more than six feet. She told me that she was considered medium height in Netherland. A year back, I had read a report about Dutch people as the tallest in the world.

The ladies were tired and wanted to go to sleep, and I wanted to see more of the city. So they took a taxi and went to the homestay, and I went to the famous park in the city where I could eat the popular ice cream of Jalalabad.

Like Osh, the environment in Jalalabad was also religious.

Women were covered, wore scarves, and the mosques were crowded with people. Like all other taxi drivers in Kyrgyzstan, the taxi driver who was taking me to that park started asking questions about where I was from and what religion I practiced. He became very happy after knowing that I was Muslim and Afghan. I was dropped at the entrance gate of the park. The park was very beautiful, green, and the people there were mostly families. I did not see couples romancing, as I had seen in Bishkek. I moved around the park, and mostly I saw elderly and young women sitting in groups talking and gossiping. At the very end, or you could say another entrance of the park, there was a canteen selling the city's famous ice cream. After eating the delicious ice cream, it was about 9 p.m. when I sat in a taxi and moved toward my homestay.

The next day I planned to visit Arslanbob, and Saskia and Eline were going to Osh. But they told me that they would meet me in Bishkek as they were flying from Bishkek to their country.

Arslanbob

The breakfast table was set with honey, jam, biscuits, boiled eggs, and green tea. I greeted Saskia and Eline, who were already sitting at the table. They had called the taxi and were ready to leave for Osh. After breakfast, I paid my night expenses of 750 som, including the breakfast and the owner of the house called CBT's car to take me to the bus station from where cars were going to Arslanbob. I thanked the hospitality of the host family and said goodbye to them.

Arslanbob is the largest natural walnut forest in the world. Mountains covered with trees of walnuts are extended throughout the area. It took me one and a half hours to get there. The driver took me straight to the office of CBT, where a CBT representative was giving information to a group of tourists. When it came to my turn, three other tourists entered the room, and we were all put together in one group. It was about 11 a.m. by this time, and we had the full day to see the walnut forest and mountains. The three tourists were from France. Two lady doctors working for "Doctors Without Borders" in France and the young man was a Ph.D. student in Hong Kong.

Our guide was an ethnic Uzbek and spoke good English. He led us through a dirt path having small houses on both sides. After a little walk, those houses were replaced by shops selling dry and fresh fruits, seeds of plants, and books with mostly elderly women and young girls as shopkeepers.

A shop on the roadside, Arslanbob

Book *Vendors, Arslanbob*

A young girl at her shop in Arslanbob

After exploring the series of shops, we came upon a large waterfall pounding the rocks, forming thick layers of foam and making a pleasant sound echoing through the nearby mountains. Some children and teenagers stood under it, enjoying the cold water while the elders were taking photos and enjoying the waterdrops which the air would spray onto their faces. To its right side, there was a small cave at the bottom of the mountain called Fertility Cave. Most of the visitors were females with a few men. It was believed that prayers of infertile people are accepted there. From there onward, we crossed a small worn metallic bridge with a rail only to its right side, over the flowing water of the waterfall. After climbing a small hill, I saw the walnut forest extended all over the mountains, and we started our journey.

Waterfall in Arslanbob

Families visiting waterfall in Arslanbob

Alan, I, French Doctor and Uzbek Guide

The guide was giving us information about the forest, trees, and the mountains. The walnut forests presented a very attractive view like a jungle in the movies. The route through the mountains would become plain sometimes, while mostly one had to know the basics of trekking. In some places, the shadow of trees would make the way look like night, and in some higher altitudes, there were green trees all around. The jungle was very vast, and the trekking path was a mix of rocky, steep, and flat terrain. The walnuts on the trees were not ripe and were on the branches.

Peter Ford mentions in his article, "Inside the World's Largest Walnut Forest," that according to the United Nations trade statistics database, 1200 tons of walnuts worth 2 million U.S. dollars were exported from Kyrgyzstan in the year 2016[16]. Whether it is tourism or sale of walnuts, Arslanbob has been contributing a lot to the local economy.

After about two-hour trekking, the French tourists decided to get some rest, and they did Yoga to remove fatigue and get refreshed. Alan, whose father was from Tunisia and his mother French, also invited the guide and me to join them. But we preferred to relax by lying in the green grass under the shadow of the tall walnut trees. Alan was guiding them on how to do yoga. First, all three stood still and breathed deep with their eyes closed, then they stood on their left leg, expanded their hands up in the air. They then did the same thing standing on their right leg. It took them about twenty minutes, and after finishing the yoga, they said they were refreshed.

[16]Peter Ford, "Inside the World's largest Walnut Forest", Roads and Kingdoms (June 14, 2017), accessed Jan.12, 2018, http://roadsandkingdoms.com/2017/inside-the-worlds-largest-walnut-forest/

A View of Walnut Forest, Arslanbob

Walnut forest, Arslanbob

Walnut forest spread throughout the area

Twenty-six-year-old Alan was a very interesting guy and during his two to three days stay in Kyrgyzstan, he learned some basic Kyrgyz. When he would talk to people in the Kyrgyz language, they would not believe that he had learned so much only in the last couple of days and would question him as to how many years did he spend in Kyrgyzstan? Because of the curious nature of Alan, he asked some questions regarding cultural differences about different ethnicities living in Kyrgyzstan, especially Kyrgyz and Uzbek, living in the southern region. But the Uzbek guide was reserved, and he did not want to discuss such topics. Apparently, there was no harm in discussing such issues, but due to the government's prohibition, people refrained because of past ethnic clashes. The history of these tensions goes back to the 1990s when a land dispute erupted between two ethnicities resulting in the killing of hundreds of people. Later in 2010, history repeated itself, and again violence erupted, this time, killings of thousands of people and the violence expanded to Jalalabad from Osh.

After spending a very tiring day of hiking in the mountains, the sun was about to set when we got down the mountains and back to our host-house where we were to spend our night. The homestay was a big house with a small garden having red and pink flowers and green trees all around. A stream with cold water was flowing inside the garden. There were three tapchans with wooden tables serving biscuits, bread, green tea, jam, and honey at the corners of the garden for the tourists. We chose the tapchan at the end of the garden. A young lady with signs of fatigue visible on her face came to us and asked about the food for the dinner. We asked about the menu, and she said so many names like laghman, plov, kordak, etc. Everybody among us requested a different dish.

"But today, we only have kordak," She replied with a yawn and closed her eyes, revealing severe tiredness by putting her left hand over her mouth. She was still waiting for our confirmation for that one-dish menu.

CBT House Arslanbob

View of garden in a CBT House, Arslanbob

After eating dinner, the two ladies seemed tired, and they left to sleep. Alan and I stayed awake until late hours and discussed multiple topics. I felt like we had known each other for years. He was a very curious person, and within a very short time he asked many questions about Afghan culture, language, and the overall situation in Afghanistan. Alan spoke English, French, Arabic, and Chinese fluently. Thanks to the host family, they provided us with hot green tea until late hours, and I was pouring the tea into Alan's cup. He was amused by my attitude and asked.

"Why are you pouring tea into my cup? I can do it myself."

"Well, I think this is because of my background, the way I was brought up in an Afghan family. I feel like a host and treat you as a guest here. Being the youngest in my family, my duties included serving the guests with tea, chocolates, and cookies, and washing their hands in the hand-wash pot before and after the meals and pouring tea into their cups whenever they would become empty. These responsibilities would get even tougher when I would go to my maternal grandparents' house during my summer break from school in the Wardak Province of Afghanistan. These jobs were very boring and were a big headache at that time, but now I see they were very important to bring discipline among children." I had many more things to tell him, but Alan's eyes were getting reddish, and I realized he needed to sleep. Because of his interest in languages, he said goodnight in the Pashto language "Kha Shpa" and we left for our rooms.

My room was big with only one bed in the right corner near the window facing the garden outside. A wooden cupboard was fitted in the wall opposite to the bed that had cups, plates, a photo of a newlywed couple and an old radio covered in a piece of white cloth embroidered with small red flowers. I understood that the room belonged to a married couple. I guessed due to peak season, the room was temporarily offered for the tourists or the husband might have been working somewhere in Russia or Kazakhstan like many of the youth did. I switched off the light, laid on the bed and smelled jasmine from the bedsheets and pillow covers. The sound of flowing water was very pleasant and relaxing.

I thought about the new friends I had made during the last couple of days. They belonged to different parts of the world, and some promised to meet in Bishkek. I wished I could host them in Afghanistan, where they could enjoy the unique hospitality and natural beauty. I wait for the day when I do not prevent tourists from entering my country but instead would suggest visits to Amir Lake and the Buddha statue in Bamiyan Province. They could sleep on the side of the lake or stay in a hotel in the newly built park, visit the ancient Jami Tower in Ghor Province; Blue mosque in Balkh Province; minarets, Friday Mosque, and citadel in Herat Province; and Takht e Rustam in Samangaan Province. They could walk around the Chalghuza forests in Paktya Province; Babur Garden and Kargha Lake in the capital city of Kabul; or the beautiful mountains and flowing river of Panjsher Province; and taste the hospitality of Afghans.

I slept very well after a long time. In the morning, I woke up with the chirping of birds. Everything was very natural. We took our breakfast together, and Alan promised that he would meet me in Bishkek on his way to Kazakhstan, where he was going to attend the wedding party of one of his friends.

After my breakfast, it was time to leave my new friends and Arslanbob for Bishkek. The journey from Arslanbob to Bishkek was about six hours. There was a German couple with me in the back seat and a tourist from the Czech Republic in the front seat. The driver was an interesting and funny person. Like all other drivers in Kyrgyzstan, he was talkative, despite not knowing his passengers' language, he was communicating. At one point, he stopped his car at the bank of a flowing river having trees and greenery to both sides where he bought a watermelon and invited us to share it with him. We accepted his hospitality and ate the tasty watermelon on the bank of the flowing river. During that six-hour journey, I came across many beautiful scenes. Snow-capped mountains, the fabulous flowing river, vast green pastures with horses, sheep and goats grazing, and small and big yurts with children playing at their sides. One would not enjoy such natural beauty traveling by plane. Sometimes the road would pass through higher altitudes while sometimes it would descend down. It was about 8 p.m. when I arrived in Bishkek.

Kyrgyz traditional Tapchan with breakfast menu, Arslanbob

The main difference that I felt between the southern region (Osh, Jalalabad, and Arslanbob) and the northern Bishkek was the level of religiosity. In Osh, people were more religious compared to Bishkek. Most of the women I saw wore long dresses and covered their heads with scarves. Moreover, young men and women were not romancing in public places. The foreign students who were studying in Osh felt envious of those living in Bishkek. Finding a girlfriend or making a friendship with girls was easier in Bishkek than compared to Osh. I remember, in Osh, when Kennie wanted to confirm the way to the main bazaar, a number of Pakistani students rushed to help us. One among them even offered his services as a guide and translator. I recognized the hidden desperation inside him, and he asked me several questions about her in Urdu after confirming my relationship with her.

Flowing river on the way from Arslanbob to Bishkek

Kunduz

The next evening I was in the Bukhara restaurant waiting for Nurlan to tell him stories of my trip. I was the last customer when Nurlan came, sat on the other side of the table, and asked smilingly, "Hello my friend, how was your trip to Osh and Jalalabad?"

"First I went to Osh, visited Sulayman Mountain, the three-story Yurt, the main bazaar and ate the delicious *laghman* there. Next, I moved to Jalalabad where I bathed in the Spring of Ayoub, and from there, I went to Arslanbob and explored the natural beauty of the walnut forest. I very much enjoyed my trip. Your country is very beautiful."

"So you did not visit Lake Sary Chelek?" he asked surprisingly.

"Well, I wanted to, but I could not manage because my friends were in Issyk Kul, and they were calling me to join them. That is the reason that I could not visit it." Nurlan was not happy that I did not visit the lake.

"How is everything with you?" I asked. "How is your job going on? What else do you do besides working here? Tell me more about your life?" Nurlan was about to answer when a waitress brought the *chay* and cleared some bills with him.

"I am from Naryn, but I have been living in Bishkek since I got admission to the university. After finishing university, I could not find a job that could fit my academic career, but luckily I found a job in a five-star hotel. I was earning a good amount of money because all the people staying were foreigners, mostly Americans and a few Europeans. During that time, I made many American friends. They were very friendly and lively people. Most of them were associated with the American Base Manas."

"How did people here perceive them? Were they happy with their presence?"

"Of course, they were happy because many people were working with them as they provided job opportunities. Some

Americans also got married to Kyrgyz ladies, which people did not like." He paused a little and then continued. "There were different reasons behind each marriage." He started telling me the story of his American friend Dick.

"Dick was a sixty-five-year-old American attached to the Manas Airbase. He was a kind, friendly and generous person. He would visit Bishkek two or three times a year and would stay for weeks or months at a time. When I worked the nightshift in the hotel's reception, he would come sit with me and we spoke on multiple topics like culture, society, politics, and tourism, etc. He was a very knowledgeable person and had information on every topic we discussed. He was a good listener too, and he listened with keen interest to the information I provided about Kyrgyzstan. He always praised the beauty of Kyrgyzstan, "Your country is very beautiful." Hearing these words I would get overjoyed and I would start telling him more about our mountains, rivers and the beautiful Issyk Kul lake. Most important, at the end of each discussion, he gave me a tip. Unlike others, I did not see him with girls or drunk, rather he was always a sober person. He was always taking good care of his health and he exercised twice a day. But then one day I was shocked when I saw him with Kunduz. I just started my work shift, and within a few minutes I found Dick and Kunduz in front of my reception desk. Dick came to me and asked for his room key. He introduced Kunduz to me and said, "This is Kunduz, my wife."

But I already knew Kunduz because she was a beautiful, polite and intelligent girl from our class. She knew very good English, and that was the reason that she always found some work during her vacation. I also knew she had a boyfriend whom she loved, and I thought they would get married. But I did not think that she would get married to a sixty-five-year-old man. That day when I saw her standing beside her husband, she did not look at me but instead, pretended to be a stranger. She did not want to let her husband know that we were classmates. Being embarrassed, I did not say anything. Dick took the digital card for opening the room from me, and that time, he was too generous. He gave me a $50 tip. That was the biggest tip I ever got. After they left, I checked their documents, and I found the age difference of about forty years. But this forty years age difference was not a hurdle in bringing them together. That day I saw extraordinary excitement in Dick's eyes. I understood what he meant when he would tell me, "Your country is very beautiful."

"That marriage was not the result of mere love, but it was also the dreams of two individuals. Dick wanted a true companion for the rest of his life, who could take care of him, who could live with him and hopefully could love him. Although he had in the back of his mind one of his friends who got married in Kyrgyzstan and then took his wife to the U.S., but she said goodbye to him the day she got a U.S. passport. Of course, Dick hoped that would not be the case with him. He only could hope because it is the hope which runs the cycle of life. In the same way, Kunduz too had a dream to go to the U.S., and take care of her parents financially. She saw the path to fulfill her dream by marrying Dick, who was both rich and American and therefore could take her to the U.S. But that had not been her dream when she was studying at the university. At that time, she wanted to study and marry the one whom she loved and live a happy life in her own country. Her boyfriend, Janat, who was also studying at that time, was a boxing champion at the national level. Her dream was very simple; to get married to Janat and live with him for the rest of her life. She had thought that she would be teaching in a school and also teach English in a language school. That simple dream was enough for her. She did not have any desire to go abroad or make lots of money. But with changing times and circumstances, her dream also changed, or maybe that was not her dream at all. It could be just her decision, a decision from a mature woman, in which she saw solutions to many of her problems. She could live without love, but living without money was difficult for her."

Nurlan took the last sip from his cup, and he poured *zelony chay* in my cup as a married couple passed in a big limousine followed by other cars from the front area of the restaurant where there was a wedding hall. Nurlan excitedly said, "Look at the caravan of this newly married couple." We watched them until they disappeared from our view. I told Nurlan that we also have Kunduz in our country, and it is a very beautiful province in the north, and thus I changed the topic of our discussion from one Kunduz to another Kunduz.

Chapter 5

Issyk Kul

Baacha, Noor, and Zahoor were in Issyk Kul, and they called me to come and join them. After spending two nights in Bishkek, the next morning, I traveled to Issyk Kul. First I went to the bus station, and from there I got into a marshrutka going to Issyk Kul. While traveling from Bishkek to Issyk Kul, I hoped to sit on a double seat and possibly have a beautiful devoshka beside.

Contrary to my expectations, a large old dedushka sat beside me who occupied not only his seat but also half of mine. Breathing became difficult and looking at his strong body, I couldn't dare to complain. He had a small bottle of vodka, which he had put in the right pocket of his coat, and about every ten minutes, he would sip from it. I tried to exchange my seat with a kid, but it didn't work.

After about four hours of traveling, I arrived in Issyk Kul. Wet with sweat, I was relieved when I got out of the marshrutka. The sun had already set, and a huge crowd of people was returning from the beach to their accommodations. Those families having kids were holding water tubes and other water toys. The couples were looking at different souvenirs, and some were buying them. Some had just come from their accommodations and were looking for a place to have their dinner. The loud music from the nearby cafes was further beautifying the atmosphere. The place where I got off the marshrutka was called Bosteri. I called my friends, and within minutes, they appeared.

The first important task was to find a place for me because they were already three in one room and did not have any more space left. We checked some places, but all were full. As it was getting dark, my friends decided to find any place just for that night, and the next day, find a better place. Luckily, three streets away from their accommodations there was a room vacant in a house. Like hundreds of other houses, that house also stayed busy with its doors opened to the tourists during summer, and after that, it would only be used for the household. The room had two single beds opposite each other. I paid 500 som for that night, locked my room, and left for dinner with my friends.

From my accommodations it was about 200 meters to the main road. On the road were shops of different items and guest houses, until you came to the area with entrance spots to the beach. After crossing those spots, you would pass through the restaurants, cafes, guest houses, hotels, and finally the beach and water. The distance between my accommodation and the beach was about two kilometers.

I saw people excitedly walking, talking and enjoying the pleasant cool weather. Some of them had already checked into the restaurants having meals or dancing to the beats of the music. Some families had brought their kids to the target shooting shops, and the little kids were shooting targets and having fun. After a little walk, we went to a small café which was more like a nightclub than a café. For a while, I forgot the lake Issyk Kul and enjoyed the lively environment. All the faces I saw were full of energy and life, and I was happily watching them. My friends were not amused; instead they were looking hungry and tired. But my feelings were different. I wanted to walk around that place and be part of that huge crowd. The cafe where we were eating became crowded with people and within a short while it looked like a disco. I was enjoying the atmosphere, but my friends looked exhausted and were ready to leave. We left the café in full swing, walking toward our accommodations.

The next morning at about 9 a.m. I woke up. I went straight to my friends to have our breakfast together. The gate of the house was open and I went straight to the door of their room. After several knocks, when they did not open the door, I understood they were still sleeping. In the meantime, I thought to go to the main bazaar to buy foodstuff for breakfast. In the street, people were walking toward the beach to get good places because later it would have been difficult to find a spot on the beach. They were holding towels and water-tubes. By the time I returned with some eggs, tomatoes, and watermelon, my friends were awake. Noor cooked eggs with tomatoes and prepared chay. After eating our breakfast, we were ready for the beach.

Issyk Kul is the world's second-largest alpine lake after Lake Titicaca in South America. It is 170 km long and 70 km wide. The word Issyk Kul means "hot lake," and because of its saline nature, its water never freezes even in extreme winter[17]. The lake not only attracts tourists from all over the country, but a good number of tourists from Kazakhstan and Russia visit this lake each year during the summer. There are different places that work as beach spots for the tourists, but the main ones are Bosteri and Cholpon Ata. I was overwhelmed by the huge amount of water that looked like a blue jewel on earth. The huge crowd of people looked amazing on the beach. They were families, couples, friends, and colleagues. Some were sunbathing, some were swimming, while others tried a boat ride, some were eating and drinking, and some enjoying the water slides. In short, there was fun and more fun. I had not seen such a vast body of water in my life, and I was in seventh heaven. I wanted to dive in the water, go deep and deeper and feel the true essence of the water. Thirst for water has always been my weakness as Afghanistan is a landlocked country. We have rivers, but Issyk Kul was like an ocean. It provided the best beach and natural environment at a much cheaper price. There were hundreds of hotels around the lake and homestays where people offer their homes to tourists. During the summer, Issyk Kul stayed busy and crowded. I spent most of my time in the water while my friends were lying under the yellow umbrella they had rented for 100 som.

It started getting cooler when the sun was about to set. Before the weather got cold, we started moving toward our rooms. In the evening we went to Cholpon Ata. It was located about ten minutes away by car. All cafes were full, and people were waiting outside for their turn. After checking some cafes, finally, we found space at Sambusa Café. It had live music, and the food was delicious too, but we had to leave after our meal for those waiting outside. During my two nights stay in Issyk Kul, I very much enjoyed myself by taking photos, walking around the beach and swimming in the lake.

[17]Bradley Mayhew, Mark Elliott, Tom Masters, and John Noble, "Lake Issyk-Kul", *Lonely Planet Central Asia*, Lonely Planet (2014) P.253

Issyk Kul Lake

Fish for sale on the roadside, Issyk Kul

American Corners

American Corners was a U.S. Embassy Program providing information about the history, culture, and society of the United States and thus worked to enhance the mutual understanding between the people of the United States and Kyrgyzstan. American Corners had centers all over the country, and everybody could participate in their events and programs. They arranged different activities like book reading, showing movies, a talking club, providing information about studying in the U.S., and different discussion and debate forums.

I got its address from Baacha, and one afternoon went there. Its Bishkek Center was in the Bayalinov Youth and Children's Library located in a huge building on Oganbaev Street, 242. They were open from 2 p.m. until 5 p.m.. Their weekly schedule was posted on their Facebook page. It was about 2:30 p.m. when I arrived and the program for the day had already begun. I entered the building, asked the receptionist about the event and climbed the stairs to the second floor. There was a big hall with computers all around on the tables attached to the walls. They had free Wi-Fi, and young boys and girls were busy in their search and research. Also books were available on the shelves, and anyone could read a book of their choice. In the middle of the hall, tables were arranged in a circle and about twenty participants were sitting. I sat silently in a corner to avoid disturbing them. The topic of the day was Democracy and Freedom of Expression. The facilitator was a young bearded man who was giving information about democracy and freedom of speech. The young participants were giving their opinions. Whoever spoke on the topic gave the example of America as the model and supporter of democracy. Some of the items that I remember the participants talking about are the following:

"Kyrgyzstan is the only democratic country in Central Asia, but still we need to have a democracy like America."

"In our country, our democracy is good but not like

America."

"In my opinion, democracy is that you should be free to express your opinion and choose your leadership."

The facilitator listened to everybody's opinion and would add or correct whenever needed.

After that part of the program was finished, some of the participants left while some went with a young lady who was already waiting for them in the hall. I did not find an opportunity to ask anyone where they were going, so I flowed with them to the next room. The young lady was sitting on a chair holding a book with twelve young boys and girls sitting in front of her. This was a book reading session. She was a volunteer Peace Corps, and her name was Larisa. Before starting, she pointed at me.

"I think you are the new one in the group,".

"Yes, my name is Muhammad Idrees. I am from Afghanistan and am studying at the OSCE Academy."

After my brief introduction, she turned to another young boy.

"Where were you? You have been absent for the past month?"

"I had exams and after that, I went to my cousin's wedding party in my native village."

"Then, you should read the previous chapters because we have been through lots of pages."

The guy nodded his head and the lady started the session by asking the participants about the previous chapters from the novel. After everybody participated in recalling some parts of the previous chapters, Larisa started reading the new pages. In the middle of the reading, she explained certain things that were new to the Kyrgyz culture. She would get the opinion of the participants and then everybody would tell her if that was practiced in their community/society. Among the participants, there was a tall, thin and bald Russian in his mid-thirties who continually interrupted her reading. His questions were mostly criticizing. For example, "Why it is like this?" "Why not like this?" and Larisa would respond to him trying to persuade him.

At one point, he strongly interrupted when Larisa was describing a gay character in the book.

"Why have you chosen this book for reading when it contains certain things that are against our culture and society?"

"We choose books randomly for reading, and we do not specify that they should contain any specific material," Larisa replied.

The tall thin man attentively listened until he had another question. "Americans want to inject bad things in our society in the name of freedom of speech. They want our people to become gays, and that is the reason that you have chosen such literature."

Larisa raised her eyebrows. "Being gay is not the choice of a person, and therefore we should not say if someone is gay, he is a bad person. A person could be gay or straight, and let's not interfere in people's personal lives."

Their discussion lasted for a while, but "Mr. Objection" was not satisfied. After the session was finished, the tall thin Russian came to me and said.

"What do you think these Americans will succeed in Afghanistan? They bomb and kill people." Before I could say anything, he replied to his own question. "No one can succeed in Afghanistan because that is the history. Americans will go back without winning the war." He shook hand with me and left the room.

The Wonderful Fine Arts Work in Bishkek

I had about two weeks left until my classes began in September, so I planned to visit the wonderful artworks in the city. The first museum I visited was the fine arts museum. My classmate, Nazgul's roommate, Jursunay, helped show me the museum and translated for me when needed. The fine arts museum had eight halls.

The first hall of the museum that we entered had empty frames. I thought that perhaps an exhibition might have recently finished and the art might have been removed from those frames, or maybe it was a new room, and they had only put up the frames so far, and then paintings would be fit inside later. Those frames looked like a horror scene of a Hollywood movie where a girl gets locked in a room having empty frames all around, and then she sees different terrible heads in each of the frames, and she tries to run away. But none of my presumptions were true because when Jursunay asked the care-taker about it, she replied that these frames themselves were the exhibit showing their history, that dated back to centuries ago. She further explained those frames, and we discovered that each frame had a history behind it and belonged to a different period of time, i.e. the 17th and 18th centuries.

Frames in the Fine Arts Museum, Bishkek

The second room that we entered was easily understandable, and it had the paintings of wild animals found in Kyrgyzstan and landscapes of the country. Then we went to other rooms with sculptures, petroglyphs, traditional rugs, paintings, and applied arts. The paintings mostly reflected Kyrgyz cultural life and life in rural areas. You could also find artworks by Kyrgyz artists there. Overall this museum reflected both the Soviet era and Kyrgyz folks. I tried to take a photo, but the care-taker told me that it was prohibited because the flash could ruin the paintings.

The next museum that I visited was the National Museum, formerly the Lenin Museum. I planned to visit the museum with Liam, Nazgul's boss's son, who had come from the U.S. to visit Kyrgyzstan and Alan. Alan called and said he was coming to Bishkek for an overnight stay and the same day, I also talked with Liam. I asked if he would like to visit the museum with us, and he agreed. I set an afternoon time with both of them to meet near the statue of Manas at Ala Too Ploshad. Once there had been a statue of Lenin, which was moved to a nearby park. Before I arrived, Liam and Alan had already met and introduced themselves to each other. Being a student of history and with his interest in Soviet and Kyrgyz history, Liam acted as a guide.

Statue of Lenin in one of the parks in the center of city

164

We entered the museum, and the entrance hall was quite big. The first hall had a few souvenirs shops and the artwork of traditional Kyrgyz folks for sale. On the second and third floors, besides paintings and sculptures, Kyrgyzstan's history was painted on the ceiling. I would not have noticed the history of Kyrgyzstan had Liam not told me to look at the ceiling. The history started from the ancient times when people lived in the mountains followed by the Soviet-era through modern times. Liam explained the different eras with keen interest.

We looked through the ancient history, and the Soviet revolution era that were both on the ceiling and then on the ground in the form of bronze sculptures and statutes. The sculptures were in a chronological sequence. Farmers sitting like slaves showing their sufferings, the uprising that was marking the beginning of the revolution and the acquisition of labors' and farmers' rights. One portion of the museum was totally reserved for Lenin, his paintings, sculptures, and photos. Besides history, that museum also had traditional Kyrgyz items like rugs, yurts, *kalpaks*, and many others. In short, if you visit this museum, you would not only get information about the history of Kyrgyzstan and Kyrgyz people, but you will also understand the history of Russia in different periods. By looking continuously at the ceiling for several minutes, I felt pain in my neck and worried it might not come back to its normal position. We spent about two hours in the museum.

After visiting the museum, I thanked Liam for his assistance, and he left. Alan wanted to meet his French friend because before he left for Arslanbob and Osh, he had put his luggage at his friend's house. He wanted to get his luggage and leave for Kazakhstan the next day, where he was attending the wedding party of his friend. From there he would fly back to Hong Kong where he was studying. So, we went there and got Alan's luggage. His friend was working for Doctors Without Borders in Bishkek, and she lived in a quite expensive part of the city. Her apartment was also very luxurious with a big hall and two bedrooms. She told Alan that he could stay with her, but he had promised me that he would visit me. We got his luggage from there and took a taxi toward my apartment. We took the luggage to my home, and then

I took him out to show him a bit of the city.

First, we went to *Yujhni Park* located at 10th *Mikrorayon*. I had visited that park a couple of times, and it was a good place for a walk, jogging, and cycling. We walked around the park, and as usual, a fat elderly Russian man was showing his feats with his six very small dogs no bigger than mice. With the help of his six small dogs, he was entertaining people, especially the kids, and at the end would ask for money in his basket. His dogs would take the money from people to that basket. That part was the most interesting for children when they would give coins to a little dog, and the dog would take and put the money in his master's basket. From there we walked a little on the main road and then we took a taxi to Bukhara café for dinner. I wanted Alan to taste traditional food, and I knew it was a good place to eat.

On the way to the restaurant, Alan asked me, "Why would you not work here after completing your studies? I know security in your country is not good."

"In order to work here, I need to have a good knowledge of Kyrgyz and Russian languages and international postings need quite a lot of experience."

After about a fifteen minutes drive, we arrived there, and Alan was impressed by its decoration and traditional environment. Later he also said he liked the food. He was going to Kazakhstan the next morning, so we came home so that he could get enough sleep. The next morning, I dropped him at the bus station. As Alan got on the bus, I said goodbye to him with the hope of seeing him again.

A couple of days after Alan departed, I got a call from Saskia. She and Eline had come to Bishkek, and the next morning they were flying back home. I met them on Sovetskaya Toktogula. Both of them looked pretty much satisfied with their tour of Kyrgyzstan. Saskia gifted me with the book *Lonely Planet* which was very helpful to me during my visits to the northern parts of the country.

Alexandra and Opera and Ballet Theatre

I was receiving messages on my mobile from an unknown number saying they wanted to meet me, but when I would try to call back, that person would not accept my call. From our communication, the person revealed that it was a "she," which further made me desperate to meet her. She knew many things about me: where I was from and where I was studying. I forgot that I should have investigated how she found my number and how she knew so much about me. But love is blind and I fell in love through texting. Every night, we would chat, exchange jokes, and sometimes our chat entered into the romantic area. But every time I would request a meeting, she ignored or changed the topic.

Finally we agreed to meet at the Hawaii coffee shop situated at a little distance from the Academy on Prospect Mira. I wore my new jeans and shirt, put cologne all over my clothes and went out with so many beautiful thoughts in my mind. That coffee shop was located in a quiet area with a quiet environment. I ordered a cup of coffee and waited for the lady to come. During the wait, I mistook another lady for my date and was about to greet her when her boyfriend joined her.

When my date did not appear after waiting thirty minutes, I sent her a text message and asked when she would arrive, but there was no response from her. I finished my coffee and ordered green tea, but still, no one appeared. An hour passed, and I sent her another message. That time I got a reply that said, "I have a severe headache. I cannot meet you today."

I was very disappointed and sad, and I didn't know what to do. I was finishing my tea but at the same time I wanted to talk to a pretty lady sitting on the sofa who seemed to be waiting for someone. I thought she might be having the same situation as I was and starting a conversation could be helpful to both of us. However, in the meantime two others came in with flowers and balloons and warmheartedly joined that lady. In a short time, a birthday cake arrived, and I understood the pretty lady was having her birthday party. I sat for a little more and thought if I could start a chat by saying happy birthday to her, but I could not dare. I left the place and headed toward my friends and told them the entire story. They all listened, but I did not know that it was them playing a kind of joke on me.

Some days later, when I went to Dolce Veta restaurant, I saw the same beautiful lady who I had seen at Hawaii café celebrating her birthday. She was with the same friends and luckily this time, they sat next to my table. They started talking, and I was busily trying to think of a way to start a conversation. The waitress came to my table with the menu, and I created an artificial scene of misunderstanding with her. Then I requested that lady at the other table help me because the waitress and I did not understand each other. I thought it could be a good opportunity to seek that beautiful lady's attention and help.

"Do you speak English?" I asked.

"Yes, please. How can I help you?"

"Could you please tell the waitress that I want chicken pizza without chicken?" I was happy learning that she spoke English, but my tongue slipped. As everything needs experience and I was immature in this game.

"Without chicken? Are you sure." She smiled meaningfully. I tried again.

"I mean without cheese," I corrected my sentence replacing chicken with cheese.

She talked to the waitress in Russian and then replied to me in English.

"I told her, and she said that it would not be possible without cheese but she would tell the chef to add a little amount of cheese."

I thanked her, and our discussion continued resulting in the exchange of mobile numbers. Her name was Alexandra, and she was from Kazakhstan. Her native town was located about 40 km from Bishkek. She had studied in Bishkek and was working with a consultancy company. She was also a yoga trainer. One day when I asked her if she could help me by showing me some historical places in the city, she mentioned the Burana Tower and museums which I already had visited. Then she told me about the opera, and ballet theatre in Bishkek. I had no idea about the theatre. She told me in two weeks Russian artists from Moscow were coming to Bishkek and they would present Swan Lake and other shows, and she would let me know about it. After about two weeks passed she called me, telling me that the Russian artists were scheduled to perform in the theatre and said that if I was interested, she could help me buy a ticket. I agreed, but I could not meet her to get the ticket from her. She had left the ticket at the reception of the theatre and told me to give them my name to get the ticket. I was a little late getting to the reception, but I got my ticket after telling my name.

It was a huge hall full of people, and the show had already begun. My seat was somewhere in the middle, and the security guy helped me find my seat. The performers' performance with the music was tremendous. Language was not a problem because they were not talking. There were only movements, gestures and emotions, and you could understand the conversation in the language of the music. The music was so pleasant and romantic that I forgot myself and I felt like everything taking place was not a stage drama but real. The performers were demonstrating the drama through their facial expressions, body language, and emotional gestures. That brilliant piece of art was a specialty of Russian Art. In the first part, there were young boys and girls dancing in pairs and the main characters were a young boy and girl, but mostly the young boy was featured. The story revolved around the main character and his love for the girl. There were also other characters, including a few of the hero's supporters, while most of the characters were the supporters of the villain who did not want the two lovers to unite. Sometimes, a wicked character wearing a black dress would also emerge in the scene and act in a disagreeing manner leading to a dispute with the main character of the drama. The movements of all the dancers, especially their flying movements and touching the ground on the tip of their toes, were fascinating. The entire presentation was so fabulous that I didn't want to even blink for fear of missing something. After about an hour of the performance, the first part of the show finished. The lights suddenly came back with the roar of applause from the audience. The performers of the drama departed in a respectful way and there was a break for thirty minutes. I realized that I was not alone but with hundreds of people watching the drama silently because that was the etiquette. Meanwhile, the red curtain covered the stage, and thus the performers disappeared from us.

The side doors of the hall opened, and people went out of the hall for coffee, *chay*, cakes, burgers, and sandwiches, etc. All the people were wearing their best formal dress because watching the show in casual clothes was against the etiquette. The attendees were couples, families, and friends. Most of the elderly couples were holding hands with their spouses and enjoying the wonderful show while some grandparents had come with their daughters or grandchildren. It probably reminded them of their youth when they would visit theatre and ballet performances.

The canteen was busy serving people. After a while, I saw some space in front of the canteen and went there to get something. I got coffee and went to one of the corners when I saw Alexandra. She had come with her mom and elder sister. I met them and realized that beauty ran in all of their family. Alexandra went to get coffee for them but I could not go beyond basic conversation as they were not familiar with English. As the break time was about to end, people were flowing back to their seats. Everyone put the rubbish in the bins, and the floor was as clean as before. I did not find any dirt or sweets and candy wrappers here and there, as everybody had put them in the right place. Everybody was seated back in the hall, the curtain opened, and the remaining part of the show began.

I had had the theatre experience before in Pakistan. In Lahore City, there were several theatres where stage dramas and dance shows were performed. But I would not call them art because all they showed were vulgar dances and dirty jokes in their dramas. I had visited Al Hamra and Al Falah theatres, which were considered the most decent ones because they work under the supervision of the government. But I did not find a work of art there. There were other theatres as well where the performances even went beyond the vulgarity and touched the essence of sexuality because the female performers took off their clothes, and sometimes the show would even end in a dispute or fight. The purpose of all those theatres was one: to make money, and to make that money they crossed every limit.

After the intermission, the costumes of the performers changed. All the girls and boys dressed in white, and I guessed that it was probably the "Swan Lake" show. The background of the stage turned into a lake with swans floating in it. On the stage, the human characters wore costumes like a happy swan, a cute swan, a dancing swan, swan in danger, swan in love, etc. There were numerous faces, emotions, and expressions. I had also changed my seat and was sitting next to Alexandra. I thought she would be helpful in case I would have any questions or need clarification, but there was complete silence in the hall, whispering could be considered disrespectful. So I watched the remaining part of the show in silence.

Ballet and Opera theatre

Afterward, I met Alexandra a couple of times, and we really enjoyed our time discussing different topics from movies to food and from sports to career. But one evening, while walking at Ata Turk Park, I heard a very strange thing from her.

"I want to drink parrot's juice," she said.

"Really! You want to drink parrot's juice."

"Yes, I like it very much, it's very tasty."

I departed and came home but was lost thinking what kind of lady was she that she liked parrot's juice. Maybe she meant blood by the word juice? Did she kill parrots for their blood? What else would she like? Should I continue my friendship with her?

That evening I was still trying to figure out the answers to Alexandra's unusual question when I heard a knock on the door. It was 11 p.m.. I peeped through the window and saw an elderly lady knocking at my door. Shivers ran down my entire body.

Who could she want? Should I open the door?

I called Hasan Lala and asked for his advice.

"Do you know her? Check your water pipes in the kitchen and toilet. Maybe she is from your neighborhood, and the water might be leaking to her apartment."

"I checked all the pipes in the kitchen and toilet, and did not see any problem."

The knocking became intense and continuous, which further made me nervous.

"Do not open the door. It is a trap. You might have told someone that you live alone or possibly have told someone your address. Such women trap foreigners for money."

When I thought about it, it was only Alexandra who knew where I lived, and she also knew that I was alone. I became sure that it was her who sent someone to trap me, get my money, or whatever I had. I heard the woman shouting and screaming and saying something which I did not understand, but I did not open the door. During that time, a lady from next door opened her door, they exchanged some words, and again the knocks started. She went down, threw some stones at the window of my room as she saw that my light was on. I kept myself calm and did not switch the light off to make her think that there was no one inside. This game continued until about 1 a.m. when finally she left. I was terrified and tired, both physically and mentally and soon went to sleep.

After that incident, I became sure that it was Alexandra who had sent someone, and I stopped meeting her.

August
The Month of Independence

August is the month of independence for many Stans, i.e. Afghanistan, Hindustan (India), Pakistan, and Kyrgyzstan. In Kyrgyzstan, the embassies of India and Pakistan celebrated their independence days at their embassies. By celebrating Independence Day, these embassies tried to enhance the sense of patriotism and unity among their people, encourage students in their studies, and deliver the message that the embassy stands with their people. August 19 is the Independence Day of Afghanistan, and I expected that our embassy would be celebrating it. Neither I nor any other Afghan colleagues of mine in the Academy received any notification. While I was curious, and thought it was no problem if I was not invited, I still wanted to participate in the independence celebration of my country. On August 19, early in the morning, I went to the embassy and found it closed due to Independence Day. I asked the security man if there would be any independence celebration anytime, anywhere, and the answer was no. I wanted to meet the Afghan ambassador and ask him the reason for not celebrating Independence Day, but the security guard told me that there was no one working.

About twelve days later, Kyrgyzstan was celebrating its independence day on August 31, and the biggest ceremony was taking place at Ala Too Ploshad. I did not want to miss the Kyrgyz independence celebration. So, I woke up early in the morning, called Zahoor, and by 9 a.m. we were at Ala Too Ploshad. It was a sunny and hot day. Everybody was rushing to the main square to see the independence celebration. Security personnel were assigned to different places all along the way. Ala Too Ploshad was usually the center for national events, concerts, or any other mega program. Before entering the main place for the ceremony, a policeman searched us thoroughly. Special guests, including foreign diplomats, high ranking government officials, and heads of

173

international organizations, were sitting near the main square guarded by alert security officials, while other people were standing and watching the celebrations from a little distance.

The legend Manas was sitting proud and glorified on his horse with a sword in his hand and watching his people celebrating the happy moments of their independence. He was happy that his country was the only democracy in Central Asia, although it was facing challenges like any other country, but still, the country was on the right track.

The podium was just in front of the Manas Statue where the President Almasbek Atambaev delivered his speech. Behind the podium, Kyrgyz yurts were placed where the performers would emerge, presenting traditional dances. I tried to watch the celebration among the VIP people, but the security personnel did not allow me, so I watched the celebration activities from a distance among other people. Despite the burning heat, I watched the entire ceremony including dance performances by little children, traditional dances, and some speeches. All the people gathered in the square were excited, and most of them had come from the nearby villages while the residents of Bishkek were staying home enjoying the weekend.

It was a sense of patriotism and love for the country that these people gathered to see their independence celebrations. A week earlier, I had seen the little children practicing for this day, but on their Independence Day, they looked very beautiful. The tune of their dances superbly matched the Kyrgyz traditional music, and their President greeted them by waving his hand with a smile on his face. I shot some videos and took some photos.

About 1 p.m. the celebration ended, and people started to disperse. Zahoor and I went to a nearby café for lunch. Jalalabad Cafe was a popular Kyrgyz traditional *Chaykhana* or cafe serving traditional Kyrgyz food.

Independence Day Celebration, Ala Too Ploshad

Independence Day Celebration, Ala Too Ploshad

Jalalabad Chaykhana

Interview with the Afghan Ambassador to Kyrgyzstan

In the first week of September, I decided to go to the Afghan Embassy again located on Zhokeeva Padovkena and meet the Afghan ambassador, Mr. Noor Mohammad Qirqin. The embassy was a large two-story building with a spacious lounge and rooms. Upon entering I was greeted by Sher Ali. He was part of the local staff of the embassy and was also studying in Bishkek. I told him the purpose of my visit and he went upstairs to talk to the ambassador. After a couple of minutes, I saw the ambassador, Mr. Qirqin coming downstairs. He looked tired or as if I had disturbed him. I told him that I needed to interview him because I was working on an article and he agreed. Later due to certain reasons, I could not develop it into an article but include my conversation with him as part of this book.

Me: When were you appointed as the ambassador of Afghanistan to the Kyrgyz Republic?

Ambassador: I have been working here for the last three and a half years (probably since 2011).

Me: When did the embassy of the Islamic Republic of Afghanistan start working in Kyrgyzstan?

Ambassador: During the mid-1990s, the embassy of Afghanistan started working in Kyrgyzstan. During the presidency of late Prof. Rabbani, the brother of Abdul Rashid Dostum (Current First Vice President of the Islamic Republic of Afghanistan) was the Charge De Affairs in Kyrgyzstan.

Me: How many Afghans are living in Kyrgyzstan?

Ambassador: In Kyrgyzstan, there were approximately 200 families (most of them living as refugees), and among them, most were accepted by the U.S. and Canada, and now live there. Now the number of Afghan refugees or asylum seekers is very small in

176

Kyrgyzstan.

Me: Does Kyrgyzstan provide any study opportunities to the Afghan students?

Ambassador: In Kyrgyzstan, the American University of Central Asia and OSCE Academy Bishkek are providing study opportunities for Afghan students. The Kyrgyz government itself is not providing any scholarships for Afghans.

Me: What kind of problems are Afghans and Afghan students facing here?

Ambassador: We usually do not deal with the issues of Afghan refugees because they are refugees. As far as the Afghan students are concerned, we did not hear any major problems from them, but sometimes when they fight, the authorities take action against them, which is not our business.

Me: Can you please tell us about the relationships between Afghanistan and Kyrgyzstan? What economic, political and cultural relationships have been established between them?

Ambassador: Currently, I am working on an article where I mention different relationships between Kyrgyzstan and Afghanistan. I talked about the details of all economic, political and cultural relationships between the two countries, and once it is published, you will know in detail.

Me: Why did the Afghan Embassy not celebrate their Independence Day while India and Pakistan celebrated their independence days?

Ambassador: The Ministry of Foreign Affairs of Afghanistan has limited funds and only for some countries, to celebrate events like independence day, and Kyrgyzstan is not included in that list. The embassies of Pakistan and India also do not celebrate their Independence Day each year. They celebrate only every two or three years.

Later I learned that these two embassies celebrated their Independence Day each year. It is not important or necessary to celebrate Independence Day in a hotel providing expensive food, but a cup of green tea would be enough if the embassy was determined to celebrate. I also learned that the monthly rent of the embassy's building was $4000. I thought the Afghan government should have their own property. Buying a proper place for the embassy would have been a good option economically rather than paying such a huge rent each month.

Later from my investigations, I learned that most of the Afghan embassies were not performing well. In the first place, most of the recruitment in the ministry of foreign affairs took place based on nepotism and favoritism. Most of the staff were relatives of the influential people and warlords. Second, their assignment on diplomatic missions was also unfair. There were diplomatic staff who did not work in the ministry of foreign affairs and were appointed directly on a diplomatic mission. However the rule is that one should work as an employee for the ministry of foreign affairs for at least three years to be eligible for any diplomatic mission. This is the reason that the Afghan embassies mostly presented a negative image. Most of the staff of the Afghan embassies are under-performing. They are not helpful to the Afghans living in those countries because of their irresponsible attitude. Many of them do not return to their country and apply for asylum after finishing their tenure.

After that brief interview, I thanked the ambassador for his time and took photos with him. He told Sher Ali to serve me tea as he went back upstairs to his office. I waited for a few minutes, and when I realized that the tea was not coming, I thanked Sher Ali and left the embassy.

With the Afghan Ambassador Noor Mohammad Qirqin

Issyk Kul in Off-Season

During my first visit to Issyk Kul, I was totally at the disposal of my friends. Since they were familiar with the place and had previous experiences, I followed wherever they would go and whatever they would tell me. I did not have any independence to enjoy it the way I may have wanted. That was the reason that I only saw the beach and nothing else. After I came back to Bishkek, I learned that besides the beautiful beach there were many touristic spots and activities like visiting the waterfalls, springs of warm and cold water, horse riding, scuba diving, and many others. In Cholpon Ata and Bosteri, there were many tourist companies, and their representatives would show you the brochure or photos explaining their trip packages. So, the first weekend after my studies started, I decided to visit Issyk Kul again. I checked with my friends, but no one was willing to join me. Finally, Zahoor agreed, and that Friday afternoon, we left for Issyk Kul. The sun had already set when we arrived in Bosteri. But we did not recognize it as everything appeared completely different from what we saw last time. It looked like a place haunted by ghosts. The shops were closed, and we did not see any people nearby. At a little distance, there was a car, probably a taxi, and a fat man was leaning against its door. I remembered from my last visit an ocean of people where we could hardly make our way among them.

"Is that the same place where we stayed last time?" I asked Zahoor in a surprising way.

"I am not sure. I think we got off in the wrong place." Then he walked toward the street going to the beachside and checked signs on some shops and said. "Very strange... How the same place looks so different. I still cannot believe it."

We were the only two standing on a roadside discussing whether we were at the right place or not and whether we should find accommodations there. In the meantime, a car stopped, and three young men started coming toward us. Staying longer was not a good idea, so before they could reach us, we walked toward the taxi driver and asked him to take us to Cholpon Ata.

Cholpon Ata was quiet and silent too, but better than Bosteri. There were a few people, and we were not alone. We were still not sure whether to stay or go back to Bishkek. We decided to check the cafes and if there were some people, then we would stay. The first café we passed by was completely empty while the second one had some customers. After seeing us, they started their live music, and we decided to stay as it was already late. First, we needed to find some accommodations which was not a problem. In between the cafes, there was a street, and there we found a room to rent for 200 som per night. In peak season it would cost 1000 or more. After putting our luggage in the room, we went out to have our dinner. After peeking into some cafes, we went to Café Sambusa, where we had been last time. There were a few other customers with live music when we arrived. In the meanwhile, as we ordered the food, a bus stopped and Indian tourists entered the café. A long group of tables were already arranged for them, and with their arrival the café became lively. All the tourists were above fifty, and they looked like a high profile delegation. The DJ realized that the guests were from India, so he starting playing Indian songs. "Jimmy, Jimmy, Jimmy… Aja Aja…", "I am a disco dancer…" and "Khatoba Khatoba…" These were some of the Indian songs popular during the Soviet time in former USSR states. Even now, they played those songs when restaurants or night-clubs wanted to add the Indian flavor. During that time, Hollywood movies were banned in these states, and as an alternative option, people watched Indian movies. The Indian guests started dancing to the beat. First, two men with thick black and white mustaches went to the dance floor and then called upon others to join them. A tall, slim lady was persuading the other lady who was both older and chubby to go with her. The lady finally agreed, and there were four people dancing and others also went to the floor, encouraging them with their clapping. After enjoying our evening with the Indian delegation, we went to our homestay to get some sleep.

It was about 10 am when we woke up. We took our lunch and breakfast together in a café and went toward the tourist companies. Unlike the season, their representatives were not busy calling the tourists. Thus they were relaxing sitting on the chairs. In front of a tourist agency, we saw a teenage couple looking for two more tourists to complete a team. We deposited the money, and after some minutes, the company's car came, and we left for our adventure.

The car first took us to see a vast landscape with flowing water. The flowing river was surrounded by the mountains having tall green trees, a fantastic view. There were also two waterfalls located a little distance from each other. The young teenage couple was expressing their love for each other from time to time, and they would not allow each other's' lips to get dried.

From there, the driver took us to a place for horse riding. There were many horses and more than enough to choose from. A brown horse that was supposed to be my buddy for an hour showed me his intentions with his vicious smile. Actually, it was not a smile because his upper jaw moved west, and his lower jaw went east, and the long teeth seemed quite scary. But I took the risk and swung into my brown horse's saddle. Brownie was initially okay when I was riding on the straight route. Then I saw Zahoor riding his horse faster and shouting at me to also go faster. But being inexperienced, when I tried to make Brownie run fast, it went wrong. He ran fast but toward the river. When I pulled his bridle, the horse's neck turned to my side while its feet were moving toward the river. He started running even faster, and I was lucky that I did not put my feet in the stirrups because if I had to jump I would have suffered a serious injury. I looked for a proper place and jumped off the horse. After my jump, the horse ran faster than before. I think it was a mad horse or maybe his mood was off. Later the owner of the horse warned me that jumping off the horse was a big mistake, which I should not have done. I did not dare to try the ride again. I chose a big rock to sit on near the bank of the river and waited for the others to come back so that we could go to another place.

Horse Riding, Issyk Kul

Flowing Water, Issyk Kul

Next the driver drove us to the spring of hot and cold water about thirty minutes drive away. It was a vast field, and the car passed through plain lands with crops on both sides of the road. The spring was a small place for about fifteen to twenty people at one time, and it had hot water, cold water, and a mix of both, all separated from one another. When we arrived, a group of elderly and chubby women from Uzbekistan occupied most of the water there. They were playing with a ball and enjoying their time. They were very friendly, and after our arrival, they invited us to join them, but space was the problem. Zahoor asked them which water we should get in first. They suggested that first, we should get into the warm and then cold water, which seemed a bit odd at that time. But those ladies emphasized their experience, and we followed their advice.

Zahoor and I could barely find space between these women while the young couple didn't miss the romantic opportunity. After spending an hour, the driver of our tour waved his hand that it was time to go back. It was already dark when we arrived in Cholpon Ata. After changing our clothes, we went out, walked along the beachside, and had our dinner in one of the cafes. Issyk Kul was calm and quiet, and most people were local or those winding up their businesses.

The next morning we checked out from the homestay and handed over the room keys to the owner of the house. We went toward the beachside. We were not going to swim because the water was cold. But instead thought riding a camel or taking photos with eagles was a good option. The camels were bored, and any price was acceptable for their owners. The camel smelled unbearable like he had not taken a bath for months. Zahoor rode a water boat, and I enjoyed the camel ride. I very much enjoyed that different experience of Issyk Kul. During the return to Bishkek, we met some female tourists from Russia. Those ladies were visiting Kyrgyzstan, and they accompanied us until Bishkek.

Camel ride

Eagle in Issyk Kul

That summer vacation was a very useful opportunity for me. I not only visited the southern parts but also the famous Issyk Kul Lake. The diverse culture and beauty of the country extended from north to south and from east to west. Moreover, I discovered that like Kabul, there was also KFC in Bishkek – Kyrgyz Fried Chicken. I ate there a few times and always found tourists taking photos with the sign-board KFC situated opposite the Beta Store-1 on Chuy. I also visited Bar Kvartira, two Indian restaurants—The Host and the Spice and Sugar—and Jalalabad Chaykhana that served traditional Kyrgyz food in the center of the city. The Host was a little more expensive than Spice and Sugar. The owner of the Spice and Sugar restaurant was an Indian lady whose son was studying medicine in Bishkek.

Kyrgyz Fried Chicken, Bishkek

Chapter 6

Dordoy Bazaar

Dordoy Bazaar was probably the largest bazaar in Central Asia. It was the hub for Chinese products, and from there, these Chinese products were re-exported to other Central Asian countries. One weekend at about 11 a.m., I got out of my apartment and asked a *babushka* on the main road where I could find the *marshrutka* going to Dordoy Bazaar. I followed her directions, and took the right *marshrutka* going to the bazaar. It drove through the city center and then out of the city where the bazaar was situated. It took me about twenty minutes to arrive in the bazaar. It was a huge bazaar with almost everything one wanted to buy, but I was not sure of where to enter. Randomly, I entered from one of the corners and started walking through the crowd of people holding their purchases and some looking for their desired products. The bazaar was in the shape of several long, narrow streets formed out of shipping containers functioning as shops. Each street was for specific products. For example, a separate street for clothes, or electronics, or furniture, etc. The shopkeepers were both men and women. The bazaar was so popular among the locals that they said that one could buy anything in that bazaar. Walking through the narrow street, I also saw some Afghan ladies selling groceries. I had brought 300 Euros with me because I had heard that the exchange rate there was better than in the center of the city. After walking through a couple of streets, I saw a place where there were shops to exchange currency, and the rate was quite better than the banks provided in the center. In the city center, one Euro was exchanged for about 65.00 som while there it was 69.50 som. So, I went to change my Euros for som, but I did not know that the profit I was looking forward to would get me into trouble.

I randomly chose the first shop in the row from the right side. I did not realize it was closed, and I misunderstood the person sitting in front of it selling mobiles and batteries as the money exchange guy. That man also pretended to be the money exchanger, and he took my 300 Euros. When I counted my money in som, there were 400 som less than the amount he owed me. I showed him the money and expressed through my gestures that four hundred som were missing, but his answer was "go away." I thought he did not understand and I asked him in my poor Russian, "*Cheterey nol nol, som*"- meaning four zero zero som (that was the level of my Russian that I could not say four hundred som), but the guy had no intention of giving me any more som. I realized his intention, but pretended that he had made a mistake, otherwise how he could not give me my money. So, smilingly, once again, I tried to make him understand that he gave me 400 som less. He said something in Russian, which I assumed was, "Don't eat my brain, I will not give you your money."

I became extremely angry, but I did not know what to do. I said that I would call the police, and his body language said to do whatever I wanted to do. I had already heard many police stories, and I knew that they would not help. I called my former colleague Rafik and told him the story. He told me to give the phone to the guy. I gave him my mobile, they talked, and I could see from the face of that man that it did not work. I got my mobile back, and Rafik told me, "Look Idrees! This guy seems dangerous, and even if you call the police, they will not get you back your money. Four hundred som is not a big amount, so the best thing is to leave that place."

I said okay and sat near his showcase, thinking about what to do next. That guy could tell that I was not going to leave him that easy. Whenever any customer would come to him, I went near and asked about my money.

" Don't think that I would just leave my money with you. I am an Afghan, and I would get my money at any cost". I tried to make him understand. I thought that by revealing my identity, he would understand and would get me my money back. He left his seat and positioned himself in a boxing style, inviting me for a fight. I said, "let's fight," but he changed his mind and sat again. I thanked God that he changed his mind because I didn't have any fighting experience and the last time I fought, I was twelve or thirteen, I think. But I was angry, and I was ready to fight at that time.

Then I did a stupid thing that I should not have done. I gave him all the money in my hand and told him to keep this money too. However luckily he gave me back my money. With this stupid act, I could have lost all of my money. Next, I showed him my student ID card and said that I would call my Academy, and they would officially complain about him, but it had not had any effect on him. After some time the real owner of that exchange shop came and at that point, I realized that I changed my money with the wrong person. I went to him and complained to him in my gestures, and he said something to the guy, probably to give me back my money. But that guy was so mean that it did not affect him.

The last option I had left was to either fight with him, snatch his mobile or stand by his showcase and tell every customer that this guy was a fraud. If I fought, I would not only have lost my money but some of my teeth too. If I snatched his mobile and tried to run away, all the shopkeepers of Dordoay Bazaar would beat me mercilessly, and the next morning, my photo would emerge in the newspaper that an Afghan thief was caught and beaten after he tried to snatch a mobile from a local shopkeeper. The administration would have also expelled me from the Academy, and I would have to return to my home without achieving anything. And for disturbing his clients, again I should have had a better knowledge of Russian, however, I could have faced serious consequences.

Finally, I made a last try. I took my mobile and took his photo, which worked, I think. He stood from his seat and told me not to take photos and agreed to give me my money. First, he gave 200, I said no. Then he offered 250 and got the same gesture from me. He was increasing the money until it became *"cheterey nol nol."* I became so happy that I wanted to give him back that amount for which I had been struggling for the last hour. I was smiling, and so was he. We shook hands and departed very friendly and happy. I still have his photo in my mobile, and now when I look at that photo it reminds me of the whole story.

If you are a foreigner in Kyrgyzstan then the secure places for exchanging money are banks or specified money exchange locations. If a problem would arise there are security cameras that will function as a witness. Later my friends told me more or less the same stories of fraudulent people in bazaars. Rustam, my colleague from the politics group, told me that once he was changing money in Dordoy Bazaar and he was given less money. He changed about $800 and was given the som equivalent of $400. Later when he counted and complained about the money, the exchanger returned som for $200, and upon several requests and counting and recounting, he finally got his exact money back. A similar story happened to some Pakistani students where they had exchanged money and were given less. Police were called, who got the money from the money exchanger but took their share as well.

Dordoy Bazaar

Meeting Obama and Putin

Meeting Obama and Putin was the most exciting, unexpected, and amazing part of my time in Bishkek. I did not expect that I would ever meet these two influential people and the presidents of the two most important countries, but anything is possible in life. Sometimes, one sees unexpected things which become the memorable moments of their entire life. Thus, Bishkek fulfilled my dream of meeting the two most important and powerful leaders of the world.

The story begins when one evening I left for visiting the newly opened "Putin Pub" located a little away from the center but in the expensive part of the city. At the entrance gate, I was searched very thoroughly and asked if I had anything like weapons or any sharp object. I had not experienced such a careful body-check before, but I thought that it might be because the pub was newly opened. Upon entering I found the pub busy and crowded. The dance floor was full of people, while others sitting on couches with tables covered with pizzas, salad, and drinks. They were eating, drinking and enjoying their time. The pub, being new, modern and mostly for elite people, had Putin's photos all around on the walls. In each photo Putin was wearing different outfits. Putin in Kyrgyz kalpak, young Putin, Putin in Mexican hat, swimming in the river, hunting, riding on a horse, and in a black suit with black shades were some of the prominent photos that I saw on the walls. I found an empty couch in the corner and ordered green tea and some salad. I was enjoying watching the dancing people and sipping the tasty green tea. In the meantime, I noticed a man of medium height wearing a white kalpak on his head comes and sits opposite to me. First, I did not think much of it maybe he did not find any space anywhere in the pub and sat to share the table, but when I took a closer look at him, I saw it was Vladimir Putin, the President of Russia. I could not believe my eyes. I confirmed that I was drinking the green tea, then I glanced around the pub, and I found the muscular tall guards spread

192

throughout the pub that assured me that it was him.

He started talking to me. I was embarrassed, thinking how and what to talk with him about. He started with politics and asked me, "How is the overall political and security situation in Afghanistan?"

I wondered how he knew that I was from Afghanistan, but I ignored that and provided him with detailed information. "Afghanistan is moving on the right track, and the new president is working hard along with the Chief Executive to get the country out of trouble and make it an important country in the region." I saw a meaningful smile on his face while I was telling all this to him.

"How can an illegitimate government move Afghanistan in the right direction?" Mr. President asked while waving his hand to the waitress.

I did not like his vicious smile and continued. "We had problems with the results of the election, but now both Ashraf Ghani and Dr. Abdullah Abdullah are determined to lead the country out of the troubles, and we see the results. Our president is an academician, and technocrat and his economic plans would make our country a prosperous one."

"You cannot solve your problems, and for every minor problem America interferes, how could you say such big statements about your country?" The waitress brought a glass of beer and set it in front of him. I remembered that I heard Putin did not drink but then thought that maybe he did sometimes. I was about to answer when he interrupted and changed the topic. "How is your study? Economics is a hard subject, especially when it contains mathematics."

I realized that he knew many things about me, and I also realized that he was keeping a close eye on everybody, not only living in his country but also in those countries which were once part of his country. It did not matter if he/she was a student, businessman, a worker or an asylum-seeker. I thought for a while that his men might have followed me wherever I went in that city.

He realized and said to me, "Do not worry, you did not visit any place which could make you a bad guy in our eyes."

I was relieved, and I asked him what he was doing there. He answered that he visits many countries and places without any prior notification, beside his official visits. I poured green tea in my cup, and he cheered with his glass striking it with my cup, and that was the first-ever experience of striking an alcoholic drink against the green tea. But I was holding my cup on top because I did not want any small drop of that "HARAM" thing to get mixed with my "HALAL" drink.[18]

He started lecturing in a dominating way that America will never be successful in Afghanistan, and they should leave the country, and Afghanistan should focus on its friendship with Russia rather than strengthening its ties with America. I did not like the way he was dictating what we should or should not do. I turned my head and looked at other people dancing and enjoying the music with their beloved ones. I was angry, and I was preparing my answer that we are an independent country, and thus we knew who to extend our friendship or who not. But I was afraid of revealing that I did not like his words or that I disagreed with him because I knew what happened to those who disagreed with him at any corner of the world. I feared that even turning my head away from him could mean a disrespectful act for which I could pay the price.

Although during our conversation, my fear was surmounting. I was excited and happy that I had met the Russian President. I got lost in thinking that tomorrow in the class I would disclose the surprising news that I had met their beloved leader. I thought about how my classmates and teachers would react to my meeting with him. But at the same time, I worried about if they would believe that I had met him as I did not have any proof. I should have taken a photo, a selfie with him or something, so I could show that to my classmates and teachers. I pulled out my mobile and looked around but he had walked off and I did not find him. Anxious and nervous, I looked around the pub some more, but found neither him nor his guards. In order to catch him, I ran toward the door while the manager of the pub ran after me with the same speed as she thought that I was escaping without paying the bill. When I got outside, I did not find him and came back disappointed. After I reentered the pub, I found the manager and the security guards alert to arrest me for escaping the café. The manager was holding the bill for a chaynak of green tea and salad. I did not find the glass of beer drunk by President Putin on the bill, or maybe he had paid for that one glass himself. I paid the bill and left the pub.

After this unusual and strange meeting, I started thinking about whether he was the real Putin or his duplicate because I had heard the stories of duplicates of famous people. I had missed the opportunity of taking a selfie with the president of Russia, which would have been proof that I was not lying or that I did not dream or imagine the whole thing. If I would tell anyone that I met Putin in a pub, people would laugh at me. Even if I would tell my very close friends that Mr. Putin not only talked to me but also drank a glass of beer cheering with my cup of green tea, they would not believe because first of all, Putin did not drink alcohol and second, cheering a glass of beer with a cup of green tea was a strange act.

After several months, the Putin Pub got closed down because of a complaint by the Russian ambassador, probably because the pub was portraying Putin in a ridiculous way. According to the ambassador, it was not ethical that a drinking place should be named after the Russian President. Although it had become one of the popular places in the city and attracted a large number of visitors.

I had also used the example of the Putin Pub during our class of international and regional trade agreements. The topic was using different approaches to attract customers. One of the approaches was using logos, to attract the customers when they saw them. I mentioned different cases like KFC (Kyrgyz Fried Chicken) where the abbreviation was not for Kentucky Fried Chicken, King Burger, where the owner had just reversed the words of the original Burger King, and the third one was Putin Pub using the name of Russian President Vladimir Putin. Actually, each of these cases has their own legal framework to be addressed, but these things were normal in countries like Kyrgyzstan. Our lecturer, Dr. Luckasz was interested in Putin Pub, and he asked me the address.

The other restaurant by the name of another most influential leader in Bishkek City was "Obama Bar and Grill" located at the center of the city. One could eat pizza, burgers, and sandwiches there. It had some big photos of President Obama on the walls while the menu also had his photo on the first page.

A couple of weeks later, while I was passing through that

restaurant, I saw an unexpected crowd in and outside. Security men were actively assigned to different places outside the restaurant while inside of the restaurant was crowded too. My sixth sense told me that the U.S. President Obama had come on an unofficial visit following his Russian counterpart's visit to ensure his country's interest in the region because Kyrgyzstan was an important country for both of them. Overwhelmed, I walked toward the restaurant to meet him. I quickly prepared some questions that I should ask. Security, radicalization, corruption, drug-trafficking, human-trafficking, and terrorism would be the topics of my discussion. I would tell him that in the United States if you can become the president and make the dream of Martin Luther King come true, we Afghans can also work for the development of our country. Afghanistan can become a transition hub connecting Central Asia with South Asia and thus become an important country. Our geo-strategic position will bring us economic prosperity, and unlike in the past, we will not suffer because of our geopolitical position. We are rich in mineral resources, which will pave the way for global investors to invest in our country. Besides our hospitality, our beautiful landscapes will attract tourists from all over the world.

With all those thoughts in my mind, I entered the restaurant and was sure I was right when I heard people talking in the American accent. I started looking for him but could not find him. Disappointed, I found a seat and thought that he might be staying in the President House, the Hyatt Regency or somewhere in Issyk Kul. I thought that maybe this was his team checking security before he visited the restaurant.

The following day, I came again to the restaurant but still did not find him. I looked at his big photo on the wall of the restaurant and was telling him the questions that I had prepared. In the meanwhile, I realized that the waitresses and the manager were continuously looking at me strangely. Before I could become further entertainment, I paid the bill for my food and left the place.

After visiting these two places, I heard that there was also a Putin Pub in Jerusalem and Dubai. But the one in Dubai was Put-in, not Putin while Obama Bar and Grill was also serving customers in the Philippines. Thus, in the capital city of Bishkek, once the names of both Russian and U.S. presidents existed but the former got closed down soon after it became popular.

[18]Anything permissible or lawful in Islam is Halal while anything forbidden or not permissible is Haram.

Putin Pub

Official Guests

It was late November when I got a message from my friend in Kabul that an official delegation was coming to Bishkek and asking if I could show them the city. They were three people coming to Bishkek on an official trip, probably to participate in the regional conference. My mid-term exam was coming up and there was a heavy load of assignments and presentations to do. But saying no was against the Afghan culture, and I could have been labeled as rude and mean. I said okay to my friend and then one day I received a call on my mobile.

"Is this Idrees? I received your mobile number from your friend in Kabul. We came on an official visit to Bishkek."

"Yes, this is Idrees and welcome to Bishkek. How was your trip?"

"It was okay. We arrived yesterday, and today we had a busy day in the conference. We are completely unfamiliar with this city. Would you please show us the city, now, if possible?"

It was 9 p.m. and it would have taken me at least an hour to reach the hotel where they were staying. I replied, "It's very late now. But I invite you and your friends tomorrow for dinner." I realized he was not happy with my answer, and I heard murmurs from his friends because he was talking over the loudspeaker.

The next evening, I went to their hotel located about five kilometers from center city. When I arrived, I saw one man talking very loudly on the phone outside the hotel's gate, and I understood from his language that it was who I was meeting. He looked to be over the age of fifty, of medium height with a big tummy and thick mustache. It was very cold outside, and light snowfall had already begun. But that man was out in his pajamas. When he finished his conversation, I went forward and introduced myself. His name was Mr. Haqiqi, and he seemed very happy to see me. We both entered the hotel's lobby, where his two other colleagues were already waiting for me. The other man had a small beard, appeared to be about the same age, and had the same

198

tummy as his colleague. His name was Mr. Khushbeen. The third man was named Kanishka, and he was a young man in his early thirties. All of them represented important departments of the government. Mr. Haqiqi offered me food, wine, whiskey or beer. He had forgotten that it was I who had invited them for dinner. They all three were about to leave when I politely asked Mr. Haqiqi if he could change his pajamas.

I took them to a local café which provided not only good food but also had live music. The café provided good entertainment in late hours, and the environment would turn into a half-disco. I explained to them the different kinds of pizzas, salads, and Kyrgyz traditional food but they seemed thirsty, and all they ordered were different drinks, while I ordered some salad and a pizza. For about ten minutes, they were sitting there acting normal but then some inner behavior started tickling them, and they started flirting with the waitresses. While ordering their drinks, I realized both Haqiqi and Khushbeen super-enjoyed when they would bring their mouths closer to the waitress's cheek. They did not eat any pizza, but ordered more and more vodka and beer, which had me worried because I was going to pay at the end.

After some time, the live music started, and the cafe was gradually transforming into a disco. Haqiqi and Khushbeen were gaining momentum, and they started moving with the beats of the music while Kanishka relaxed at the corner of the couch. Knowing their intentions, I warned them that people come here with their spouses, friends, and girlfriends and any misbehavior can lead to serious problems. In the meantime, I went to the washroom, and when I returned, I could not believe my eyes. Mr. Haqiqi was somersaulting in the middle of the dance floor, followed by a unique vibrational dance while Mr. Khushbeen was busy clapping to give him more momentum. All the other people were standing aside, entertained and astonished because they had not seen such feats in any circus in their life. Before he collided with the DJ and speakers, two security guards came and took him to his table. Mr. Haqiqi was exhausted and had sweat coming down from his bald head and the thick mustache. People started going back to the dance floor, but the vacuum that was left by Haqiqi could not be filled again.

Mr. Kanishka was half-asleep, but Mr. Khushbeen did not

return from the dance floor, and instead went to another table of ladies where his flirting crossed the limits. I saw him in a situation where language was not a problem. I took him from that table, but he shouted. "Please do not take me from this table. You see, she wants me to sit there. She likes me." I knew that at the end of some kisses, I would have to pay their bill too.

"You should be careful because these ladies have connections with the police. They trap people, especially foreigners, call the police and take money from them." I wanted to make him scared by mentioning the police while the lady whom he was busy with looked at me with one eye and puffed the smoke of cigarette into the air.

Mr. Khushbeen said, "You know the chief of police was at the conference today, and he became my friend. I have his mobile number, and I can call him if there will be any problem."

I was puzzled by his reply and became confused as to what to say next. I brought him to our table, but by then, Mr. Haqiqi once again had found his way to the dance floor. The second time he was entertaining the crowd with his *Gonjeshkak*[19] dance. I felt a severe headache because controlling these two uncontrollable men became a challenge. Thankfully, Mr. Kanishka slept after a few more toasts. After bringing back Mr. Haqiqi, I decided it was time to leave. I took them from the café, got everyone into a taxi and headed for their hotel while they kept insisting on staying because there was still time until morning.

That was the weirdest experience, but I learned a good lesson to be careful in the future. I felt sorry for the Afghan delegations that come to attend the important conferences and seminars and spend most of their time in discos, and nightclubs, drinking alcohol and looking for prostitutes. They do not return to their country and apply for asylum during their visits to Europe, U.S., Canada, and Australia. When I shared my experience with one of my Afghan friends who was selling *chay* in Dordoay Bazaar, he told me more or less the same story.

"One summer I was walking around the beach in Issyk Kul, when I saw a group of people gathered around a tall muscular man completely naked shouting out dirty stuff. I understood what he was saying but luckily no one understood his language among the crowd. He was dead-drunk and his underwear was lying at his feet.

I went to him, introduced myself and told him to take care of his underwear. Later, I heard that he belonged to Afghanistan's ministry of interior and was a high-ranking official."

[19]One of the popular local Afghan dances mostly seen at weddings and other ceremonies.

Happy New Year

Ata Turk Park remained my buddy throughout my studies in Bishkek. My different memories of frustration, tense moments, enjoying the weather, meeting someone, thinking about the research topic, and many others were connected to this park. Ata Turk Park had two entrance gates from the Akhunbaev Dushambinskaya, and at the second gate, there was the statue of Mustafa Kamal Ata-Turk[20]. The park had a running track, playground for children, water-fountains, and grassy areas with wooden and metallic benches. At the end of the park, there was a monument in memorial of the Afghan-Soviet War followed by an area of trees and bushes, giving it the look of a mini-jungle.

One afternoon, Zahoor and I went to the park for a walk. It was Sunday, and the park had mostly children with their parents or grandparents. We wanted to go to Cosmo Park, which like Bishkek Park was not a park but a big shopping mall. While passing by the monument in the memory of Afghan-Soviet War, we saw an old couple standing by it. They were reading the writing on the rocks in front of the monument.

The monument was of two soldiers, one with an AK-47 hanging down his shoulder, and in his arms a wounded soldier. The wounded soldier was shown in such a way that it looked like a woman in the soldier's arms. For this reason I mistook the wounded soldier for his beloved one. War is always associated with many disasters, irrespective of whether you win or lose. The second thing I had assumed was a soldier returning from a war meeting his beloved one. In both cases, I assumed the second soldier was a female. Later when I asked some locals about the description of that monument, they told me that it was a wounded soldier in his arms.

The old couple was watching the monument silently and I asked Zahoor to talk to them and ask them the purpose of visiting that place. Like many other people, they had come to pay tribute to those soldiers who lost their lives in the Afghan-Soviet War from 1979-89. They paid their tribute by presenting a bouquet of flowers. I was inspired by their act. I thought maybe a member of their family had been killed or wounded in that war. But the answer was no. When they heard that I was from Afghanistan, I did not see any expressions of pride, guilt or sorrow in their faces. After presenting flowers, the old couple went on their way holding hands in an affectionate way.

[20]Founder and first President of Turkey.

Ata Turk Park

A Monument in Ata Turk Park built in the memory of Afghan-Soviet War

Next, Zahoor and I walked toward Cosmo Park. An old ethnic Russian with a long chin and muscular body sitting on a wooden stool was playing an old accordion. He had put a small tray near his stool to collect coins from generous ones. I put some coins in the tray. The old man's mood became happy, and he changed the pieces of music. When I looked down at his tray, I saw there were a few coins, probably 20 som. My generosity of two notes of 50 som further had activated him and he played a few more music tunes. I listened to his music for a few moments and then I moved toward the entrance gate of the Park where Zahoor was talking to another old man with a telescope charging 50 som per person to look in it. I went near them to see the moon. I looked back, and saw that the first old man was collecting his accordion along with the stool and tray. The telescope guy had a small white beard and was an angry man. We tried a few times, but all we could see was darkness, with nothing visible. We tried for the third time, but there was nothing seeable. After our protest, the old man became angry and asked for his money. In order to avoid his further anger, we gave him the money and thanked him for showing us the moon. I was dubious whether it was a real telescope or just an instrument that was no longer usable. Maybe that telescope was the means of his earnings, giving him the strength not to think that he was a useless person but earning for his family. We should have pretended like we had seen the moon.

A telescope for seeing the moon near Cosmo Park

With some sad feelings, we entered the park to eat something for dinner. After eating, when we got out, both of the old men were toasting with vodka sitting on a bench. That is life. Sometimes we see and perceive things differently than they actually are.

The New Year celebration had begun in the city. Inside and out the big shopping malls were decorated with different colored lights highlighting 2015. Most of the shopping malls had Christmas trees decorated with colorful lights with a Santa entertaining the kids and had different attractive gifts placed in their front areas. On New Year's Eve, it snowed during the day, which made the evening chilling cold and was getting colder as late night approached. I crossed Bishkek Park where some young Indian boys and girls were taking photos with the electronic billboard showing the digits 2 0 1 5 installed. Inside the park was the most crowded I had ever seen.

That night was different from the nights during the rest of the year. When I checked the time, there were still two hours left before the year would change. I visited a couple of cafes to spend my time and possibly eat something, but they all were full. I moved toward the Ala Too Ploshad, where hundreds of people had gathered for the New Year celebrations. The main square had a stage for a concert, and the organizers were busy installing electrical connections and other logistic arrangements. After a while, the local singers started practicing their songs. Tittering with the severe cold, it felt as though my cheeks were frozen. I was making my way among the crowd when I felt a hand on my shoulder and turned to see a mass covered with heavy winter clothes with only eyes visible holding a small bag of documents and files.

"What are you doing here?" he asked me. But I did not recognize him without him removing the muffler around his face. It was John. Had I seen him any other night alone, I might have gone unconscious of fear because he did not look like a Homo sapiens in any way.

"I have come to see the New Year celebrations. Have you also come here to see the celebrations?"

"I worked late in the office, and today I did not realize how fast the time passed. When I came out of the office and passed through the square, I saw it full of people, and then I realized that it is New Year's Eve."

The crowd at Ala Too Ploshad started a countdown when ten seconds were left for the year to change. Fireworks cracked across the sky after the New Year emerged with screaming and whistling from the crowd. The presenter delivered the happy New Year message to the crowd, followed by singers singing merry songs.

"Let's greet people with Happy New Year." John walked away from the crowd and moved toward the area where there were fountains. He greeted every girl without a male with "S Novim Godom" meaning Happy New Year. Almost every girl replied with the same words and John felt proud. It was probably the only night of the year where his voice was heard, and he received replies with smiles. We walked around the fountains where communication was easier than the crowd near the square.

"Oh my God!" John suddenly shouted, which made me worried.

"Is everything okay?" I asked. His facial expressions told me that something was wrong.

"The hostel closes after 10 p.m.. Now I either have to climb through a window to the fourth floor, but if I fall or…" He looked at me and waited for my reply.

"It is okay. You can come and stay with me. My flat-mates have already left Bishkek, so you can stay in any of their two rooms."

He accepted my offer, and we took a taxi to my apartment. After John removed his socks, an unbearable smell spread all around the apartment. I showed him to his room, and all night I heard him greeting Happy New Year messages, and after he went to sleep the sound of his snoring disturbed me one room away.

After seeing the New Year celebrations, I had to go back to Kabul where I needed to start my internship. I had two and a half months to complete not only the internship but also submit my final thesis, which was the most important part of my master's studies. We were also given a choice to choose our supervisor. He/she could be any professor from the Academy or from other academic institutions. I talked to Prof. Greg, who already had taught Research Methods and Designs and International Financial system in the second and third semesters, respectively. He agreed, and until I left for Kabul, I discussed my topic a couple of times with him. Prof. Greg was helpful and friendly, and without his help and guidance, I might not have completed my thesis. For the internship, I contacted the UNFPA Kabul Office and talked to my former supervisor and the Country Representative about giving me an internship opportunity there. Luckily, they agreed and accepted my request.

Two days before my departure for Kabul, Liam called and told me that his sister Lillian had also come to Kyrgyzstan for a brief visit and asked if we could meet sometime. We agreed to meet the coming evening. Lillian was working with UNDP in Bosnia. We had a very good time together, and talked about different topics from Afghan to Kyrgyz culture. Most of the things that I told them seemed to make them excited to visit Afghanistan. For example, our discussion went from bride kidnappings to weddings in Afghanistan.

"In Afghanistan, weddings in rural areas are different than in the main cities, and both have their own charm. A couple of years ago, I very much enjoyed one of my cousins' weddings in my native village (Wardak Province). As I belonged to the bride's side, a day before the wedding day, female relatives of the groom came to my uncle's house for the Henna ceremony. They had brought Henna, dresses, jewelry and other gifts for the bride. After dinner, the ladies pasted Henna on the bride's hands. They were singing songs, playing dayerah or daf[21] and dancing. It was a party only for the ladies. Meanwhile the male members from the bride's side were busy cooking meat from a cow they had slaughtered late that afternoon.

A week before the wedding day, my other cousin had written the invitations, which were handed over to the village barber. Despite being illiterate, he remembered the invitation for each house and every village. The village barber took them to all the people from the same village and relatives and friends living in other villages. The village barber, called Dam in the local language, is also responsible for beating drums at people's weddings and other ceremonies of joy. Besides these activities, he also cuts the hair of every person in the village and circumcises boys. In the past, he also worked as a dentist by pulling out teeth. In return, he gets grains and other food products obtained from the land of each household.

The next morning at 9 a.m., the flow of guests started. The food was soup made from the meat called shurwa, which had been cooking on the light fire since the previous night. It was served with fresh fruits from the garden and salad. The bread was broken into small pieces and then put in the shurwa, and meat was served separately. Guests came, ate the food and went, and it continued until 1 p.m.. There was no limit on guests. Many of the guests the host family did not know because they had just heard that food was being served at a wedding, so they came. As my uncle's house was located on the main road, I saw some cars stop by, and the passengers got out to eat a free lunch.

All this was normal in a village wedding in Afghanistan. While in cities the wedding ceremonies differ. First, most of the wedding ceremonies are held in wedding halls. There you provide the number of expected guests coming and choose the menu of food to be served. The wedding hall administration has the capacity to feed more in case the guests increase in number. Normally the number of guests for a normal family is between 700 to 1200. But there are people that have between 2 to 5 thousand guests. Moreover, for a normal wedding from its start until the wedding day an average cost could be $30,000 to $40,000 in cities. This includes buying dresses and jewelry for the bride, the cost of a wedding hall and food during the wedding day, and the amount of money called bridewealth which is paid in cash to the family of brides varies in different regions ranging from $2000 to $20,000."

I realized my story was getting longer, but both brother and sister were keen to listen. Everything they saw in Kyrgyzstan and my stories from Afghanistan were different from the culture they had come from.

[21]A dayerah or daf is a medium-sized frame drum mostly with metal ringlets attached to it.

Chapter 7

The Changing Kabul

After spending one year in Bishkek, I was going back to Kabul and was very excited to see my parents, relatives, and the streets of my city. After arriving at the Kabul airport, a unique smell followed by the noise of talking people welcomed me, and I felt like I had not been out of my country.

After only one year, I was not expecting some very prominent changes, but I saw changes starting from the airport. The first change that I saw was outside the airport's terminal. A long blue board having the fares to every place had been installed, which meant that one no longer had to negotiate with the taxi drivers. All you had to do is go and see the fare on the board and get into a taxi. I was impressed seeing that change. Second, the road from Pul-e-Sokhta to Darulaman had been asphalted. Before leaving for Bishkek, because of the condition of the road, most of the taxi drivers would not like to take me when I would tell them the address to my house, and those willing would charge Afs. 50 to 100 more.

After reaching the Pule e Sokhta area, there was a traffic jam, and I saw the disastrous situation of drug addicts. I found their number had increased compared to the previous year. They walked here and there like zombies begging for money and food. They approached every car and were bloodied and shaking while some of them were holding drug paraphernalia in their hands. Most of them looked terrible, and their long dirty hair and beards along with their dirty clothes gave them a further scary look while a few were looking normal but still identifiable as addicts. These normal-looking new **zombies** would look the same as their seniors within months because that is the rule of the game. Their dirty, burned hands were approaching us, sliding over the window, knocking non-stop. I wound up the window and locked the doors to avoid any disturbance. They looked exactly like the zombies in the Hollywood movies moving toward their targets, following them until they get them and then break them into pieces.

210

All of this reminded me of when my family first moved to that part of Kabul City. At that time, being new in the area, most of the things around were also new for me. I would wonder how all these people passing through this place were not even slightly worried about the presence of these *zombies,* but then I got used to their presence and accepted that bitter reality. These *zombies* had been living in or around the famous *Pul e Sokhta* bridge, which means the burned bridge in the local language, located in the west of Kabul. I do not know how it got this name, but when I saw hundreds of zombies living under it or around it burning themselves with drugs (heroin, opium, and others), I began to understand that its name absolutely fits its current scenario. The idea of a *zombie* is fictitious, but one can see them in most parts of Kabul City. Not one, two or three but in hundreds while their actual number is in millions all over the country.

After the end of the Taliban regime and the establishment of the democratic era in the country, the number of these *zombies* increased very rapidly. This is not a simple business where the government would eradicate its production in months or years, but the drug-mafia behind it is so powerful that year after year, the government could not stop it. *Pul e Sokhta* bridge had been built on Kabul River, and once upon a time, water used to flow, giving a beautiful look as it would pass through the center of the city. But for more than three decades, the flow of water has stopped, and drainage water from the households has found its way to it. The smell of filth is unbearable, and the *zombies* or drug addicts have further polluted the environment. All the area in or around the bridge has turned into a drug addicts' epicenter. The area under the bridge is now full, and they can be seen all around it too. There are shops and vendors selling fruits and vegetables around the bridge and at a short walking distance, there are residential areas. People living nearby cross the bridge once, twice or maybe more times a day. They meet these *zombies* begging on the way. People from the nearby areas also come to buy cheaper fruits or vegetables from the vendors near the area surrounding the bridge.

One can see *zombies* in different situations begging, cleaning the windows of the cars for money, selling stolen items, helping their *co-zombies* inject heroin, washing under the sewage water, eating, and sleeping. The problem is not only the presence of

211

these *zombies* begging for money, polluting the environment and making this place a major hub for heroin and other illicit drug sales but there is a bigger risk that a person shopping could accidently injure and infect themselves walking over used needles lying around.

Drug addiction is one of the main industries where we are progressing outstandingly. During the past couple of years, the number of drug addicts has increased rapidly in Afghanistan. Afghanistan has become one of the leading countries in producing and exporting heroin to Europe, Central Asia, and Russia, where it is in high demand and continues to be a lucrative business. In Afghanistan, the money from the heroin trade goes to the drug-mafia, including warlords and the militants fighting the Afghan Forces. Currently Afghanistan is not only one of the leading producers but also among the leading drug consumers in the world. There is likely no family or household not dealing with this problem directly or indirectly, and thus, the problems are not only limited to the user, but his/her family and friends suffer more or less the same. These zombies were also responsible for spreading dangerous diseases like Hepatitis-B and C, along with HIV.

There are different causes for this problem. The most important one is its large scale production and its easy availability. The government has not been successful in stopping its production and sale, while tribal elders and religious leaders having an influence on the society also did not play their role. The other causes include depression, frustration, unemployment, bad network of friends and difficulties of life. A quite good number of these drug-users got addicted while in Iran and Pakistan. Moreover, drug addiction in children is also one of the concerns in our country. Mostly, people give drugs as medicine to their children to relieve pain from wounds or diseases that they suffer.

After arriving home, I learned that my father had retired. Thus, the usual fighting between my mom and dad, that started late in the afternoons, could now erupt at any time. But the main change I saw was the change in government. Before I left for Bishkek, Hamid Karzai was ruling the country, and after I came back, the government of unity had established with Dr. Ashraf Ghani as the President and Dr. Abdullah Abdullah as the Chief Executive, and Hamid Karzai's status changed from current to the former president. The government seemed determined to eliminate corruption and had recruited young talent into the system. The new president also seemed firm on restoring the ancient Silk Route and exploring the country's natural resources.

Moreover, at the end of 2013, there were rumors that after the withdrawal of the U.S. and its allied forces, Afghanistan would go back into chaos, and civil war could start in the country, but all those rumors proved false and the new government was trying to meet people's expectations. One of the emerging problems was the rise of ISIS, which had spread another layer of fear among Afghans besides the Taliban. Likewise, due to multiple reasons, thousands of people were fleeing the country to Europe in search of a secure and better life. They were using different routes, and most of those routes were going through dangerous waters. Thus it was the growing insecurity that led to the problem of migration.

In my former office, where I started my new internship, there were also noticeable changes. Before leaving for Bishkek, UNFPA had completed SDES in Bamiyan (2011), Daikundi and Ghor Provinces (2012), while in 2013 the survey activities like training, media campaigns, the hiring of surveyors and publication of manuals and guidelines were in progress in Kapisa, Parwan and Kabul provinces. When I came back, UNFPA had already collected the data from these provinces, and the process of data analysis was in progress. My former supervisor Tia assigned me with a new supervisor Mae, and she assigned me data analysis work. Jawed had been promoted from assistant to associate level, and Khan stayed the same, busy with his GIS and other technical activities[22]. The office also had new staff because the survey was being implemented in many provinces at the same time. Besides my data analysis work, I also worked on my dissertation.

The reason behind choosing UNFPA for the internship was that I already knew the nature of work and was hoping that my supervisor would be flexible and not overload me with work so I could focus on my dissertation. However, I had lots of work as the survey was at its peak and I struggled between my time with internship and dissertation. During that time, I was regularly exchanging emails with my academic supervisor Prof. Greg. He advised, corrected and assigned me with new tasks along with deadlines. I progressed well during that period, and finally the time arrived when I had to fly back to Bishkek.

[22]Jawed and Khan were my colleagues and friends at UNFPA office Kabul

Kot e Sangi Bazaar, Kabul

Road going to Kargha Lake and Paghman hillside

11th Mikrorayon

On March 13, early in the morning, I arrived back in Bishkek. This time, the Fly Dubai Airline from Kabul to Dubai was full of those Afghans going to the U.S. on the special immigration visa (SIV). This special immigration visa is granted to those Afghans who had worked for the U.S. government or the International Security Assistance Force (ISAF) in Afghanistan from 2001 onward[23]. They had separate queues at the Kabul airport, and the IOM staff was there to help them as some of them did not know how to move ahead with all the procedures as it was their first time traveling abroad. Thousands of people were benefiting from this opportunity to start a new life in the United States. During the entire flight, there was noise, mostly children crying and their parents yelling or spanking them to stay calm. At Dubai airport's terminal, once again the IOM staff was there to guide them for their next flight.

Unlike the flight from Kabul to Dubai, the flight from Dubai to Bishkek was calm and quiet because most of the seats were vacant. There was no one nearby, and two rows toward the front, I saw two kids about three and five years old standing on their seats. Their mother was talking to them in an affectionate manner. I had not seen such kind of conversation before. A few hours ago I was seeing different children and mothers, and that language spoken by the parents was violent. But here, there was the language of love and affection.

"Mom, I want to open the window."

"No, it's a plane. People do not open its windows."

"Why not?"

"Because it is dangerous, the plane might fall, and we all will be killed."

Her younger son became quiet after listening to his mom's answer, and her elder son said, "I want to press this button."

"No, do not press it because after you press that button the waitress will come, and she would ask you what you need. But you

215

do not need anything." He postponed his act of pressing the button while standing on his seat.

In third world countries, parents and teachers do not pay proper attention to grooming children's physical and mental health. That is the reason that their proper mental and physical nourishment does not take place, and for Afghanistan the case is even worse. From child labor to child abuse and early child marriages, all pose serious threats in shaping their personalities. Even in the well-educated families, children cannot talk in front of the elders as it is considered a disrespectful act. In schools, they cannot ask questions or ask for clarification, and that is why many things stay unclear and unanswered until they grow up. I wondered how our society could provide a suitable platform for the children and young ones so that their physical and mental health can develop properly. The scenes of children and their parents from both flights were going through my mind, and I felt grieved for the huge difference in attitudes and behaviors.

I did not remember when I fell asleep but soon the voice of the air hostess awoke me to be prepared for the landing. Like the previous time, my visa was upon arrival, and I went straight to the consular affair office's window while other passengers went straight as most of them were Kyrgyz, and a few non-Kyrgyz had visas on their passports. The officer took my passport, and in the meanwhile, a couple came and stood beside me. The chubby lady with a round face was wearing a loose white shirt with black patches, a long black coat with blue jeans while the skinny man wearing glasses in dress-pants looked weak and pale like he had just been released from a prison.

The officer gave us forms to fill out and became busy in processing my visa. The form was simple. It asked some questions like the purpose of my visit, address in home-country, telephone number, contact address in Kyrgyzstan…

I started filling in the form when I heard the lady yelled at the man. "Where is your pen? Did you not bring your pen?" The man searched the pockets of his coat and pants in a panic but did not find anything. I quickly filled out the simple form and gave the pen to the man, and the lady calmed down. In the meanwhile, I got my passport with the visa stamped and paid the $70 when the man asked her for some information on the form.

"Do you not know? Every time I have to tell you." The lady shouted louder than before, and the man was standing like an innocent prisoner. After a while the lady said, "Ah! What clean and fresh air." She breathed hard. She was inside the closed building of the airport but had sensed the clean fresh air.

The man was filling out the form while she made gestures like he could not even do that simple thing. She looked at me and asked, "Where are you from? The U.S.?"

"No, I am from Afghanistan, and I am studying in Bishkek. Where are you two from?"

"I am from Brazil and this is my British boyfriend. We both work in a private finance company in Dubai. Now we want to see Kyrgyzstan. I heard a lot about this country."

I looked at her boyfriend, who was standing quiet and looking helpless, listening to our conversation. He was actually filling out the form for her because being British, he did not need a Kyrgyz visa, and he could stay in Kyrgyzstan without a visa for sixty days. While she had to get her visa upon arrival at the airport and thus had to fill out that form. I wished them happy holidays and got out of the airport.

I called Noor and asked about their new address. My doctor friends had also changed their accommodations. Noor and Baacha, along with their two other friends Younis and Hanif, had shifted to Asanbai, located a little away from the center but close to the mountains. They lived on the eighth floor of the building. Zahoor was living with his cousin Khurshed in another apartment, and only Hasan, along with Liaqat preferred to live in the hostel. After arriving, I slept for some hours, and then at lunchtime, I was introduced to Younis and Hanif because I had not met them before. I asked my friends to find me a single-room apartment. Although they insisted that I should stay with them, but I needed a calm place to finish my dissertation.

In Bishkek, if you are looking for an apartment, you either read the advertisements in the newspapers or deposit 500 to 1000 som to a real estate agency, and they find a place. Noor was looking for me in the newspapers, and during these three days, we checked out seven or eight apartments. One day when Noor and I went out to see one of the apartments nearby, we met John, who was also looking to find an affordable place because he did not want to live in the hostel anymore.

"I know about an apartment, and if you agree, we can rent that. The apartment has two rooms, and the monthly rent of one room is 500 som."

I was surprised to hear an apartment could be so cheap, and with this calculation, two rooms would be 1000 som. I showed a willingness, and Noor asked him a couple of questions about the location and inside of the apartment.

It was in the 5th Mikrorayon which was near to my Academy too.

"Let's see and check the apartment," I said. "If it is okay, we can share the apartment one room for each of us."

"The problem is that we would share one room because the owner of the apartment lives in the other room."

After revealing this important point, I changed my mind because I did not want to share the room with anyone at that stage of my studies. Later I learned that John had rented that apartment. But the problem was that the old owner was an alcoholic and bringing vodka at any time of the day or night was also included in John's responsibilities. But then something tragic happened, and the owner of the house died. Police interrogated John in the investigation until the forensic reports confirmed that the old man had died because of excessive alcohol drinking.

Finally, I found a single room apartment in the 11th Mikrorayon, about a five minute walk from the place where my friends lived. The apartment was new, well furnished with new furniture, attached toilet and bathroom, and a kitchen having all necessities. Although its monthly rent was a little expensive, wasting more time on looking for an apartment was not wise.

The DomKom was a chubby ethnic Russian babushka who did not like me at first. Noor introduced me to her, but after realizing the situation, he suggested I give her a gift. The next day, I bought her a dress and gifted it to her, and from that day onward she not only became good with me but started taking care of me. She would always ask me if I had any problem.

My apartment was situated in a four-story horizontal building with six entry places to each unit of living. It had four apartments on each floor, and I was living on the second floor. Each unit had wooden benches which would have been mostly occupied by the babushkas spending their time gossiping. The front area of the building was both a playground for children and a park-type area, and behind it was another building having the same features as the one I described. I also remember a few of my neighbors. On the fourth floor, beside the Domkom lady, another old lady about sixty-years-old lived with her mother. She would come down for a walk with her chubby cat with a leash around her neck. To my right was a Kyrgyz man married to a Russian lady, and to my left was a Kyrgyz family and the babushka of the family would mostly watch outside from her window. On the ground floor, an ethnic Russian woman over fifty lived with her dark-skinned daughter and two granddaughters with the same color. The difference in color was because the woman had married an Arab from Dubai, but she was now divorced.

The big problem she had was her addiction to alcohol, which I did not realize at first. One day, I heard someone vigorously pounding on my door. When I opened the door, she was standing vigilant, asking for 50 som. I could not understand the reason behind collecting the money but assumed that she asked for the money for the cleaning charges by the municipality team. I did not have change, so I gave 500 som and made her understand to bring me back the remaining money. After a while, she returned with some bottles of vodka and two photo frames. She showed me her shopping, and I realized that my remaining money was gone. I became very angry, and I complained to the Domkom lady and told her my story. Being already familiar with her, she became furious and took me straight to her apartment's door and started aggressive pounding with her powerful hands. The woman did not open the door but exchanged some words with the Domkom lady that made her further furious. Her intentions scared me, and I withdrew from my stand. I said to her that it was okay, I did not want my money. But Domkom felt sorry for me and later, whenever she would see me, she asked me about the money whether I had gotten any of it back.

Outside of the building, a few yards to the right was adinatsit bazaar. It was a small bazaar with shops on both sides of the street containing different items from the grocery to fruits and vegetables, medicine, cosmetics, and a bread baking shop. Besides these shops, there were also vendors, mostly elderly women, selling eggs, milk, yogurts, and handmade woolen socks. Among them was a Tatar man of medium height and Stalin-style mustache. Whenever I would go there to buy some eggs, let's say four, he would make me buy eight or ten because of his tremendous marketing skills.

"I need four eggs."

"Only four? You are a strong Afghan, you should eat good food and more eggs." Then he would put ten eggs in the plastic bag.

There was also a chubby Uighur lady wearing a scarf selling milk and yogurt at the back of her car, mostly in the morning. A little farther was an old ethnic Russian lady selling swine meat, and early in the morning, one could see their chopped-off heads and limbs. The shop from where I bought vegetables and fruits and the bakery shop were opposite to each other. I had very friendly relationships with all the shopkeepers except the guy from the bakery-shop.

Whenever I bought bread from his shop, I heard words from him that made the other customers laugh. I realized they were bad or insulting words. Sometimes he would not give me the bread by saying "finish" while I would see them "not finished." But I had no other option but to ignore him. Then I tried to talk to him in the Kyrgyz language and make his attitude better toward me. I would greet him with "salam" and then would say Bir Naan (one bread) or Eki Naan (two breads), and in the end, I would depart, saying Rahmat (thanks) to embark his national or Islamic spirit, but nothing worked. Finally, I got used to his behavior.

That small bazaar represented a very good example of multiculturalism and mutual harmony. People belonging to different ethnicities and religions were selling their various products in a peaceful and friendly environment. Nobody was criticizing anyone based on religion, race, or ethnicity. I forgot to mention one other shop which sold fish, beer and kwas and the owners of that shop were two tall ethnic Russian sisters. The elder sister was of the same height as me, and the younger was taller than me. Very early in the morning, when I would go for a jog, which happened rarely, I found them cleaning and sweeping in and outside of their shop. During the day, all they focused on was their work. Sometimes I wanted to have a chat with them, but seeing them busy would change my mind. One day I told them, "I don't think I could find ladies of your height in Afghanistan." Both of them took a pause, thought for a while and asked, "Why not?" I was about to answer when other customers came, and I left the shop.

In the Russian language, kwas is a kind of drink made from dry bread and is very popular in Slavic countries and the former Soviet Socialist Republics. It is a non-alcoholic drink having an old history in these countries, and its roots trace back to the 10th century A.D. This drink has also been mentioned in Russian literature. In summer one can find this drink along the roadside with other cold drinks. Besides bread, this juice has other flavors like lemon, honey, and other fruits. I did not like its taste at first, but when John told me its uncountable health benefits, I drank it sometimes during the summer. According to him, it was the best heat killer in summer. As summer was very hot in Bishkek, people sold different kinds of cold drinks in bazaars, roadsides, and shopping centers. The other traditional juice or cold drinks included ayran, which is yogurt, while chalap is the diluted form of ayran. Kumis was also popular, which was the fermented mare's milk, and jarma was made from crushed wheat.

After John was declared innocent in the murder case of his apartment's owner, he, along with his friends, moved opposite to my friends' apartment. His love stories and memories of Bishkek were very interesting. In every Mikrorayon he had a loved one and, thus, was the new one. Based on the love at first sight principle, John fell in love with Natasha, but Natasha was living with Sergey. She would always be either with Sergey or following Sergey, and John was following Natasha. But because of his fear of Sergey, he would not dare to go near Natasha. John knew that in the presence of Sergey, he could not get Natasha, but he was not losing hope. In the presence of Sergey even saying "Privet" was difficult for him and both John and Sergey did not like each other. Sergey was always everywhere with Natasha. Park, shop, car... There was not any place where Natasha went without Sergey. Therefore Sergey was like a bone in Kebab in John's way, and he did not know what to do with him.

John tried to befriend him and offered him meat but faced a strong reaction from Natasha because Sergey was a vegetarian.

John even tried to kidnap Sergey, but Sergey foiled his plan and informed the entire neighborhood. Now the neighborhood knew the intentions of John and warned him that in case any harm came to Sergey, it would be John who would be responsible. John had used all his cards, and it was Sergey's turn to take his revenge on him.

Sergey knew that John could not do anything because he had already exposed him to the entire neighborhood when he tried to kidnap him. After that, Sergey would wait for his enemy in the nearby bushes every day and looked for a suitable opportunity to take his revenge. One day when John was on his way home, Sergey was hiding very quiet in the bushes. When John came near, Sergey attacked him and bit him on his butt. After a defensive struggle, John was able to get him off, but Sergey did his work and left for his home. After coming home, John's friends realized the situation. One of his friends suggested taking John to the hospital to get treatment with anti-rabies medicine because he thought that Sergey might be mad. After taking him to the hospital, John was prescribed six anti-rabies injections, two a month.

[23]"Special Immigrant Visas for Afghans – Who Were Employed by/on Behalf of the U.S. Government", U.S. Department of State – Bureau of Consular Affairs, accessed May 15, 2018, https://travel.state.gov/content/travel/en/us-visas/immigrate/special-immg-visa-afghans-employed-us-gov.html#overview

Graduation Ceremony

April 5 was the deadline for the submission of our dissertation, and upon late submission, a specific percentage of marks would be deducted on a daily basis until April 10. After that, no dissertation would be accepted.

The biggest advantage of living near my doctor friends was that I was free from cooking and would go to them for lunch and dinner. I did not have to think about cooking my food, and thus, I had enough time to spend on my dissertation. During that period, Prof. Greg was guiding me, and I would incorporate his suggestions and advice. To get the degree, you need to pass all course-work exams, state exam, and the dissertation. On April 14, we had our state exam and my dissertation defense on April 22. In short, I succeeded in both tasks, and then it was time to prepare for the graduation day celebration. We received our caps and gowns from the Academy to be worn on that day.

April 29, 2015, was the day we had waited for during the last one and a half years. We had different times of happiness, worries, tensions, and jealousy but everything had its own taste. I remember, sometimes, the load of studies or assignments would get so high that I would get lost as to how to accomplish so many tasks. That was the time when even going to Bishkek Park or walking in Ata Turk Park was so enjoyable that their impressions still echo in my mind. Later after graduation, I had time to go anywhere I wanted but it was not very enjoyable. Time flew very fast, and the first day in the Academy always moves through my mind.

Our graduation day celebration was held at a five-star hotel, Jannat Regency, located about fifteen minutes from the center of the city. Each student was allowed to bring a guest or two by depositing 1500 som per person. The problem for me was how to minimize the number of my friends whom I wanted to invite to the graduation party because during that short time period, I had made many friends. I contacted Rafik and Gerald. Rafik accepted my invitation, but Gerald was not in Bishkek, he was on a mission to Batken, and had already received the official invitation from the Academy. So without Gerald, I had six guests to attend my graduation ceremony. The other five were my doctor friends Baacha, Zahoor, Noor, Younis, and Hanif. Hanif could not participate because he had exams that day.

Rafik showed up for a short time because his father was traveling somewhere, and he had to say goodbye. The event was in the Royal Ballroom of Jannat Regency. Each graduate had come with his/her parents, spouse or other family members. Everyone was happy. Parents were happy because they were seeing their children grown up and would soon occupy important positions in their countries. The married ones had come with their spouses and kids. The jolly kids playing in the hall gave a lively look to the party.

The chief guest of the ceremony was the foreign minister of Kyrgyzstan, Mr. Erlan Abdyldayev. Representatives from the international organizations, diplomates of the embassies, and professors of universities were also invited to the ceremony. At about 6 p.m. the ceremony started with the speech of Dr. Pal Dunay, Director of the OSCE Academy. He narrated the achievements of the Academy in the academic and research arenas and thanked the donor communities and the government of Kyrgyzstan for their assistance and support. John McGregor, the deputy head of the OSCE Center in Kyrgyzstan and Mr. Erlan Abdyldayev, congratulated the graduates, wished them all the best in their careers and assured their cooperation in the future. Afterward, the distribution of degrees began. Every graduate looked fresh and enthusiastic because they were enjoying the fruit of their hard-work for the last one and a half years.

Following receiving the degrees, all graduates, chief guests, and the Academy's staff took group photos. Mr. Qasemi represented the Afghan embassy. He was the second secretary and quite a talkative and jolly person. He introduced himself to most of the guests and gave them his business cards. After eating our dinner, some short games were played, and each student was given a special mug with the name of the student and his special characteristic written on it. For example, on my mug, it was written, "Most friendly." Each title given was based on the majority of votes, and the voting took place through email by the Academy a couple of weeks prior. The party finished at 10 p.m. marking the end of our important academic chapter but opening many doors of academic and professional successes to every individual.

Receiving MA degree from the John McGregor, the deputy head of the OSCE Center in Kyrgyzstan

Graduation Day

Graduation Day

From Left, Rafik, me, and Prof. Greg

From Left, Noor, Zahoor, me, Qasemi, and Baacha

Chapter 8

The Victory Day

Old men, dressed in military uniforms with medals on their chests and flowers in their hands, either with their spouses, children or grandchildren were walking toward a specific direction. People along their way met them with respect, and some presented flowers to them. I saw some little children who greeted them with flowers and then passed on very proudly to those accompanying them. That was the late morning scene that I saw when I went to do shopping at the nearby bazaar, but I did not understand the reason behind the story.

Late afternoon, I went to Victory Park, also called Youjhnee or Southern Park, located about fifteen minutes from my apartment for a walk. Twice or maybe three times a week, I would go there for a walk or cycling. Unlike any other normal day, the park's look was different. Mostly I saw children along with their families, couples, or teenagers who spent their late afternoon time in the park. But that day I found a large crowd at the tall tower in the middle of the park. When I went near, people were busy arranging the stage like an important event was taking place. Old veterans with their shining medals were sitting proudly in the first row. A few of whom I had already seen that morning. The youngsters would come and take selfies with them while the little children presented them flowers. Unfortunately, I could not figure out what that all was about. The first idea that came into my mind was that a film was being shot, and they needed those old veterans for their shooting. But soon the stage was arranged, and it looked like a concert was going to start.

A lady in military uniform came to the stage and started singing a song. I had seen her when she was coming to the park. She was in a hurry and running toward the park. I thought there might be some security incident, but I did not know that she was a famous singer. Had I recognized her, I would have definitely taken some photos with her. But I could not understand why the old men in military uniforms and medals on their chests were being given respect and honor. She sang two songs and the movements and cheering of the crowd revealed that she was quite popular among them. Next was a middle-aged man with curly hair, and the front half of his head was bald, but the remaining half at the back were long touching his shoulders. He also sang two songs on the stage, and I assumed that he was also a popular singer. In his last song, I only understood the names of the provinces of Kyrgyzstan and I guessed that he was praising the beauty of the country in that song. At the end of the day, each of the veterans walked toward their home with their family members.

After I went back home and asked my friends, I learned that May 9 is the Victory Day. The history of that day goes back to the defeat of Nazis by Soviets, and therefore, that day is not only celebrated in Russia but in some other countries too where Soviets had ruled. In fact, thousands of Kyrgyz people participated in that war, and probably thousands had died, and therefore, the day was not only to show their loyalty to Russia but they also had their own connection to it. Had I known about Victory Day earlier, I would have visited Victory Square near the center of the city where military parades pass. Or I might have visited Philharmonic hall to watch dramas or live performances or at least I could give some flowers to the veterans living in and around my neighborhood. But it was all because of my ignorance and lack of information that I even could not take a single photo with them and who knows whether I would find this opportunity in the future. If, in the future, I did find the opportunity to participate in any victory day celebration, would any veteran still be alive because they were already over eighty?

That was the day for which these veterans waited all year like children waiting for the New Year or Eid. They understand that each year, the number of their comrades decreased. That was the only day when they felt proud, and they thought they were not useless. That feeling kept them alive for the rest of the year waiting once again for this day to come.

May 9, Victory Day celebration

Cricket in Bishkek

Cricket, invented by the British, is mostly played in the former colonies of Great Britain. The Soviet block and its former Republics are unaware of this sport. In Kyrgyzstan, the game cricket was brought by Indian and Pakistani students studying there, but still, Kyrgyzstan did not have any official cricket team. Every year in Osh and Bishkek, cricket tournaments were organized, and students studying in various universities participated in those tournaments. In the year 2015, Indian and Pakistani students arranged a cricket tournament, and my friends' team was Salaar Cricket Club. I was offered a place on the team at the start, but was busy with my dissertation writing. After I graduated, I was free, and I had time to play, relax, and enjoy my time with friends. But based on the rules I was not allowed to join my friends' team because I was not enlisted before. The only option left was to be its supporter.

The sport cricket was not known to Kyrgyz people, and therefore, whenever they would see Pakistanis or Indians playing that game, they would stop and watch it with curiosity as to what type of sport it was. That tournament was arranged in Polytechnic University's playground situated in Akhunbaev Dushambinskaya, and the daily fee was 500 som. The team that I supported was doing a good job, and at the end of each victory, we would celebrate by cooking *plov* and meat at home or would go to Tokmok to eat *shashlik*. In total, fourteen teams participated from Indian and Pakistani students. We enjoyed every game until the semifinal, where our team lost, and our guys went home defeated.

MUHAMMAD IDREES

Salaar Cricket Team after qualifying for the Semi-final

When the Salaar team had qualified for the semifinal, the team and its supporters arranged a one day trip to Issyk Ata. Issyk Ata is a valley surrounded by green mountains and alpine meadows. It is located about 40 km from Bishkek. All of us together were sixteen men in four cars, and we camped at one of the places at the bank of the river. We had taken with us rice, meat, big pots for cooking, plates, and coal for burning. That get together was financed by an Afghan businessman who had married a Kyrgyz lady. Initially, the idea was to take two sheep and then grill them along with the rice. That idea had been circulating for the last two months. After a couple of weeks, it became one sheep, and finally Mr. Businessman bought 7 kilograms of meat, which he thought was more than enough for sixteen guys. That businessman was a very smart person, and giving a party like this was not a bad idea because these students were useful to him in many ways as he did not speak Kyrgyz or Russian languages. He had a good relationship with Afghan and Pakistani ambassadors and Kyrgyz officials, and he often arranged parties for them. Those parties were completely different than the one he arranged for us because he was a businessman with a business mind.

Now you are probably wondering what kind of business he was involved in. It was a medicinal plant that was found in the mountains of Kyrgyzstan, and he exported that plant to India, where there was a high demand. The search for that plant had

232

started in Afghanistan a couple of years ago, which moved to Tajikistan. After stripping off the mountains of both countries, he was in Kyrgyzstan. Later I discovered that the reason behind his marriage was also a business deal because once you get married to a local girl, you are entitled to many opportunities. After a brief communication, when he realized that I was not of any use to him, he did not extend the conversation. But I really enjoyed the Afghan *plov* and my time in the mountains.

One month before my friends' departure, they arranged another trip to Kashka Soo. I could not differentiate between the places. Same green mountains and alpine meadows but on this trip we were eight people with two cars. They already had prepared rice with meat, and we took them in big pots to the mountains. Eating *plov* and meat at the top of the mountains with green pastures all around helped us enjoy the true essence of nature.

Nearby, horses and cattle were grazing, and their movements would further romanticize the environment. After lunch, Baacha and I went toward the two yurts located in the area surrounded by the mountains. A little girl was playing with a brown puppy at the back of the yurt. A middle-aged woman and her husband were sitting on a broken and rusted iron bed with its two legs tightened by rope to its main part. A little farther were a young boy and girl playing chess on a wooden table about half a foot above the ground. They had a guest too, her husband's Russian friend who was sitting on a wooden stool next to her husband. There seemed to be a close connection between the woman's husband and that Russian guest, and later I knew that connection was vodka. When we reached them, they became alert, unaware of the reason behind our meeting. But what was the reason? Very simple, I wanted to know about life in yurts, and I asked Baacha to help me with translating.

The woman answered, "We live in yurts as part of our old Kyrgyz tradition. In summer, a yurt is cooler, and our livestock grazes in the nearby pastures and mountains. After the summer ends, we dismantle the yurts and move to our houses."

"Where are you from?" she asked me.

When I answered Afghanistan, the Russian guest sitting on the stool became very happy and told me that he had many friends in Afghanistan because he spent a year as a soldier there.

"I had friends Tahir and Rahman. If you know them…"

How could I know Tahir and Rahman from a population of more than 30 million? Who knows if they were still alive or not? Every Soviet soldier who had spent some time in Afghanistan had some memories and mostly good from the Afghan people and Afghanistan.

After a little chat, we departed from there. On the way back, our car stopped for a moment in front of the president's house, as an act of respect. If you do not make a stop, you would be caught by the traffic police through cameras and would have to pay a fine of between 1000 and 1500 som. Our friends in the other car did not make a proper stop and were stopped by the traffic police a little away from the president's house and fined 1000 som.

Kashka Soo Mountains

Lunch in Mountains

Chatting with a Krgyz family living in Yurt

Little boy and girl playing chess, Kashka Soo

Some days before the graduation ceremony of my friends, a terrible incident happened to one of their colleagues who had graduated from Osh Medical University and had come to Bishkek to attest his documents before leaving for Pakistan. He lost all his documents and passports in a taxi. The problem was that he had not used a call taxi—a taxi from the company having a specific number. He had used a taxi on the road and stopped it for a ride. That taxi driver did not notice the documents, or maybe other passengers took them or maybe any other case, but this affected not only the owner of the documents but his friends in Bishkek too.

Every day from morning until evening, they would go out to find the documents. They filed a case with the police, made announcements on radio and television, and tried any other possible way but with no result. Finally, he officially documented his case in the Pakistani Embassy and started the process to get out of this problem. Every day he would go to government departments for legal procedures to get the new documents. After a struggle of three weeks, he got new documents and passport and was eligible to travel back to his country.

Jinny and Lilly

It was a hot sunny day, and I was standing outside Tsum Center, thinking about who to call. I had a problem with my mobile, and I went to Tsum Center to fix it. I went inside and showed my mobile to two of the mobile repair shops, but they told me many things that I could not understand. In front of Tsum, I was about to call someone to come and help me translate when two girls approached me. The taller, wearing a short skirt but big shades said "hello" and started talking to me in English while the other girl, shorter in height wearing jeans, was standing quiet. After replying with the same hello, she asked where I was from. Usually, I answer this question with "Afghanistan." My friends think this is the worst answer to move forward because the very first things that come into their minds were war, *Kalashnikov*, or hashish. I dodged the question and said that I was studying in Bishkek. At that time, a breeze blew and was strong enough that the tall girl held her skirt tightly like she had read my mind. But my mind was as clear as glass.

"Won't you invite us for a cup of coffee?" she said, smiling.

She was quicker than I thought because I was not expecting this. I forgot for a while the purpose of my visiting Tsum Center and accepted their proposal to invite them for a coffee. There was a coffee shop on the other side of the road. Based on the ladies' first principle, I followed them, but the breeze did not blow again.

When the menu arrived, I was embarrassed by the way they were ordering because it was more than a cup of coffee. Once again, I was impressed because they did not even consider if I could bear such a burden. I excused myself for the toilet and made some rough calculations to see if I was able to pay the bill, but I returned without any conclusion. The one wearing the skirt was Jinny, and the other wearing jeans was Lilly. After eating the food, I paid the bill, and my mood changed. But while departing, I received kisses on my cheeks from both of them, and my mood changed again - the other way around.

Two days later I received a call from Jinny.

"Do you know that tomorrow is my birthday?" How could I know, but I made a polite answer.

"You did not tell me, or I would have definitely known."

"Okay, tell me what will you buy for me as a birthday present?"

Again she had come directly to the point. I got a bit puzzled and then replied. "Well, I do not know, but I will buy something."

"See you tomorrow at 11 a.m. at Sovetskaya Moskovskaya."

I was a bit surprised when she told me about her birthday party but she did not invite me. Instead, she told me to meet at 11 a.m.. The next day at Sovetskaya Moskovskaya, Jinny appeared wearing high red heels, and a skirt a few inches shorter than the one she was wearing the first time I met her. I felt the dress was not proper because I heard some young men greeting her with some not so good words. She took me straight to a dessert shop and asked me to buy a cake for her birthday. My eyes were looking for a lower price, but she chose the most expensive one. After buying the cake for her birthday, she threw out the idea of having lunch and again I accepted.

"Thank you very much for your gift. Now I am going home to take care of guests coming for my birthday."

I was walking with her when she gave me a goodbye kiss and departed. It was an unacceptable situation when someone talks about her birthday, makes you buy a birthday gift and then leaves you without inviting you to the party. I returned home angry and did not understand what kind of attitude and behavior that was. After a couple of weeks, I received a call from Lilly, and she told me that she had her birthday the next day. I already doubted them in my mind, but that time I realized that these two girls were making a fool of me by playing the birthday game. I made an excuse and said that I was busy. I should have understood them from the very beginning because how could Jinny and Lilly be the names of Kyrgyz girls.

My doubts proved right when after a couple of days, Jinny called me and asked me to lend her some money. I said sorry and said goodbye to both Jinny and Lilly. Later John told me that birthdays were one of the tricks that ladies used to get money or gifts from men. Jinnys and Lillys exist everywhere, and they use different ways and techniques to get their prey.

I had not recovered from the birthday incident when Alexandra called me on my mobile but I did not answer. I was dubious that she wanted to trap me again. After carefully watching these two cases, I became further suspect that there was a connection between these ladies. Jinny and Lilly might belong to her gang, and they wanted to trap me or get my money. After not answering her call, I received a message.

"I am going to Russia next week because I have found a job in Saint Petersburg. If you want, we can meet for the last time."

First, I thought not to meet because I could face any possible number of problems, but then after talking to my friends, I was given an NOC (no objection certificate).

After sitting for about thirty minutes, Alexandra broke the ice.

"Why did not you call me during all that time?"

I could have asked the same question from her, but I came directly to the point. "Look, first, you send that old lady to my apartment, and then Jinny and Lilly to trap me. If you wanted anything, you could have asked me directly. Moreover, your desire for parrot's juice [blood] also made me scared of you."

"What? What are you talking about? I did not send anyone, and I did not want anything from you. In fact, I was in Saint Petersburg for some months for my company, and now I am going to shift there permanently. Regarding the parrot's juice, I mistakenly used parrot for carrot."

After that, once again, there prevailed the atmosphere of silence. That was my last meeting with Alexandra, and then she left for Russia. That was my short love story, which finished before it started.

Good Bye My Friends

After Alexandra's departure, my friends also started packing for their homes. They had their graduation ceremony on June 25th. That was the day they had been waiting for the last six years. They had also invited me to the event. The ceremony was arranged in the main hall of Kyrgyzstan State Medical Academy (KSMA). The huge crowd of students in formal dresses revealed that the day was special.

Inside the gate of the university, there were hundreds of graduates wearing caps and gowns belonging to different parts of the world. Flags of different countries were hanging in the hall, representing the countries of the students graduating from that university. After entering the hall, some students were busy taking photos, a few organizing the stage and most of them occupying the seats as the event was ready to begin.

All over the hall, colorful balloons gave lively colors to the event. Rector and two senior professors were sitting on the stage while other professors and staff were sitting in the first row beneath the podium. First the Rector and the two senior professors delivered their speeches followed by the short speeches of student presidents from both Pakistan and India. Then they started the distribution of degrees to the students. The announcement of each name was followed by clapping of all sitting in the hall. Some close friends would even stand while some would get alerted to take photos. This session lasted for about an hour, and those getting their degrees from the dais would receive flowers and gifts from their friends. Some had come with their girlfriends who were checking the collars, coat, and hair of their beloved ones. Their joys were worth-seeing when they saw their beloved ones receiving the degrees. The overall event was well-organized, and everybody was happy. There was no food or refreshments served because of the month of Ramadan. Their academic journey to achieve a medical degree had come to an end. Next they had to attest their degrees from Kyrgyz governmental departments like the Ministry of Education and Ministry of Foreign Affairs of Kyrgyzstan and then from the embassies of their respective countries.

I was sitting in the last row watching the entire ceremony. Two seats to my right was a Kyrgyz girl also watching in silence. At one point, when an Indian guy was receiving his degree, that lady left her seat and walked to the podium. She took several photos of that guy. After he received his degree, they hugged each other, and she presented him with flowers, and then both of them came back to the row of chairs where she was sitting before. I looked at the degree of that Indian guy, and it was red, meaning that it was a distinguished degree. After the distribution of degrees was completed, the name of that Indian was again announced, as he won the award for the best student. Once again that lady left her seat, went near the podium, and took photos of him. This guy was Sahu, an Indian and belonged to Uttar Pradesh. Like many other Indians, he had also come to Kyrgyzstan to pursue his studies in medicine.

Before my friends left Kyrgyzstan, we spent happy times together, especially in the last couple of months. We went to the mountains, parks, city center and enjoyed the best of our time. That year, I was also very comfortable in Ramadan because I would sleep during the day, and go to my friends for fast breaking. They stayed busy preparing the food, which was not ordinary but a mix of different dishes.

On July 14th, it was time for my friends to leave Kyrgyzstan. I accompanied them to the airport. After spending six years in that country they really loved Kyrgyzstan. On that day, about twenty other graduates were leaving Bishkek. A few had their girlfriends with tears in their eyes at the airport. They had scheduled their flight from Bishkek to Dushanbe, Dushanbe to Kabul, and then onward to Peshawar and Buner, where they went by road. Finally after two days of traveling, they would be in their homes. In Pakistan a new chapter of their life was waiting to begin. They had to pass Pakistan Medical and Dental Council (PMDC) examinations arranged for the Pakistanis who studied abroad. Passing PMDC examinations was a big headache. Some students took years to pass that exam, which had three parts. There were reports of corruption that students had to pay bribes to pass the test. That would be very horrible if students did not study medicine properly and got the authorization to treating patients.

Among my friends, only Zahoor stayed for a month more, and we spent some memorable time together. During the last week of Ramadan, I visited two mosques (Hazrat Aisha mosque in the 12th Mikrorayon and Central Mosque) and ate my dinner together with the local people. There was a long Dastarkhan with juice, bread, fruit, and rice served for free. I also met Nurlan there. When I asked who financed the food, Nurlan told me that usually, money came from the charities.

Breaking the fast at Hazrat Ayesha Mosque in 12th Mikrorayon

Iftar in Central Mosque

One day before Eid, a security incident took place, and it was reported that some terrorists were killed before they carried out their activities on the Eid day. There were different reports about that incident. Some were saying that the Russian intelligence forces participated and killed the attackers in one of the apartments in Bishkek city. Another was that there was a dispute among the former intelligence mafia and the current ones. Therefore security was tight on Eid day. Police and intelligence staff were performing their duties at different places near Ala Too Ploshad, and they were searching the suspicious ones coming to Eid prayer.

After the prayer, people started to greet Imam Maqsad for respect and sacredness. They were struggling among the big crowd of people to kiss the hands of the Imam. I noticed among Kyrgyz people that they blindly believed in their religious leaders. In most cases, the common people gave respect to every person with a beard and religious appearance. The good thing was that they worked under the tight control of the government. Although, a handful of Kyrgyz in and outside the country were joining the extremist elements, which I will discuss in the last part of this book.

People greeting the religious leaders after the Eid Prayer

Afghans in Kyrgyzstan

I did not find any concrete data about the number of Afghans living in Kyrgyzstan. In my interview with the Afghan ambassador, I asked him about the data, but he did not have the precise numbers. He roughly said that an estimated 200 Afghan families lived in Kyrgyzstan, and most of them had been granted asylum in the U.S. and Canada, with the remaining granted Kyrgyz citizenship. Afghan asylum seekers started coming to Kyrgyzstan at different times, from the 1990s until the present. For the last couple of years, because of the current wave of insecurity in Afghanistan, a few Afghan families also moved to Kyrgyzstan. Their purpose was the same, to flee insecure Afghanistan and find their way abroad for a better life. Besides asylum seekers, there were a handful of businessmen doing business and students studying there.

The month of July was hot and wet, and after each rainfall, the weather would get very pleasant. At the end of July, Zahoor and I planned to visit Kant, a small town located about 20 km from Bishkek. One afternoon at about 2 p.m., we got into a *marshrutka* going to Kant. Zahoor had lived for about one year there when he first arrived in Kyrgyzstan, and he wanted to refresh his memories before going home. After a thirty minutes drive in the *marshrutka,* we were in Kant.

I realized Zahoor was struggling to remember the town because he had not visited for the last five years. We walked through different streets in search of the place where Zahoor had lived. Finally, and coincidently, we came across the football stadium and thanks to his memory, he started to recall the streets and other locations. In the stadium, boys were busy playing football, and some young men were running on the track. There was a man over forty, lying on the green grass listening to the legendry Afghan singer, Ahmad Zahir's songs and his children playing while his wife was reading a prayer in another corner a little distance away. Zahoor recognized him and told me that he was from Afghanistan and they had befriended him when he was living in Kant. Zahoor was expecting a hello, but he seemed so much lost in that song or probably pretended to do so that the meeting did not take place. After crossing the stadium, there was the railway track. We crossed the track and entered into a kind of colony having different residential houses. He showed me his apartment where he and his other friends had lived. He then took me to a house and asked about a *babushka* with whom he and his friends would drink tea. Zahoor told me that he would prepare milk-chay for her and practice his Russian with her. Her grandsons were busy loading a car with luggage, and they told him that she had died a year ago. After hearing that bad news, tears came in Zahoor's eyes as he had some good memories with her. He started asking questions about why and how she died, but her grandchildren were not in the mood to provide details, and thus we left that place.

We then walked inside the colony and found some Afghan children playing there. After introductions, we learned these boys belonged to four different families who had recently moved to Kyrgyzstan from Kabul. They had applied for asylum. The result would be either acceptance to the U.S. or Canada, or they would be given Kyrgyz citizenship. But all this takes about five to ten years, depending on the nature of the case. Their male members of the family were working in the Dordoy bazaar selling green and black tea. These families belonged to the new migrants who left Afghanistan because of insecurity and dreamed of a bright future in the U.S. or any other country.

After a brief chat, we bought ice cream for them, and while eating, a lady passed by us. "Did not I tell you not to accept anything from strangers? I will report that to your parents," she warned the children angrily when they had just started tasting the ice creams.

"I bought them the ice creams; they did not ask me to do so," I interrupted after seeing the anger on her face.

"Well, you know people here mind when children ask people to buy them anything, especially when they are strangers. That is why we always stress to them not to ask for or take anything from people they do not know. I saw them a couple of times before, asking people to buy them chocolates or ice creams." She said these words and went on her way without bothering to prolong the conversation with a person from her country.

"First, give us our money then teach us manners." One among them with curly hair shouted in a bit louder and angry voice.

"What kind of money does she owe to you?" I asked him.

"Her husband took money from many Afghan families and promised that he would bring us to Kyrgyzstan in a plane, but he lied and brought us by road. He owes us $5000," the boy replied.

"If you did not come by plane, then how did you come here?"

"I do not know. First it was a plane, then car."

I understood coming to Kyrgyzstan was not easy, and one had to go through many ups and downs. But the lady's advice was right because I remembered when I gave some som to a child in my neighborhood. He took the money but faced many questions at home. Later I met his aunt, who had come from the U.S. to visit her parents, and I asked this question of her, if it was okay to give money to children. She said, "Ah, it was you who gave him the money. All of us at home became so annoyed, wondering who gave him the money and why?"

Making children addicted to money is not good anywhere in any society. They would rather be appreciated with gifts or learning materials that could help them in their mental growth. I understood that giving money to children was an unfamiliar act, but in Kant those children were from my country, and therefore I thought it should be okay.

Things differ from society to society and culture to culture. After I got back to Kabul, one day, I discussed that topic with my friend Hafiz who was living in Baltimore, Maryland and had come to Kabul for a couple of months along with his children. I told him that in Bishkek, I communicated with children, old people, young boys, and girls without any hesitation and they had no fear from the foreigners. I could talk to children in my neighborhood. I could communicate with them. I even bought ice cream for them. He said that in the U.S. the situation was different.

"People usually do not communicate with strangers, and parents are very strict with their children, especially when it comes to communicating with strangers. Parents strictly watch their children, and they can even complain or call the police against any stranger for a suspicious act. In the U.S., parents train their children not to talk to strangers and not to accept anything from them. Once I was in a doctor's clinic with my son for a normal medical checkup when a little girl started talking to me. She was a very smart and cute girl. She asked me, 'Did you have such a doll when you were kid? My doll is very beautiful. She can talk and sing.' I was answering with yes and no answers and then her mother interfered and told her in an affectionate tone, 'Do not talk with strangers because who knows if that person is good or bad.'"

Back in Kant, Zahoor showed me a café which was once a disco and told me he had been there twice along with his friends. It was getting dark, and we needed to finish our adventure. We made our way to the main road. At the small bus stop *marshrutkas* waited for the passengers. We got into a *marshrutka* and left for Bishkek. After arriving back in Bishkek, we got off the *marshrutka* and crossed the road to get another *marshrutka* to our accommodations. After a little walk, five policemen suddenly appeared from the bushes and came toward us like we had committed a serious crime. They quickly checked our documents and wallets, followed by a couple of questions, but did not find anything wrong. Finally, they gave us back everything and departed in a friendly way. But during the search, they had taken 1000 som from each of us so skillfully that we did not realize it until we got home. At that time, we thanked them and were impressed by their kind and friendly attitude.

In Kyrgyzstan one should also be careful of police because they can create problems when they know that you are a foreigner, and in fact, the locals can also suffer. Vita (a young taxi driver who became my friend in the very last month) told me that one day his father withdrew money from the bank. Some policemen mistook him as a foreigner (though he was Russian but with a foreign look) and interrogated him as to why he had such a big lump of money. When they were sure that his father would not give them anything, they even threatened him that they would make a case against him that he was planting a bomb in the market. Later, his father called his family members, and with their intervention, the problem was settled.

Two days before Zahoor was scheduled to leave Kyrgyzstan,

we planned to go to the Hawaii café located in the Tokmok region, about 40 km from Bishkek. It was a big café or in other words a restaurant with a pool of water with boats, a small garden, live music and some statues of animals. By visiting that place, you can have peace of mind by relaxing in the garden, taking a boat ride and enjoying live music with some good food.

I talked with Vita, and he took us there. Vita was a trustworthy person, and during the last month, wherever I would go, I called him, and he charged a reasonable price. He was a calm and cool guy and spoke only when we would talk to him. When we arrived there, it was getting dark. We quickly took photos in the lawn with the animal statues and at the bank of water to keep it in our album as proof that we had visited. The restaurant had two halls, one in open air and another covered, and both of them had live music. That was my last trip with Zahoor, and the next day he left for Pakistan.

Chapter 9

Karakol

Since the previous year I had visited the southern parts of the country, the next year, I decided to visit the remaining parts. In early August, I left for Karakol, which was about an eight-hour drive by *marshrukta* from Bishkek. It took me four hours from Bishkek to Issyk Kul and then another four hours from Issyk Kul to Karakol. Karakol was a calm and beautiful city. I arrived there at about 4 p.m., and the first thing was to find an accommodation. I went straight to the CBT office, where tens of tourists were leaving the office, and there, I learned they had no space. The other option was to look for a hostel or guesthouse. I met some tourists in the bazaar, and they told me the names of a few guesthouses, Amir and Jamilia, but when I arrived, there was no space at either. But one did not have to worry because in Karakol there are lots of hotels and hostels at lower prices. I checked into the Issyk Ata hotel located near Alybakov Street. The room was small but clean, with an attached toilet. It had a wooden cupboard and television as well, and the cost for one night was 250 som. I put my luggage in the room, took a shower and then went out with my camera to discover the city.

Earlier I had gotten information from the tourist guide book *Lonely Planet*. The street in front of the guesthouse was very quiet and calm. To the right, it joined the main road while to the left was a residential area. I knew from the book that somewhere near was Pushkin Park, but I did not know exactly in which direction. During those silent moments, I saw a man riding a bicycle, and one could hear a hissing sound whenever he pedaled from quite a long distance. When he came near, I asked him about the address of Pushkin Park. He told me to walk a little to the left and then turn right, and I would find it.

The afternoon was so quiet that once again, I thought that time passed slower than in Bishkek. I followed his directions, and on the way, I met two children looking bored who were seeking good company. Both of them were of the same age, maybe twelve.

One was chubby with small eyes and a round face and looked to be Kyrgyz, and the other was skinny with freckles on his face, he looked Russian. I communicated with them in Russian and told them that I wanted to go to the park. They were very friendly and were not afraid of strangers, or their parents had not told them to stay away from foreigners. Being a grown-up child, I very much enjoyed their company. In Pushkin Park, there was a tank and a monument with names of soldiers who had lost their lives in the war of Afghanistan. That was the second place, after the monument of Ata Turk Park that I visited, built in memory of the Afghan-Soviet War. After taking some photos, toward the end of the park, we did some target shooting and then went to Zoo Park. Zoo Park had different kinds of birds, wolves, eagles, deers, yaks, dogs, and cats. It also had a stream flowing, which gave more beauty to the park. Even in the park, the atmosphere was quite calm, and the animals were peaceful. Besides us, there was a couple with two little girls visiting the zoo. We all three enjoyed ourselves, but when we wanted to go out of the park, we found the main gate locked. The caretaker lady called her colleague to bring the key, but her colleague did not appear. We climbed the main gate and walked back through the park.

These two little boys told me many things which I did not understand despite my best effort. At the end of the day, when I gave them some money, I felt they were eager for the next day's adventure as well, but I could not promise them because I had to visit some places which were a little far from my hotel. I had already done some research about the restaurant, and I went to the Kench café for dinner. It was a small, well-decorated cafe with visitors both inside in the hall and outside sitting in the open space, and the prices for food were reasonable. I sat inside, where two groups of foreigners were occupying other tables. The first group included five men dressed officially, and they looked like employees of an international organization. At the other table, there were two ladies, looking tired, from trekking probably. Overall, the atmosphere of the café was calm, and the sound of a television could clearly be heard. I ordered *shashlik* with chips and salad, and the food was very tasty. After a while, the other people left the café, and I was alone. At about 10 p.m., I went back to my hotel.

At the entrance, there were some drunk men enjoying their party. The gate was closed. I got worried because waiting at the gate could get their attention, but thankfully, the old lady administrator showed up after several rings of the bell.

The next morning it was about 9 a.m. when I woke up. I took a shower and changed my clothes. First, I went to the colorful old Orthodox Church. Although I had tried to visit it on the day I arrived, I was too late, and it had already closed. But the following day, I was on time, as it was about 10 a.m. when I arrived. I met two other tourists from Russia. With them was a local Kyrgyz lady who was studying at the American University, and as she had a holiday, she was working for a tourist company. Those tourists were looking at everything with a keen eye and discussed details about its construction and functions in the past. Luckily, that Kyrgyz lady provided me with some translation.

"The church was entirely made of wood with no nails used. The church was originally made of stone then destroyed, and the current wooden form was built in 1895."

Inside, the church was very beautiful. It was the first-ever church I visited. There were photos of Jesus and Mary, and candles lit in all its corners. One other old local lady had come for prayer. After visiting the church, I went to the museum situated a very small distance from the church. It was a small museum divided into two types of items i.e., traditional Kyrgyz and ancient stuff like handmade rugs, carpets, coins, komuz, and yurts, etc., and preserved animals like wolves, foxes, bears, eagles, leopards, deers, and different birds.

Inside View of a Museum, Karakol

After visiting the museum, I left to see the historical Dungon mosque. On my way I went to another mosque mistaking it for Dungon. This mosque actually resembled the mosques in the villages of Afghanistan, both in shape and size. Later I checked my guidebook and learned that the Dungon mosque was situated a little farther away. On the way, I ate delicious *kordak* as my breakfast and lunch together. After eating, I went toward the Dungon mosque. It was one of the sightseeing places for tourists visiting Karakol. It took six years to build and was completed in 1910. That mosque was wooden, and like the Orthodox Church was also believed to be built without using any nails.

Before I got into the main gate of the mosque, two tour buses stopped there, and passengers started flowing inside. These tourists were Russian speakers, probably from Russia or Kazakhstan. After the tourists left the mosque, I decided to read my prayer, but before I entered into the praying hall, one person —probably the caretaker of the mosque—stopped me. After telling him my aim of reading prayer, he allowed me in but was not sure and continuously watched me. When I was leaving the mosque, he waved his hand, indicating I should come to him. He told me to sit with him and asked about my nationality and job. When I told him that I was from Afghanistan and studying in Bishkek, he gave me a very long lecture on terrorism in his broken English. I had to leave Karakol the next day, but before I left, I wanted to visit the beach there, so I said goodbye to him.

Dungon Mosque

I was looking for a taxi that could take me to the nearby shore and bring me back to my hotel. In front of my guesthouse, I talked to a taxi driver, and he agreed to 700 som. It was a drive of about twenty minutes to the nearby shore or beach. I just wanted to see how the beach looked there.

The road to the beach was beautiful, and surrounded by a nice mountainous view. On the beach there were three or four groups of families preparing to depart because the sun was about to set. There was one chubby old lady, and her granddaughter was insisting that she should jump into the water. The grandma was reluctant at first, but then she agreed. At first, she started shivering after she jumped into the water, but then she got used to it. Whenever she would jump, her jelly-belly would make several vibrations and movements, and her skinny granddaughter would enjoy seeing her grandma in the water. That sight of the beach was different from the main Issyk Kul beaches. There it was calm, natural and one could enjoy being free from the noise of people.

Most of the people who come to Karakol go for trekking and sleep in their sleeping bags in the mountains while enjoying the peaceful beach and a calm environment. I took some photos, saw the view of the sunset, and came back to my hotel after dark.

I ate my dinner at the same Kench café, and it was about 10 p.m. when I returned to my hotel with an ice cream I had bought for the old caretaker lady. But that time she was replaced by another old lady. She was very happy seeing the ice cream unexpectedly in the middle of the night. The next day, at about 10 a.m., I packed my luggage and checked out of the hotel. I went straight to Fakir Café to eat my lunch where a wedding ceremony was already in progress. I sat in the center of the café while that gathering was taking place in the right corner where several tables were joined together. It was probably not a bride kidnapping because the bride and groom looked very happy, determined and prepared for their new life. There was a charming spark in their eyes, and their family members wished them a good life.

After about a four hour ride in a *marshrutka*, I was in Bosteri, Issyk Kul. On the way before reaching Bosteri, there was a traffic jam because the Kazakh President Nursultan Nazarbayev had come to Issyk Kul. Security personnel took a position in different places. When I arrived, it was noon, and the first thing I did was to find a place to stay. In Issyk Kul if you want a good room near the beach, it could cost you from 1000 to 2000 som. While away from the beach or homestay can be from 300 to 500 per night. I got a room neither near nor far from the beach at 1000 som.

This time I was alone and memories of last summer returned when I had come with my friends. Unlike Karakol, I felt lonely in the huge ocean of people lying on the beach, playing, and enjoying themselves. I did not know what to do. I bought a yellow tube and swam in the water. Waves would take me up and down, and I was moving away from the beach toward deeper water. There came the point where the people lying or walking on the beach seemed smaller like ants, and I was far away from them. I had the blue water around me with a blue sky above. I was away from the noise in a natural environment and was alone. But all those relaxing movements that I was enjoying were because of that yellow tube which I bought for 100 som. I would not have enjoyed myself so much without the help of that tube.

I was also continuously watching my bag I had left with a family on the beach. Now I could not see anything, and knew I should get back to the beach. I started moving back to where I had started my journey. After getting near the beach, where several others were enjoying swimming, a little girl noticed my tube. She asked her mom to buy it for her, and she was right because with the help of it, she could enjoy more than without it. That yellow tube helped me feel the depth of the lake where my sense of creativity was provoked, which made me spend more and more time there.

But in my mind there was a problem, that bag had all my possessions, my money, and camera, and therefore I could have lost it. I would not have lost only money and clothes but the memories of my traveling. That little girl was continuously asking her mom for that tube. Finally when I reached the coast, I gifted that yellow tube to her. Although that little girl was not the only one who wanted it, as I had seen more eyes on it but that girl was more deserving.

After experiencing the water, I thanked the family who watched my bag. I went toward the cruise ships along the coast where for 500 som they would give you a ride to a deeper side of the lake where they provided a life jacket and could enjoy the water. I paid 500 som and took a seat in the front part of the ship. The center of the ship was covered, and tables and chairs were arranged like a café or restaurant. The ship waited until it got full and then left for the voyage. It also had music, and played different songs during the voyage. First the ship rode slowly and then it got some speed and took us to the center where all around us was water and more water. Most of the passengers traveling on the cruise were young and beautiful girls with a few men and probably two or three *babushkas*. When the cruise reached the middle of the lake, it stopped suddenly with a hissing sound followed by a continuous ringing siren. With the sound of the siren, all people started running toward the back of the ship. I thought it was an emergency situation and got worried, wondering what would happen to us and how we would be rescued. I sprinted among the crowd of young girls when my foot bumped against something and…

If you think that I fell in the lap of a young beautiful lady, you are wrong. Nothing like that happened. If you think that a beautiful lady held me before I fell, again, you are wrong because it did not happen. But a very strange thing did happen. In order to keep myself from falling, my hand looked for anything, and accidentally grabbed the skirt of a young girl and stripped it off of her. Terrified and nervous, I prepared myself for kicks and beating by her shoes because that was the norm in the city from where I belonged regardless if the act was intentional or unintentional. Now you may think that I was beaten by her, but once again, you are wrong. I saw a very unexpected behavior from her. She came close to me, held my hand and helped me stand again.

"Are you okay? I hope you are not hurt?"

I was not expecting that kind of behavior from her at all; tears oozed out of my eyes because that was the first time I received so much respect from a girl.

After reaching the last part of the ship, I saw children, men, and women quickly putting on their life jackets. There, I understood the reason behind the siren. It was sounded to call to the rear of the ship, put on the life jacket, and enjoy the water of Issyk Kul. My nerves eased, and in the meanwhile, I saw the young lady whom I had met by accident. She was wearing a bikini, waved her hand at me, and jumped into the water.

Afterward, I started watching people diving into the water. Everybody getting into the water was interesting. For example, a mother of three sons got into the water with her eldest son of about eight-years-old. But the younger two were reluctant to get in. Their eldest brother started playing in the water to encourage his younger brothers, but they were scared. Their mother was insisting there was nothing to be scared of, this made her second son agree to get in. His mom was holding him until he became comfortable. Then, the eldest invited his younger brother, who was in the lap of his aunt, and after many encouraging shows by his elder brothers, he finally agreed. Getting down with the help of the stairs, the little boy looked like he was about to cry. But as soon as he touched the water, he shouted. His mother held him, and he enjoyed the water in his mom's lap.

Two large elderly sisters jumped in together, and the result of their jumping was terrible. The two brothers stuck to each other because of the waves produced from the jump. The others also got worried because it had created a Tsunami scenario. But everybody had life jackets and thus no one was harmed. I did not try that part of the adventure because I did not feel comfortable. I just watched people in the water enjoying and taking photos. After experiencing the cruise, I came back to my room before the sunset, took a shower and changed my clothes. Then I went out again to eat dinner.

Cafes were rocking with the sound of the music, and people were enjoying their walk and meal. After eating my dinner, I sat on a bench in the open area where people were walking all around. After some minutes, a skinny man with a beard came near and lit a cigarette.

"Do you smoke cigarettes?"

"No, I do not."

"Where are you from?"

"Afghanistan."

"Ah, then, of course, you smoke hashish, do you have some?"

"If I do not smoke cigarettes, how can I have hashish?"

"I have some that is very good. If you want, I can bring some to you."

After realizing that I was not the type that he was looking for, he moved to the next bench where two young couples were sitting. He started his conversation with the cigarette and moved to hashish. The group agreed to smoke hashish with him, and he went to bring it for them. After he brought back the hashish, the group starting preparing it for their cigarette when all of a sudden, ten policemen arrived and arrested that group while the bearded man was gone. There were screams and cries, and the police handcuffed them and took them away.

I got up from my bench and moved toward my room. I learned from this story that hashish was not only used for smoking but also to trap people and then get money from them.

The next morning I went to Cholpon Ata and walked around the beach there. The atmosphere in Cholpon Ata was calmer than Bosteri. The weather was cloudy, and it rained a few drops, so people left the beach earlier. The same evening I left for Bishkek.

In the Land of Manas

In late August, I got my degree from the Academy, and the next step was to attest or verify it from the relevant government departments and the Afghan Embassy in Bishkek. I had also to attest the degrees of my three friends (Masood, Jawed, and Waheed) who had already finished their studies and were working in Afghanistan. I visited many offices doing the legalization of the documents, but the problem was that they needed the physical presence of my friends or a legal document along with their signatures. But I did not have their signatures nor were they physically present. Our Academy's assistant, Victoria told me about Slang Translation Company, where my problem was solved, and my friends' degrees were attested. Later I took them to the Afghan Embassy, and after paying fees, I verified the degrees, and thus, was done with my degree from the Academy and Kyrgyzstan.

I started preparing to go to my country as the mission I had come for was successfully completed. But before leaving Kyrgyzstan, I wanted to see the remaining notable places in the country. In the first week of September, I planned to go to Talas, located in the North-East of the country. Talas is the city of the legendary hero Manas and the famous writer Chingiz Aitmatov.

The distance from Bishkek to Talas is about 300 km, a six hour drive. The road goes through high mountains where sometimes you can even touch the clouds. At higher altitudes, the weather gets very cold. Despite the very high altitude, the road was good and wide, and even in summer, you can see snow on sides of the road. On both sides of the road, you can see yurts in different places selling kumis, dry yogurts, and milk. At one point on top of the mountains, where we had just crossed the second tunnel, the fog got so dense that the driver could not see even one meter ahead of him, and at the same time it started raining. The last one hour drive was with great difficulty, and it was about 8 p.m. when I arrived in Talas City.

On the way to Talas

I had already called the CBT Office in Talas, and their representative had talked to the driver, and he drove me to the homestay in Talas. The house owner was a very kind man, and he told me that his wife could prepare eggs and potatoes if I wanted. But I preferred to go to a restaurant. I called the same driver whom I had come from Bishkek with, and he and I went together to a nearby café. We both ate kordak. Besides us, there was a big party at the corner of the restaurant, probably a wedding-related party. After eating dinner, the driver dropped me at my homestay. The house had working Wi-Fi, and the owner showed me the toilet and kitchen in case I needed anything. The room was very luxurious, with everything new and clean.

In the morning I found the outside of the house very beautiful. It had a green lawn, trees, and a yurt, which gave a traditional touch to the house. The owner of the house was busy cleaning the yurt when I told him that I wanted to see Manas Ordo. The owner took me to the place where cars were going to Manas Ordo. Manas Ordo was a historical park containing a museum, the tomb of Manas, and the hill attached to the park. Manas Ordo historical park was a beautiful park surrounded by green trees with Manas's huge statue holding a sword in his hands with the statues of his companions to his right and left. The poem Epic of Manas, believed to be a thousand-year-old poem, highlights the struggle, heroism, and leadership of the legendary hero. It was Manas's capabilities that he united the Kyrgyz and regained their captured lands back from the Chinese[24]. Besides Manas international airport in Bishkek, there was a road and university named Manas, near our Academ. His statues mostly of him sitting on a horse with a sword and shield, can be seen throughout the country. The other famous personality associated with Talas is Chingiz Aitmatov. Born on December 12, 1928, he wrote both in Russian and his native Kyrgyz language, and his work was translated into more than 150 languages. His works mostly depict love, kindness, human emotions, devotion, and wisdom. Besides his literary work, he was also Kyrgyzstan's ambassador to the European Union, NATO, UNESCO, Belgium, Luxemburg, and the Netherland[25]. Chingiz's famous pieces of writing include Jamilia, The Day Lasts More than a Hundred Years, The White Ship, The Dreams of a She-Wolf, and The First Teacher; and I was going to visit their native land.

[24]Jeffrey Heys, "Manas", Facts and Details, (April 2016), accessed March 22, 2018,
http://factsanddetails.com/central-asia/Kyrgyzstan/sub8_5c/entry-4772.html
[25]Mark Yoffe, "Chingiz Aitmatov", The Guardian (July 14, 2008), accessed May 12, 2018,
https://www.theguardian.com/books/2008/jul/15/culture.obituaries

Kyrgyz Traditional Yurt in a CBT House, Talas

CBT Host House in Talas

The long road went straight to the museum, and then at the back of the museum was a hill. While climbing there, you could see the whole view of Talas Valley. The valley looked green and beautiful. I was sitting alone on top of the hill and enjoying the entire view. The view was very similar to Bamiyan Province in Afghanistan when you see it from the Buddha. Actually, most of Kyrgyzstan resembled Afghanistan. Once I was showing some video shots of Bamiyan Province to my classmate Aijan, and she did not believe that was not Kyrgyzstan.

I was sitting on top enjoying the view when I saw two ladies climbing up the hill. They were over forty and climbing quite slowly. After reaching the top, I learned that they were originally from Talas but had moved to Bishkek, and then they were visiting their native land. Before their arrival, I was taking selfies, and when they climbed up, I requested them to take some photos of me. We got down off the hill together.

View of Talas Valley from top of the hill

Talas Valley from top of the hill

I wanted to visit the museum but that day it was closed for cleaning and repair work, and therefore I was not able to see it. To the left of the museum, a few yards away was the Gumbez of the legendary hero Manas. When I reached the Gumbez, one man was reciting the verses from the Holy Quran, and the local visitors were listening. One lady reminded me to hold my hands together with respect because of the recitation, and I followed her reminder. That was the tomb of the Manas, whose statutes were placed all over the country. Manas was the symbol of respect, honor, pride, and dignity and has a special place among Kyrgyz people. After visiting the Gumbez, I passed by the main statue of Manas holding a sword with his accompaniers all around. I moved toward the main road, to catch a local minibus going toward the city.

Talas Bazaar

The city was beautiful, quiet and clean. I walked through the city and then went to a local café for my lunch. I was done with Manas Ordo, and I did not hear of any other important place to visit, I decided to go back to Bishkek the same day. I came back to Bishkk with the same driver.

Hill of Manas

Manas Museum

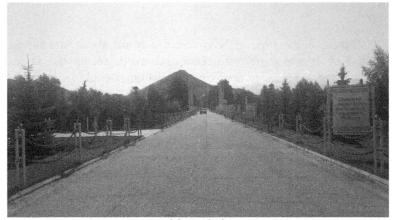

Manas Ordo

Tomb of Manas

Kochkor and Naryn

During all my time in Kyrgyzstan, I heard about visiting the Issyk Kul. It was a beautiful lake and worth seeing but in my opinion, visiting it more than one or two times could be boring. I did not hear of other places like Arslanbob in the south and Naryn in the north. However, in my last days in Kyrgyzstan, I planned to visit Naryn. I researched Kochkor, as it is on the way to Naryn. I planned to go to Kochkor and from there to Naryn.

It was about 2 p.m. when I left for Kochkor. After about a four hour drive, I arrived. In Kochkor bazaar, I found some tourists shopping and buying foodstuffs. I asked them about the CBT Office, and they gave me directions as it was attached to that small bazaar. I went to their office but it was closed. There was a mobile number written on the door. I called the number, but there was no answer. It was getting darker, and I was worried about finding a place for my overnight stay. After calling several times a man answered and said that he would be there in ten minutes. I waited for about an hour, but he did not show up. Again, I started calling him, but he did not answer. I went out to find a place. At the northern end of the bazaar, there was the Adamkaly hotel, and I went there and checked in for one night.

Kochkur was a favorite place of tourists because they found some good mountainous places for their trekking. I was not interested in trekking, so I did not find any other interesting thing there. After putting my luggage in the hotel's room, I went out for a walk followed by dinner. I found the bazaar calm and quiet. Only one café seemed to be working in the bazaar. When I entered, the waitresses were watching television. The café was about to close, and I was the last customer there. The only dish left was *shorpo*. During our talk, they told me that they wanted to learn English and work in Bishkek. That was their dream of settling in Bishkek. I got lost in thought for a while thinking about how dreams differ. Some people have very big dreams of having a big house, lots of money, an established business, or becoming famous, while some dreams are very simple. But the important thing is one should have a dream because it is the dream which keeps us alive, which makes life interesting and meaningful. I left the café with a wish that their dreams come true.

Yurts on both sides of the road

The next morning I left for Naryn. The distance between Kochkor and Naryn was about a three hour drive. It was about noon when I arrived in Naryn, and I went straight to the CBT Office. Gulira was an active coordinator of the CBT office in Naryn. She listened to me that I would be staying in Naryn for three nights and scheduled me to see as many places as I could. She called the driver to take me to Tashrabat that very first day. The drive to Tashrabat was about one and half hours and we mostly drove on a dirt path. We got a flat tire on the way, which was fixed by the driver.

Tashrabat was a Caravanserai of the 15th century built by stone. This Caravanserai was part of the ancient Silk Road, where travelers would stay for a night or more. That Caravanserai was built on a foothill with mountains and hills all around. Inside of the Caravanserai was both large rooms in the shape of halls and small rooms for travelers. The driver and the lady caretaker stayed outside the gate. Because of the frequent visits, that place was no longer interesting for them. After I entered the inside, it took me a thousand years back, and I found it filled with tens of people.

Their horses, donkeys, and camels, along with the luggage, were in a separate place in one of the corners of the Caravanserai, and their servants were taking care of them. Outside, the moon was full, and it reflected the picture of a day. Camels, horses, and donkeys were taking rest as they were tired from the entire day of traveling. Inside the rooms, some people were busy eating *shorpo* along with bread, while some were drinking black *chay*. Some were discussing the routes and wondering if there would be any problem, probably of thieves or wild animals, while passing through their territories, and some were discussing the upcoming weather. The old workers sitting in a corner were sipping *chay*, looking at the traders. The young teenage worker of the Caravanserai came to me and asked for what I wanted. I ordered black *chay* because it was cold, and the black *chay* could give warmth to my body. I was a thousand years back, when the voice of the driver brought me back to the 21st century, I asked him to take some photos of me.

At a little distance from Caravanserai were yurts where tourists stayed. Inside each yurt, there could be six to ten beds depending upon the size of the yurt. The yurts, mountains, and caravanserai were presenting a romantic view, and one could get lost in its beauty. The air was clean, life was simple, and everything was natural there. On the way back, I saw herds of yaks grazing in the mountains, and it was almost sunset when I arrived in Naryn City. I called Gulira, and she told the driver to take me to the place where I was to stay. That homestay was a two-room apartment. I stayed in one room, while a French tourist who was a professor of history stayed in the other room. He had also visited Afghanistan, and he knew some basic Dari too. He told me that he had planned to visit the Pamir region of both Afghanistan and Tajikistan, and that was his favorite region to travel. According to him, that part of Pamir situated in Afghanistan was the most beautiful region in the world. The tourists went from Tajikistan's soil, and they did not need an Afghan visa. When I asked him if that part was safe and secure, he replied that the region was safe because it was almost inaccessible from Afghanistan, and tourists mostly went there from Tajikistan. After a brief chat, he left for his dinner somewhere outside, and I stayed in the house.

When he came back, I asked him about the restaurant he had

been to, and he told me the address of Khan Tengri restaurant. He told me the address in a very technical way that I did not fully understand. I always believe in asking people rather than looking at maps wherever I went, and it worked for me. I went along the bank of the Naryn river to the main road. After crossing the road, I asked a couple I assumed were rushing for their home, and after getting directions, I moved on to a small street. After covering some distance to the left was Khan Tengri restaurant. It was a big restaurant having both inside and outside areas for eating and relaxing. As it was a little cold, I went inside and there once again a party was going on with live music. So I not only ate my dinner but enjoyed live music while watching the dancers. By 10 p.m. I was back in my room.

Caravanserai, Tashrabat

Inside of Caravanserai

Outer view of Caravanserai

Inside of a Yurt

The next morning, at 8 a.m. I had already missed four calls from Gulira. At 9 a.m. when I finally received Gulir'a call, she asked, "Are you still sleeping? Get prepared for the adventurous horse riding in the mountains, and the driver is waiting for you in the car."

The owner of the apartment where we were staying was our neighbor, and she arranged a breakfast with bread, jam, *chay,* and eggs. The French tourist had already taken his breakfast and had left the apartment. I ate my breakfast quickly and got ready for the trip. The driver was someone different, and he could speak English and was very friendly. After about a two hour drive, we reached a place surrounded by green and tall mountains. There were four yurts in pair form. The owner of those yurts was Mr. Isken. He was a fifty-three-year-old, and a joyful and friendly man. First, I was given yogurt, honey, and bread in the yurt, and then I went outside with Isken to choose the horse. You may recall the last time I rode a horse in Issyk Kul. That experience made me afraid of horses, and therefore I was reluctant in choosing. Isken told me not to get worried as he would be with me on another horse. The only thing I could ask was for a calm horse, and there was the brown mare. Besides his two horses and me, Isken's dog, who was missing his left toe, also accompanied us. Isken told me that whenever he takes tourists to the mountains on a horse ride, the dog accompanies him. Running with three legs, the dog would sometimes get ahead of his master while sometimes following his master. When I asked Isken about the missing toe of the dog, he replied that one night a wolf came and attacked him. He fought bravely, but still fighting with a wolf was not easy, and the wolf ate his toe. Isken liked talking about the dog, and I told him some real stories about dogs in my bad Russian.

"When I was a kid, my dad would tell us the story of his dog. His parents were living in their native village while he was studying in Kabul, so whenever he would go home on weekends, the dog would know, and he would wait for him on the main road. When he would leave for Kabul, again the dog would be very sad and would accompany him to the bus stop. At that time, the story seemed exaggerated, but later I discovered that dogs really do possess special senses."

Another story was about my friend's uncle, who had a dog. His master was working in another city, and one day, he died in that city while his dog was at his home in his native village. My friend told me that the dead body of his uncle was not brought home but to the main Hujra. The dog realized that his master was dead and before his master's body arrived, the dog was already there waiting eagerly until the dead body of his master arrived. Moreover, the famous Hachiko story is known to almost every dog lover.

In another movie "Artist," (an old black and white movie), a little dog saves the life of his owner when, at one stage, his owner, who is also a famous artist, burns all of his work and the fire spread all around the house. The dog gets out and gets the attention of the policeman with his different acts and gestures. Finally the policeman goes with him and finds the apartment of the dog's owner full of smoke. He goes inside and gets out his owner and saves his life.

Isken's dog was ahead of us, and he was constantly keeping his eyes on us because he was not certain of the stranger with his owner. I felt like a king when I was riding the horse, especially when it was walking on the thin edge of the mountain, and the sound of the flowing river was echoing in my ears. Isken and I enjoyed the horse ride on the high mountains of Naryn. But I was a bit scared because we were moving higher and higher in altitude.

Isken told me that he loved the village life and the reason behind his strong health was clean air and natural food. He also disclosed the secret behind his manpower, that the horse riding strengthened it. If that was true, then it should work for a donkey ride too, and then I remembered John, who had once told me that he had a good experience riding donkeys when he lived in his village.

After spending three hours in the high green mountains, it was time to get back because we were supposed to be in the city before sunset. I had taken with me some stationery, including pens, pencils, color pencils, erasers, sharpeners, and chocolates. I distributed them between the grandchildren of Isken, and later I gave some to the children of my driver. These small gifts made them very happy. We took photos, and Isken told me that I was the first-ever Afghan visiting these remote areas in Kyrgyzstan.

On the way back, the driver took me to a small place with deers, ibexes, barasinghas, and yaks. There were other tourists too, giving chewing gums to the deers. The driver was a very friendly guy and was honest in showing me as many interesting places as he could. Upon my request, Gulira had changed my accommodation because it had no internet. The new place was also a two-room apartment. In one room a group of two tourists slept, and in the other room, I was alone.

Naryn

Herds of sheep and goats, Naryn

A FantasticView of Naryn

Isken and his family

With Isken

The next day, I wanted to meet Nurlan, who had become my friend in Bishkek. Naryn was Nurlan's native village, and before leaving for Naryn, he told me to visit him as he would be in Naryn during that time. I called him, and he told me the address. As I was leaving the next day, I wanted to just pass my hello to him. In his native village, he had many horses, cows, and sheep. He had also land for cultivating different fruits and crops, and he also sold them in the open market. In short his village life was like heaven. During lunch he said, "In Kyrgyz culture, when a guest is very special, we kill a horse. When just special, we kill a sheep, and when nothing at all, we give him/her normal food."

I looked here and there and started eating the "normal food" happily. Later he showed me his sheep, horses, cows and his garden. I really enjoyed my time with him, and before sunset, I got back to my apartment.

The next morning, I called Gulira and told her that I wanted to go to Kochkor through Song Kul Lake. Gulira arranged a driver who would take me to Song Kul Lake first, stay there for a while and then drive me to Kochkor. That time, it was a third driver, but very smart one. He was not alone, as he had his girlfriend with him whom he had promised to show the Song Kul Lake. I did not have any problem with his girlfriend joining that trip, but the problem was that he was continuously busy with her, and I could not find the time or opportunity to ask about the name of places or any other information. Moreover, in some places, they would disappear while I would wait for them in the car. I felt like I was their driver and guide, taking them on a trip to Song Kul Lake.

The road to Song Kul Lake was also mostly a dirt path. It went higher in the mountains, and you would feel most often like you were bouncing at certain places. The distance from Naryn to the lake was about a two hour drive. The road passed through very high altitudes where the driver stopped and took photos with his beloved one. I had the only option to take selfies. After the drive of about two hours, we reached the lake.

The lake was very wide and the water covered a large area, but a very strong wind was blowing. There were a number of yurts near the bank of the lake. We ate *kordak* in the yurt, and I paid for my driver and his girlfriend too, which made me angry. Not because I paid for the driver, and not because I paid for his girlfriend, but because my *kordak* was far less rich and hearty as compared to their *kordak*. Later, as I walked on the bank of the lake, I saw two Germans with their van that was their home. It had a kitchen, toilet, bathroom, and almost everything. At the back of the van there was a bed with blankets, mattress, pillows, and a sleeping bag. Toward the door, there was a refrigerator and stove. I asked how did they come from Germany to Kyrgyzstan and was that cheaper than staying in hotels or motels. They replied that they drove wherever driving was possible and launched the van on a ship where there was a sea route and paid on the basis of a meter. They were packing their luggage and moving to another place.

In the meanwhile a *marshrutka* arrived full of tourists. The driver of the car first greeted the dog who belonged to one of the yurts there. I was scared of that big dog since I arrived there and I was continuously asking the owner of the yurt if the dog was quiet, calm and harmless. But the driver of the *marshrutka* hugged the dog and was friendly with him within seconds. The weather was getting colder, and the sky was also cloudy while the cold breeze blowing made it unbearable to stay outside the yurt. My driver and his girlfriend went very far to the water of the lake. After they came back, we decided to leave as we might be late. Before our departure, a very young lady riding a horse super-fast came and said something to the owner of the yurt and then went inside. It was about 2 p.m. when we left for Kochkor after saying goodbye to the yurt families. At about 4 p.m. I arrived in Kochkor. The weather had become rainy, and I took a shared taxi toward Bishkek and at 8 p.m. I arrived in Bishkek.

On the way to Song Kul Lake

On the way to Song Kul Lake

On the way to Song Kul Lake

Chapter 10

My Campaign for Kyrgyzstan's Tourism

During all my time in Kyrgyzstan, I encouraged my friends and colleagues to visit that heaven on earth. I even gave them offers that the accommodation would be on me, and I would be their guide there. My efforts to campaign for Kyrgyzstan finally bore fruit, and my former supervisor Tia agreed to visit Kyrgyzstan. Although I had already informed her that June, July, and August are the best months to visit Kyrgyzstan, because of her tight schedule, she could not plan to visit it during these months. She came to Kyrgyzstan in mid-September. Initially, she had planned to stay for a week, which was okay to visit some main places in the country, but one day before her arrival, she informed me that her stay was only for two days. Two days were not even enough for Bishkek City. Anyway, I started thinking about what important and interesting places we could visit in those two days. I made a schedule that the first day we would go to Burana Tower in the morning and then would move around Ala Too Ploshad in the center and would probably visit some shopping malls or parks. The next day I planned to visit Al Archa National Park in the morning and Hawaii Café in Tokmok in the evening.

Early in the morning, at about 4 a.m., I went along with Vita to get Tia from the airport. At about 5:30 a.m. Tia appeared with a smile on her face. For these two days, she stayed at my apartment, and I stayed with my friend, Abid, who was in the final year of his medical studies and the president of the Asia Youth Organization. I dropped Tia at my apartment and told her to get some rest, and when she had enough sleep, we could go out to see the city. It was about 9 a.m. when she sent me a Skype message. The distance between my apartment and Abid's apartment was about a five minute walk. We decided to go to Tokmok and visit the historical Burana Tower. I called Vita and it was about 10 a.m. when we left Bishkek for Burana.

280

Tia was on her vacation and she had already spent a week in Qatar where it was so hot that she had to wait all day for the sun to disappear so she, along with her family, could get out to see the city. That day the weather was cloudy but no signs of rain. After reaching the tower, I briefed her about the tower and stated its history. But Burana Tower did not impress her, and she said that the way through the tower was like going to any village in Afghanistan. Then I climbed up through the narrow and dark stairs to the top where I took photos. Tia did not climb up because of the problems from the narrowness of the path.

On the top, there was a lady tourist who was taking photos and filming her own videos talking about the tower and Kyrgyzstan. She also recorded my opinion and feelings about Kyrgyzstan after knowing that I was from Afghanistan. After climbing down the tower, we took photos around the tower and the ancient petroglyphs and stones. We also visited the museum and then left for Bishkek after our brief trip.

Tia wanted to meet Rafik and Gerald. I tried Gerald's number, but it was off, and then, when I called Rafik, I learned Gerald was off on a mission abroad. With Rafik, we confirmed dinner in the Bukhara restaurant on Chuy. Tia had a Skype conference at 4 p.m., so we went back home. But when she arrived, she had received an email that it was canceled.

At about 6 p.m. we went to Bukhara café. We had our dinner together with Rafik and had a good time talking about the experiences of working in Kabul. The next morning it was raining, which interrupted our plans, and therefore we could not go to Ala Archa National Park and Hawaii café. Until almost noon, the rain did not stop, and we thought that we might have to spend our entire day in the room. But after that it slowed down a little giving us an opportunity to go out to see the downtown part of the city.

First, we went to Tsum Center, where Tia bought some souvenirs, and from there we walked to Ala Too Ploshad. We took photos in front of the parliament and white house and then we visited a couple of parks around the area. From there, we moved to Bishkek Park and walked to the center of the city. The sun had disappeared when we got in a taxi toward our home. Tia had to leave for Kabul early in the morning. I told Vita the time to come and take us to the airport.

The next day when we arrived at the airport, people were standing in rows to check their luggage and get their boarding passes. They were not respecting each other's turn, and a kind of pushing and pulling was seen there. After standing there for thirty minutes, we did not move a single step.

"Here it is even worse than Kabul. For the last thirty minutes, we are standing at the same point." Tia expressed her anger and then moved a little ahead to stay in the queue and then a couple of minutes later found her way to the officer issuing the boarding pass.

"I want a seat near the window."

First, he ignored her, and later, when he saw her UN passport, he called upon his friend "Smotret Diplomateka" (Look diplomatic passport), and then he listened to her very well and helped her wherever she wanted to be seated. After stamping her passport with "Exit," Tia waved her hand and disappeared from me.

Good Bye Kyrgyzstan!

Before leaving for Afghanistan, I needed to go to a dentist for my teeth because I was feeling pain in three teeth in my lower left jaw. I asked for help from Victoria, Dina (my teacher), and Abid. Victoria told me that she did not know because it was long ago that she had been to a dentist, and she did not even remember the address of the clinic. Abid took me first to his Iranian friend, and when he checked my teeth, he said that I had problems with eight other teeth, which I did not know. He was checking my teeth so mercilessly that I got scared of his rough hands, and I did not continue with him. Dina told me about a lady dentist Tatyana who was working in the Sun City Clinic, located a little distance from the center. Coincidentally, Abid's second choice was also a lady dentist named Tatyana but working at the Dentist Tree Clinic. First I went to Tatyana no. 1, working in the Sun City Clinic. She checked my teeth and told me that my lower three teeth had got holes near the roots because of my aggressive and improper brushing. According to her, I should leave them as they were but change my brushing habit, and I should fill my upper two teeth. I could not decide at that time, and I thought I should go to Tatyana no. 2, to see if she could come up with a better idea. I went to Tatyana no. 2 and she told me exactly the same by Tatyana no. 1. The difference was that Tatyana no. 1 was directly telling me in English while Tatyana no. 2 told me all this through Natalia, who was working as an admin and translating for me. So, Tatyana no. 2 made a simple filling to the first tooth while she did the RCT (Root Canal treatment) to the other one, which she should not have done unless a normal filling could not work.

Teeth treatment is a very important and sensitive issue, and its treatment should be done on time; otherwise the issue will get bigger and bigger. The other issue related to its treatment is that in the western world, the dentists take care of the instruments for teeth treatment. They are sterilized and free of germs and bacteria, while I was not sure dentists in Bishkek were doing proper sterilization of their instruments because it is a very long and time-taking process.

After my treatment was finished, Tatyana told me to pay the bill with Natasha at the reception. When I approached the reception desk, I found a lady who I knew by the name of Natalia there, and when I asked about Natasha, she smiled and said: "I am both Natalia and Natasha." First I thought she was kidding, and later I knew about these two names for the same person, and Natasha was short of Natalia. I could not know the logic behind how Natasha could be short of Natalia because both names contain the seven letters.

After attesting my degree from the Kyrgyz government and the embassy of Afghanistan, I started to schedule my trip back to Afghanistan because my visa would expire on September 31. Initially, I had the idea to get the transit visa of Uzbekistan and travel through its transit route. I would have had the opportunity to see a bit of the country or at least I would have had a brief idea for my next visit. In August, I went to the Uzbek embassy in Bishkek and talked to the responsible person for a transit visa. But the response was that I had to apply three to four months before my planned date of departure, and even then, there was no surety whether I would get the visa. So that route did not work for me. The next option was to go through Tajikistan. The Tajik embassy was able to provide transit visas. I went there two weeks earlier before my visa expired, but there I discovered that the visa stamping machine was not working. Either I had to wait for weeks so they could get a new machine from Tajikistan, or I could apply through their embassy in Kazakhstan, which was again difficult because I needed the visa of Kazakhstan first. Therefore, the only option left was to travel by plane.

I booked my flight on September 21. I had spent almost two years in a country which once was totally unknown to me. These two years of my life was a very interesting experience for me, and I learned many things. I saw how people lived there, how hospitable and loving the people were and what challenges they were facing in their country. I saw and experienced many new things, but still there were somethings which I could not do although I had planned to. For example, I did not visit the main church in Bishkek, where I could watch how the Orthodox

Christians attend church. I wanted to spend a night in a yurt but I could not, although I ate in the yurt in Naryn and Song Kul Lake and I even laid on one of the beds in a yurt at the Caravanserai, so I could tell people that I had been there. But still, spending a night until the morning would have been an exciting experience. I also could not visit Lake Sery Chelek despite that being on my target list.

On my departure day, Vita took me to the airport from where I flew toward Kabul. Kyrgyzstan hosted me for almost two years, and those two years were one of the best times of my life. I believe that one day, this country will emerge on the world's map as a prosperous country. The plane took off, and I left behind the gorgeous mountains firm and proud. Good Bye Bishkek and Good Bye Kyrgyzstan. I hope to see you soon!

"Radicalization and Violent Extremism in Central Asia and Afghanistan"

My wish of seeing Bishkek again happened within a short time, and after two months, I was back in Bishkek. I applied to participate in a conference on Radicalization and Violent Extremism in Central Asia and Afghanistan arranged by the SaferWorld with the support of the U.S. Embassy, and I was accepted.

I was to deliver my presentation on the issue of the growing trend of radicalization and violent extremism in Central Asia and Afghanistan. The organizer of the conference had also invited regional and international experts on the topic to discuss possible solutions to the problem. But for me to participate in the conference, there was the problem of a visa. The SaferWorld organization had started processing my visa. Based on the regular process, I would get the reference visa, but that was a time taking process, and I would have missed the conference. Thus, I had only one option left: to go to the Kyrgyz Embassy in Kabul to grant me the visa.

Azamat, the consular affairs officer saw my invitation letter both in Russian and English, checked my passport, and asked me about my previous visits, then went to another room. I assumed he went to speak to his senior. He then came back, bombarding me with questions regarding SaferWorld like the address of its main office in Kyrgyzstan, its activities, and many more. After I gave him some basic information about the functions of the organization and the address in Osh City, Azamat expressed his concern.

"Do you know that the foreign NGOs were involved in the unrest events of Osh?"

"Well, you can check their website. They work legally in

Kyrgyzstan with the permission of the government."

He again checked the invitation letter and checked their website on his computer but was still reluctant to grant me the visa.

In order to persuade him, I visited the embassy several times. Most of those times, I waited outside the embassy's building until Azamat would receive my call and would let me in, and once again, I would face the same questions. During that time, the guards on duty took pity on me and advised me of some other ways to get the visa that I should have tried from the very first day. During one of my visits, while I was waiting outside Azamat's office, I saw some cartons of pomegranates had arrived. A few of them were bulging out but tightened with a transparent tape followed by muscular men in traditional Afghan clothes. They drank chay with the Ambassador, and then the Ambassador himself gave their passport to Azamat to stamp them with a visa. There I realized the power of pomegranates, and later the guards outside told me that one among them was a member of the parliament along with his friends. Finally, when there was only one week left before the conference, I told Azamat that I was already working on a research paper, and my participation in the conference was important. I stressed that if I was not given the visa, I would mention the uncooperative attitude of the Kyrgyz Embassy working in Kabul. That appeared to work because they granted me a two-week visa.

On this trip, I had no worries like previous times that I would be interrogated at the Kabul airport because I had Kyrgyz visa stamped on my passport. My flight was scheduled through Safi Airways from Kabul to Dubai, and from Dubai to Bishkek through Fly Dubai. At the Kabul airport, I was told to get my luggage in Dubai, and from there, I had to transfer the luggage myself to Fly Dubai Airline going to Bishkek. In Dubai, I learned that I should contact Marhaba Service Center for the transferring process.

The lady from Marhaba Center first told me that I should pay $70 for the luggage transfer, but then she told me to check with section D located nearby regarding the luggage transfer. As I approached that section, I saw two ladies sitting behind their desktop computers. The one with white skin was busy putting makeup on her face while the other, dark-skinned and large, yelled at a Pakistani man in Arabic and then she shifted to English.

"What is this?" She threw the passport back to him, which fell on the ground. When I looked at the passport, it looked like someone had chewed it and then threw it out. I thanked God that I did not go to her, but the one who was supposed to listen to me was still busy with her makeup, and I silently stood to not make any disturbance. Finally, she finished her makeup and turned to face me.

"How can I help you?"

"My flight is from Kabul to Dubai through Safi Airline and from there to Bishkek through Fly Dubai. I was told at Kabul Airport to go to the Marhaba Help Center to transfer my luggage onto the next flight, but the lady at the Marhaba Center desk sent me here."

"Give me your passport and ticket, please."

She checked the computer and returned to me a short time later. "Do not worry. You do not need to pay any amount, and you will get your luggage at Bishkek Airport."

"So, I do not need to pay any amount?"

"No, Sir." I was relieved and then went to the waiting lounge for my flight.

When I got into the plane, it was quite empty, with only a few passengers. I saw a few other Afghans that I assumed might be participating in a conference. As the plane was so empty, I could sit anywhere.

After arriving in Bishkek, I cleared customs but could not find my luggage. I became worried because my suit for the conference was in that luggage. I registered my complaint, and the customs official told me that they would call me when it arrived. Outside the terminal, SaferWorld had sent its car to pick me up. The driver took me to a hotel where I was to stay and also attend the conference.

It was my first participation in any conference, and thus I was very much excited. In the reception, the guy checked my name and passport and then gave me the electronic key card for opening the door. I put my carryon aside and started checking the room. It had a double bed, attached bathroom, television, a table and chair for reading, a small refrigerator full of both soft and hard drinks, and a cupboard. There was also a small lockbox that I mistook for a microwave oven at first glance because its inside was very warm. Even later, I was not so sure and would check my wallet to see if the money inside was okay.

I believed I was in a four-star hotel until Abid visited me and deducted one star from it. Being tired, I slept for some hours, and after I woke up, I called Stefan, who was the coordinator and representative for SaferWorld about any prior activities. He told me that I should get some rest. The conference would begin the next day and if I needed anything I could call him.

My participation in that conference was the result of my interest in the topic that covered radicalization, terrorism, extremism, etc. During my years studying in Bishkek, I discussed that topic with my friends and colleagues. We talked about how the overall situation in the country was. Besides many other problems like corruption, weak governance, poverty, and unemployment, the growing trend of radicalization and extremism was also a serious concern for the Kyrgyz government. The number of Kyrgyz people joining ISIS was reported, and the government was taking measures as to how to control that growing threat. Inside the country, the overall atmosphere seemed okay, but still, the situation was not like it used to be.

One day when I was discussing the same topic with Gerald, he told me that in Osh some of the shopkeepers had received warnings not to sell alcoholic beverages, which had spread a layer of fear among the shopkeepers. But misunderstanding or exaggerating the issue was another problem, and that was the reason men keeping a beard or women who wore a hijab could apparently be considered as evidence of radicalization according to some people, which was not right at all.

One day a colleague of mine told me about an interesting incident in her office. She was working in a private company. She said that both Russians and Kyrgyz were working in that company. But one day, a Kyrgyz guy told a Russian girl to dress appropriately because, according to him, her dress was not proper. She argued with him that she was not a Muslim but an ethnic Russian and had the right to wear whatever she wanted and he did not have the right to interfere in her personal matters. The problem went bigger until other colleagues, and finally, the manager interfered.

On the first day of the conference, the lady registering the participants seemed familiar, and after talking to her, she said she was one of our Academy's graduates. After registering, I was introduced to the SaferWorld and U.S. Embassy staff.

The coordinating lady was from the U.S. Embassy. I forget her name, but she introduced me to the U.S. Ambassador. "This is the guy from Afghanistan who reached us in the very final moments."

The U.S. Ambassador, Ms. Sheila Gwaltney, greeted me and asked about my education, job, and the overall situation in Afghanistan. The conference started with the opening speech of the U.S. ambassador, and then participants started their presentations. Different participants had a different understanding of radicalization and extremism, and each one presented the issue in their own context. The second day included some group work, where the issue was discussed in detail, and then recommendations from the participants were filed as possible solutions to the problem. There were several reasons and causes for this growing trend from poverty to unemployment, from illiteracy to the lack of Islamic knowledge, education, and misinterpretations of Islamic teachings. The government of Kyrgyzstan was very serious about stopping this growing trend by designing solid policies and keeping an eye on their citizens and foreigners living in the country. Kyrgyzstan's government had also started an effective measure of testing the Islamic knowledge of the imams of the mosques.

In 2014, the Muslim Spiritual Board had made it compulsory that all imams pass tests on Sharia law and the Arabic language because they found some imams lacked this knowledge[26]. In conclusion, different solutions such as the role of religious scholars, coordination between the Central Asian countries and Central Asia and Afghanistan, controlling drug and human trafficking, strengthening the institutions and eradicating corruption and spreading the proper understanding of Islam were suggested.

After the conference ended, I stayed for two more days with Abid. I visited my previous accommodations and refreshed my memories. I wanted to meet the Domkom in the 11th

Mikrorayon, but I could not find her in the front area of the apartment where she would sit. I visited Yujhni and Ata Turk Park, and it seemed very different to me at that time. After spending about a week in Bishkek, my flight was scheduled through Turkey and then from Turkey to Kabul.

Istanbul Airport was very big, and I had a layover of about ten hours there. Turkish Airline from Bishkek to Istanbul had a very comfortable flight, and the food they provided was very tasty. But before boarding the plane, I wondered how to spend those ten hours. First, I started walking inside the terminal. I went to the big bookstore, but their books were very expensive. I then moved toward the restaurants and cafés and chose one of the cafes to sit in for a while. I ordered coffee and a chicken burger, but the food was very expensive too. I would say that it was about three to four times more expensive than in the terminal at Dubai Airport.

Afterward, when I checked the time, only three hours had passed, and seven hours were remaining. I went to the lounge and preferred to wait there. After a while, three Russian ladies sat beside me. I started a conversation with them, and they told me that they were going to China for business. Soon they left the lounge, as the time of their flight arrived. Three hours were left when I moved to the lounge for the Kabul flight. That place was filled with Afghans, mostly students, people seeking medical treatment, and businessmen going back to Kabul. We sat in the plane, and it was about to take off when we got the news that it had some technical issue. We were taken back to the terminal, and after waiting for about an hour we got into another plane, which looked exactly the same as the previous one.

Unfortunately, again an old large man, probably English, sat beside me, and he reminded me of the old dedushka traveling from Bishkek to Issyk Kul. In front of me an Afghan had a young lady beside him. He started his conversation with her by promising many of this and that in Kabul. They both were enjoying their time. I was feeling sleepy. I watched a little of an Indian movie and then the smell of Turkish food brought me awake. I ate the food and was active for about an hour and during that time I watched another movie. While watching the movie, the time moved so fast, that only a few minutes were left before the plane would land at Kabul Airport.

[26]"Kyrgyzstan Testing Clerics' Knowledge of Islam", Eurasianet, (May 28, 2015), accessed June 14, 2018, https://eurasianet.org/s/kyrgyzstan-testing-clerics-knowledge-of-islam

Glossary and Abbreviations

Aazaan - Islamic call to prayer.

Adinatsit Bazaar – Bazaar in the 11th Mikrorayon.

Afghani – The currency of Afghanistan.

Ait or Eid – Eid is the Islamic festival and Muslims celebrate it two times a year; Eid Al-Fitr that comes after the holy month of Ramadan and Eid Al-Adha which is celebrated on 10th of the last month (Dhu Al-Hijja) of the Islamic calendar in the commemoration when Allah asked Prophet Ibrahim to sacrifice his son (Prophet Ismail). Before Prophet Ibrahim sacrificed his son, Allah sent a sheep to sacrifice instead and accepted his sacrifice. Since then, Muslims celebrate this day by sacrificing animals (cows, goats, sheep, and camels), and the pilgrims perform Hajj (pilgrimage) in Makkah—the holiest city of Muslims in Saudi Arabia.

Ait Merik Bolsun – Happy Eid.

Ala Archa National Park – It is a nature park with an area of about 200 sq. km in the Tian Shan Mountains at about 40 km from Bishkek. It has a flowing river surrounded by green mountains providing a good picnic spot and a nice place for hikers, trekkers, mountain climbers, and skiers (in winter). The word

Ala Archa means "Variegated Junipers."

Ala Too Ploshad – It is the main square in the city and a favorite place of the people to meet, walk, cycle, and for hanging out. Important public events also take place there. To all four sides of this square there are important public buildings like the White House, parks, and museums. At its very center, you can see the statue of Manas on a horse with a big Kyrgyz flag to its right. Opposite to Manas statue, there are water fountains and sitting places where people relax and take photos.

Avtavagzal – Bus station.

Ayran – A drink of yogurt (salty).

Babushka – Grandmother.

Bagh e Babur – This is a historical park in Kabul built by the first Mughal king Babur where he is also buried.

Bagh e Bala – It is a picnic area located on a green hill with trees all around near Kart e Parwan area at a distance of about 5 km from Kabul City.

Bazarchik – A small bazaar or market.

Beshbarmak – This is a dish with boiled mutton, nodules, and onions, having parsley and coriander on top. It is served in the form of soup. Literally Beshbarmak means five fingers because of the shape of the nodules.

Bir – In the Kyrgyz language bir means one.

Bolani – A flat-bread from Afghanistan, baked or fried having potatoes, spinach, pumpkin, or the green weed called *gandana* inside similar to Russian *Pirojhki* or *Turkish gozleme*.

Borsok – Pieces of dough fried in oil – a flavor of Kyrgyz tradition.

Caravanserai – In past caravanserai served as a place built for the travelers along the roadside where they stayed during their journeys.

CASA-1000 – The Central Asia-South Asia power project.

Chalap - Diluted yogurt with water.

Chalghuza – Afghan pine nuts.

Chaykhana – A tea house. In the past chaykhanas not only provided tea but people also took rest while traveling from one place to another. These chaykhanas were popular along the Silk Road linking China, the Middle East, the Indian subcontinent, and Europe.

Chaynak – Kettle.

Cheteeri nol nol – Four zero zero.

Dam – Barber.

Darulaman – Is a locality in the south-western part of Kabul in District 6.

Darulaman Road – A small road (about 3 km) located at the south-west of Kabul connecting the Dehmazang area with the Darulaman.

Dastarkhan – A sheet of cloth on which food is served in a traditional way.

Dayerah - A dayerah or daf is a medium-sized framed drum mostly with metal ringlets attached to it.

Devochka – Little girl.

Devoshka – Girl. Can also be used for girlfriend.

Dedushka – Grandfather.

Dirham – A unit of currency in the United Arab Emirates.

Dolce Vita – An Italian restaurant in Bishkek.

Domkom – A person having the responsibility to take care of the entire building and in return, he/she gets some benefits for his/her services.

Dordoy Bazaar – A wholesale and retail market mostly of Chinese goods in Bishkek.

Dyadya – Uncle

Eidi – It is usually the money or gifts given to children or youngsters by elders on Eid day.

Eki – In the Kyrgyz language eki means two.

Ferdowsi – Abul Qasim Ferdowsi was a Persian poet of the 10th century who wrote the famous Shahnamah (Book of Kings).

Gashish – Hashish.

Gonjeshkak – One of the popular local Afghan dances mostly seen at weddings and other ceremonies.

Gumbez – Tomb or mausoleum.

Haft Mewa – Literally means seven food, a kind of fruit salad along with its syrup made up of seven dried fruits in a big pot. The seven dry fruits include raisins, walnuts, almonds, *senjed* (the dry fruit of the lotus tree), pistachios, hazelnuts, and dry apricots and is traditionally served on the day of Nowruz.

Halal – Anything permissible or lawful in Islam.

Haram – Anything forbidden or not permissible in Islam.

Henna – It is a dye pasted on female hands in various patterns at special occasions like wedding ceremonies, birthdays and the Eid celebrations.

Henna Ceremony – It is a solo female ceremony where young ladies paste henna on the hands of the bride and themselves a day or two before the wedding day.

Hujra – In Pashtun society every village has a common Hujra which works as a social center where mostly the elders get together and talk about daily life, discuss problems to find solutions, and greet guests from the other villages.

Iftar – Breaking the fast in the evening after the call to the Maghrib prayer is made during the month of Ramadan.

Imam – Islamic leader who usually heads a mosque.

Iskender Kebab – Thinly cut grilled lamb meat basted with hot tomato sauce along with yogurt, fresh tomatoes, bread, and chilies.

Issyk Kul – Is one of the regions in Kyrgyzstan, and the lake Issyk Kul is located in this region with an area of 6236 sq. km. Issyk Kul Lake is the tenth largest lake in the world by volume and the second largest mountain lake in the world behind Lake Titicaca in South America.

Jalalabad – Capital City of Nangarhar Province in Afghanistan and a southern city in Kyrgyzstan.

Jarma – It is a cold beverage derived from cereal diluted with yogurt.

Kaaba – It is the holiest and most sacred cube-shaped building (of Muslims) located at the Masjid Al-Haram in the city of Makkah, Saudi Arabia. Muslims face Kaaba for reading their prayers.

Kabuli Plov —Rice cooked with meat, raisins, and carrots.

Kak dela – How are you.

Karahi – Karahi is a popular Indian and Pakistani dish made of tomatoes cooked together either with chicken or mutton. Actually karahi is the name of the pot in which this dish is cooked.

Kazan Kebab – Lamb meat grilled and steamed with potatoes.

Keffiyeh – A head-dress worn by Arabs consisting of a square of fabric fastened by a band around the crown of the head.

King Burger – A Pakistani restaurant – an inverted form of the famous Burger King.

King Jamshed – One of the greatest Persian kings.

Kompot – Beverage that is obtained by cooking fruits like apples, apricots, cherries, and peaches, etc. with a large amount of water.

Komuz – Kyrgyz music instrument like guitar.

Kordak – A Central Asian dish in which fried mutton is prepared with potatoes and onions.

Koritsa – Chicken meat.

Kote-Sangi – An area located in the west of Kabul at District 5.

Kwas - A popular non-alcoholic drink in Slavic countries made from dry bread while it has other flavors like lemon, honey, and other fruits. One can find it near the roads and inside shopping malls during the summer.

Laghman – Is popular Kyrgyz food made of long noodles, potatoes, carrots, onion, coriander, meat, and spices. It is also the name of a province in eastern Afghanistan.

Leposhka – Bread.

Maghrib prayer – Is the prayer that is prayed just after sunset and is the fourth of five daily prayers.

Manas — Kyrgyz legendary hero who united his tribes against the Chinese warriors and got back their lands.

Mantu – Dumplings with minced beef or mutton along with onion inside, topped with yogurt and vegetable sauce with split peas or beans.

Masala – A mixture of ground spices used in Indian Subcontinent cuisines.

Mashrutka – A small vain used as public transportation.

Mikrorayon – Micro-regions. An area or region with lots of apartments. Different regions are divided into different mikrorayons 1, 2, etc. In Kabul there are also mikrorayon apartments from 1 to 4.

Milk Chay – Milk tea.

Minbar –Is a pulpit in the mosque where the imam stands to deliver sermons or speeches.

Mujahedeen – Holly warriors.

Mullah – Islamic cleric who usually lead prayers in mosque.

Naan – bread.

Narudni – Chain of supermarkets open twenty-four hours.

Nyet – No.

Ogan – Fire.

Orozo – Fasting in Kyrgyz language and also a female name.

Paghman District – Is located in the western part of Kabul Province with green hills and waterfalls making it an attractive spot for tourists.

Philharmonic Hall – It is one of the main places in the center of the city where music performances and public events are organized.

Pirojhki – Flat dough filled with potatoes, meat or cabbage.

Pishpek - The wooden paddle used for making Kumuz – mare's fermented milk.

Ploshad – Square.

Plov – A dish of rice with mutton or beef along with fried

shredded carrots and raisins.

Privet – Hi/Hello

Prospect Mira or Prospect Manas – Name of the road.

Pul e Sokhta – This is an area located at the west of Kabul famous for the bridge built on Kabul River. Nowadays, the area is famous for the drug addicts living under the bridge.

Qargha Lake – Is a water reservoir having picnic spots all around located at a distance of about 10 km from Kabul City.

Rahmat – Means thanks in the Kyrgyz language.

Ramadan - The ninth month on the Islamic calendar in which Muslims observe fasting from morning until evening for the whole month.

Rayon – district or region.

Salah – In Islam salah means prayer, which is obligatory upon Muslims five times a day.

Salam – Is an Arabic word literally meaning peace but is used in greeting in most of the Muslim countries.

Samsa – A typical Central Asian *samsa* or *samusa* is a baked dish of bread with minced of onions, chicken, beef, or mutton inside.

Sary Chelek Lake – It is a mountain lake located in the Jalalabad Province.

Shahnamah – A long epic poem written by a famous Persian poet Ferdowsi in the 10th century.

Shashlik – A dish of skewered and grilled pieces of meat.

Shisha – Also called Hookah is an instrument used for smoking flavored tobaccos or cannabis.

Shorpo – A soup of lamb meat and vegetables like potatoes, onions, and carrots.

Shurwa – Is a traditional Afghan soup along with potatoes and meat. The soup is served separately in a bowl in which bread is put in pieces while the meat and potatoes are put on a plate.

Shyrdak – Handmade traditional Kyrgyz rug.

S Novim Godom – Happy New Year

Tablighi Jamaat – A group of people preaching Islam in peaceful ways and are active almost all over the world.

Tanduri Chicken - A chicken dish prepared by roasting chicken marinated in yogurt and spices in a tandoor or oven.

Tikka Kebab – A dish of beef, mutton, or chicken meat grilled using skewers on burning coals.

Tokmok – A city in the Chuy Province toward the east of Bishkek.

Voyeval – Fought

Vy Ochen Krasivaya – You are very beautiful.

Ya Hocho – I want.

Zdrastvoyty – Hello.

Zdes Astanavitsa – Stop here

Zelony Chay – Green Tea.

Abbreviations or Acronyms

AUCA – American University of Central Asia.

CBT – Community Based Tourism.

CSTO – Collective Security Treaty Organization

GCSP – Geneva Center for Security Policy.

GIS – Geographic Information System

IOM – International Organization for Migration.

ISAF – International Security Assistance Forces.

ISIS – Islamic State in Iraq and Syria.

KIA – Kabul International Airport.

KSMA – Kyrgyz State Medical Academy.

PMDC – Pakistan Medical and Dental Council.

NATO – North Atlantic Treaty Organiztion

NUPI – Norwegian Institute of International Affairs.

OSCE – Organization for Security and Cooperation in Europe.

SCO – Shanghai Cooperation Organization.

SDES – Socio-Demographic and Economic Survey.

SIV – Special Immigrant Visa.

UNDP – United Nations Development Program.

UNESCO – United Nations Educational, Scientific and Cultural Organization.

UNFPA – United Nations Population Fund.

UN Women – United Nations Women is an organization for gender equality and women empowerment.

References

"Bishkek City." Oriental Express Central Asia. Accessed May 20, 2016. http://www.kyrgyzstan.orexca.com/bishkek_kyrgyzstan.shtml.

Catherine Putz, "What About that Proposed Second Russian Base in Kyrgyzstan?" The Diplomat, (March 07, 2018). Accessed March 25, 2018. https://thediplomat.com/2018/03/what-about-that-proposed-second-russian-base-in-kyrgyzstan/.

Commissionerate Afghan Refugees (CAR). Khyber Pakhtunkhwa, Peshawar. Accessed Nov. 29, 2017. http://www.kpkcar.org/carnewsite/CAR/index.php/page/about-us.

Dinara Murzaeva. "Kyrgyzstan-Turkey Relations: Cooperation in Political and Educational spheres." Review of European Studies, Vol.6, No.3 (2014). Accessed Dec. 22, 2017. http://www.ccsenet.org/journal/index.php/res/article/view/395 11/21896.

Dinara Taldybayeva. "Prospects for China-Kyrgyzstan Economic Relations in the Framework of the Silk Road Economic Belt Project." HKTDC (March 28, 2017). Accessed Oct. 14, 2017. http://china-trade-research.hktdc.com/business-news/article/The-Belt-and-Road-Initiative/Prospects-for-China-Kyrgyzstan-Economic-Relations-in-the-Framework-of-the-Silk-Road-Economic-Belt-Project/obor/en/1/1X000000/1X0A9JIX.htm.

Ford Peter. "Inside the World's largest Walnut Forest." Roads and Kingdoms (June 14, 2017). Accessed January 12, 2018. http://roadsandkingdoms.com/2017/inside-the-worlds-largest-walnut-forest/.

Franco Galdini. "Kyrgyzstan Violence: Four Years On." Aljazeera (July 01, 2014). Accessed Oct. 08, 2017. https://www.aljazeera.com/indepth/opinion/2014/06/kyrgyzstan-violence-2010-201463016460195835.html.

Hays Jeffrey. "Manas" Facts and Details, (April 2016), Accessed March 22, 2018. http://factsanddetails.com/central-asia/Kyrgyzstan/sub8_5c/entry-4772.html.

"History of the Academy." OSCE Academy in Bishkek. Accessed May 16, 2016. http://osce-academy.net/en/about/history/.

Kucera Joshua. "U.S. Checked in Central Asia." The New York Times. Accessed Nov. 17, 2017 (Nov. 04, 2013). https://www.nytimes.com/2013/11/05/opinion/us-checked-in-central-asia.html?rref=collection%2Ftimestopic%2FTransit%20Center%20at%20Manas.

"Kyrgyzstan Testing Clerics' Knowledge of Islam." Eurasianet. (May 28, 2015). Accessed June 14, 2018. https://eurasianet.org/s/kyrgyzstan-testing-clerics-knowledge-of-islam.

Mark Yoffe. "Chingiz Aitmatov." The Guardian (July 14, 2008). Accessed May 12, 2018. https://www.theguardian.com/books/2008/jul/15/culture.obituaries.

Mayhew, Elliott, Masters and Noble. "Lake Issyk-Kul." Lonely Planet Central Asia. Lonely Planet (2014) P.253.

"New Year's Celebrations Nowruz." Asian Art Museum. Accessed March 03, 2016.

http://education.asianart.org/sites/asianart.org/files/resource-downloads/Nowruz_Teacher_Packet.pdf.

Ovozi Qishloq. "Who Was Kurmanjan Datka, and What Does She Mean to the Kyrgyz People?" Radio Free Europe (Dec. 31, 2014). Accessed Jan. 04, 2017. https://www.rferl.org/a/qishloq-ovozi-who-was-kurmanjan-datka/26770979.html.

"Peshawar, Pakistan." World Heritage Encyclopedia. Accessed Nov. 17, 2017. http://www.worldlibrary.org/articles/peshawar,_pakistan.

Philip Shishkin, Restless Valley, Yale University Press, New Haven and London (2013) p.4.

"Special Immigrant Visas for Afghans – Who Were Employed by/on Behalf of the U.S. Government." U.S. Department of State – Bureau of Consular Affairs. Accessed May 15, 2018. https://travel.state.gov/content/travel/en/us-visas/immigrate/special-immg-visa-afghans-employed-us-gov.html#overview.

"The World Factbook, Kyrgyzstan." CIA. (May 17, 2016). Accessed May 20, 2016. https://www.cia.gov/library/publications/the-world-factbook/geos/kg.html.

Made in the USA
Middletown, DE
27 October 2020